Sibbele Hylkema ofm

Cowries among the Me or Ekagi

Comparative Anthropological Studies in Society, Cosmology and Politics

edited by

Prof. Dr. Josephus D. M. Platenkamp
(University of Münster/Germany)

Prof. Dr. Bruce Kapferer
(University of Bergen/Norway)

and

Prof. Dr. Guido Sprenger
(University of Münster/Germany)

Volume 8

LIT

Sibbele Hylkema ofm

Cowries among the Me or Ekagi

The Impact of a new Currency on a Group of Central Highlanders in Papua, Indonesia

Edited by Anton Ploeg

LIT

∞

Gedruckt auf alterungsbeständigem Werkdruckpapier entsprechend
ANSI Z3948 DIN ISO 9706

Bibliographic information published by the Deutsche Nationalbibliothek
The Deutsche Nationalbibliothek lists this publication in the Deutsche Nationalbibliografie; detailed bibliographic data are available in the Internet at http://dnb.d-nb.de.

ISBN 978-3-643-90200-9

A catalogue record for this book is available from the British Library

Klosbachstr. 107
CH-8032 Zürich
Tel. +41 (0) 44-251 75 05
Fax +41 (0) 44-251 75 06
e-Mail: zuerich@lit-verlag.ch
http://www.lit-verlag.ch

LIT VERLAG Dr. W. Hopf
Berlin 2012
Fresnostr. 2
D-48159 Münster
Tel. +49 (0) 2 51-620 320
Fax +49 (0) 2 51-23 19 72
e-Mail: lit@lit-verlag.de
http://www.lit-verlag.de

Distribution:
In Germany: LIT Verlag Fresnostr. 2, D-48159 Münster
Tel. +49 (0) 2 51-620 32 22, Fax +49 (0) 2 51-922 60 99, e-mail: vertrieb@lit-verlag.de

In Austria: Medienlogistik Pichler-ÖBZ, e-mail: mlo@medien-logistik.at

In Switzerland: B + M Buch- und Medienvertrieb, e-mail: order@buch-medien.ch

In the UK: Global Book Marketing, e-mail: mo@centralbooks.com

In North America: International Specialized Book Services, e-mail: orders@isbs.com

TABLE OF CONTENTS

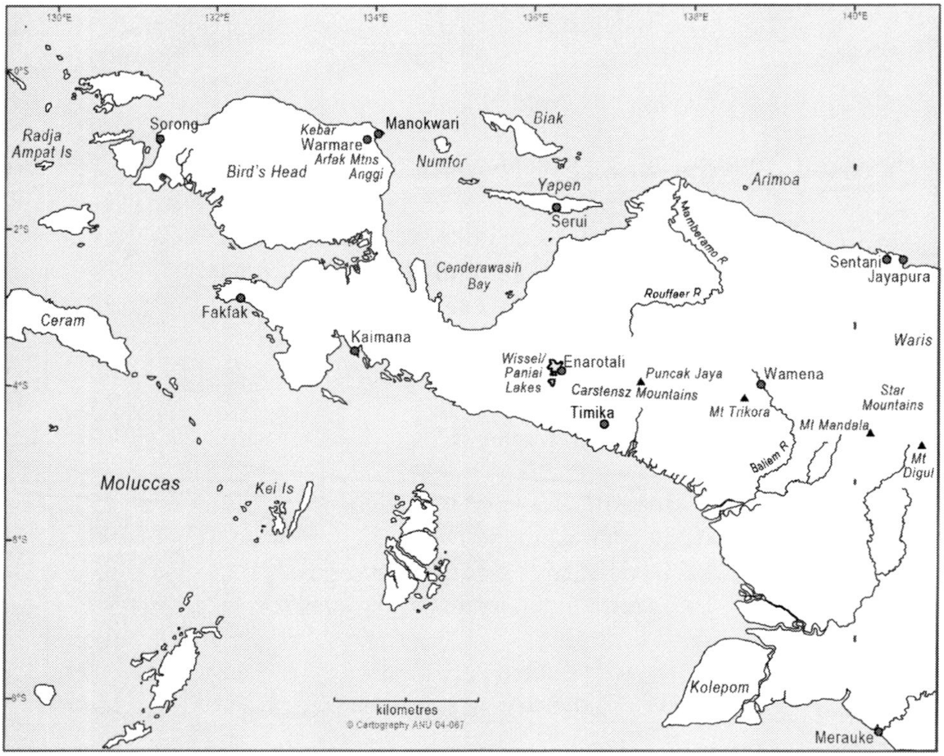

Map 1 Papua

Map 1 is taken from *The Sweet Potato in Oceania: a Reappraisal*, edited by Chris Ballard, Paula Brown, R. Michael Bourke and Tracy Harwood. I thank the Cartographic Services of the College of Asia and the Pacific of the Australian National University for allowing me to use it.

Map 2, the Me habitat, is in part made by Hylkema. I found it among his papers and recognised his hand writing. I presume Hylkema used an existing map and added the geographical names. While almost all his texts are in Dutch, in this map he used for lakes the abbreviation 'L', and for rivers 'r', as if he expected English viewers. It is unclear to me how this came about. The contours of mountain ranges are indicated by dotted lines and mountain peaks by crosses. The map I found was a copy and many names had to be rewritten to make them legible.

PREFACE, by Anton Ploeg

While preparing this book for publication I was assisted and encouraged by a number of people and institutions. I mention first Sibbele Hylkema's family who trusted me with editing Sibbele's work at a time they did not know me. They have been most patient and provided me with additional information each time I requested it. I mention especially Sjoerdtsje Hylkema, Sibbele's sister, who helped me decipher her brother's handwriting.

I also thank the administrators of the Dutch province of the Franciscan order for allowing me access to Hylkema's manuscripts. I single out Joost van Heijst, the secretary of the provincial board, and J. Steenkamer ofm, the archivist of the province. Several of Hylkema's colleagues provided me with additional information. I mention especially Jos Donkers and Joop Sierat.

Toine van Hemelrijck, then a staff member of the anthropology Department of Radboud University, Nijmegen, kindly undertook the scanning of Hylkema's manuscripts. Marijke Weerheym, of Studio Natatoma, made Hylkema's map of the Me territories legible, in Hylkema's hand writing. While the idea to use this map for the book's cover is mine, it was the graphic design firm *De Getemde Muis,* that made the idea a reality. Stéphane Breton gave instructive comments on part 4 of the manuscript. Members of the Sterenborg family helped out with identifying biblical references in Hylkema's texts. Dave Hardy, corrected the English of parts 1 and 4 of the monograph, and Rosemary Robson translated Hylkema's text. That was an arduous undertaking, given his complex use of the Dutch language. I thank her for persevering to the end. And I am grateful to René van der Haar, Centre for Pacific and Asian Studies, Radboud University Nijmegen, and to my wife, Magda Bolt, since they solved the last problems.

MAP 2 The Me habitat, with geographical names entered by Sibbele Hylkema

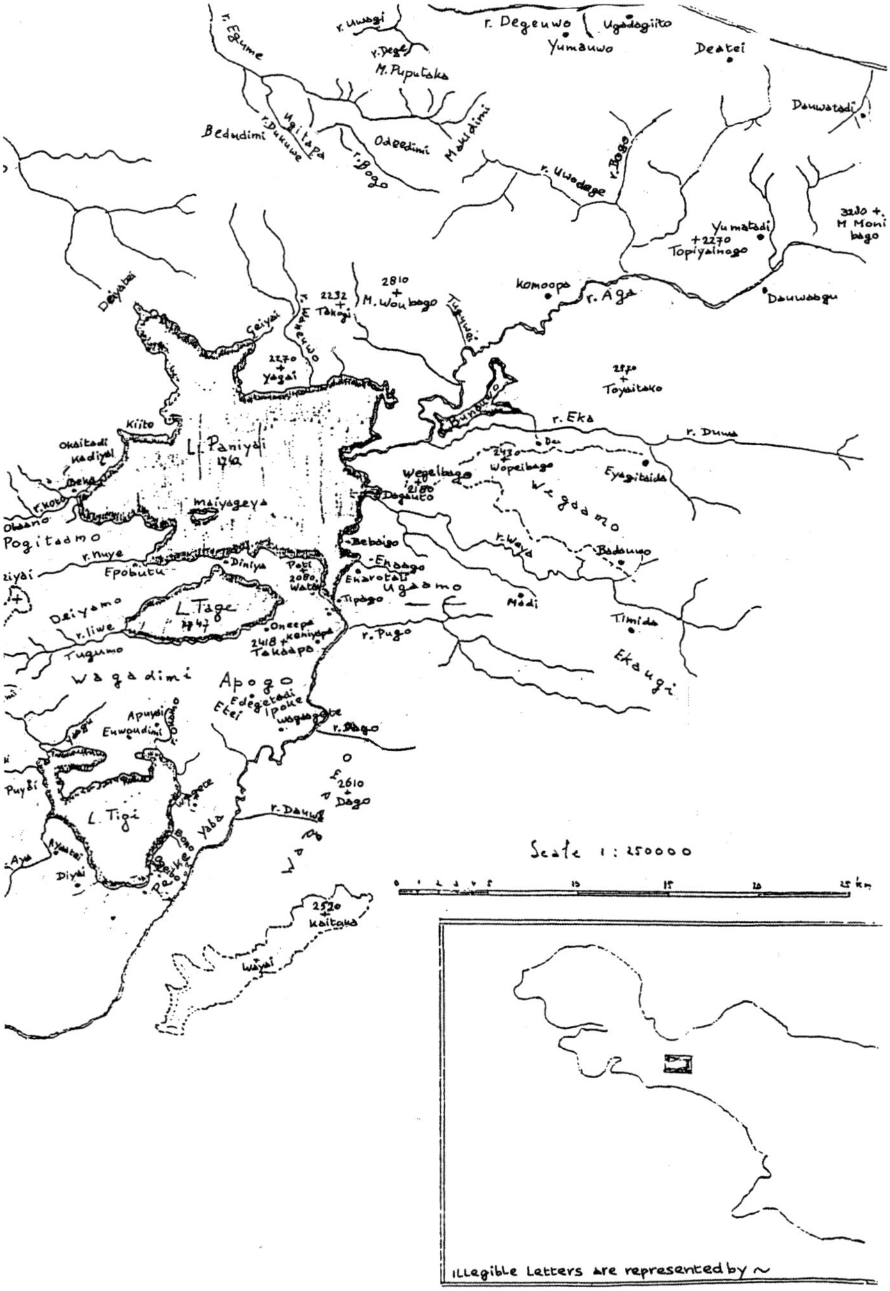
r. Egume
r. Uwagi
r. Degeuwo
Ugadagiito
Yumauwo
Deatei
M. Puputaka
Bedudimi
r. Dukuwe
Ugitapa
Odeedimi
r. Bogo
Makidimi
Dauwatadi
r. Uwadege
r. Bogo
3200 +
M Moni
bago
Yumatadi
+2270
Topiyainago
Deiyabai
2232
Takogi
2810
M. Woubago
Komoopa
r. Aga
Dauwabagu
Geiyai
2270
Yagai
2870
Toyaitako
r. Eka
r. Duwa
Kiito
Okaitadi
Kadiyai
L. Paniyai
1740
Wegeibago
Wopeibago
Eyagitaida
Dagauto
Maiyageya
Pogitadmo
r. Nuye
Epobutu
Diniya
Bebaigo
Ekaago
Enarotali
r. Weya
Badauwo
Deiyamo
L. Tage
1747
Tipago
Ugaamo
Madi
Timida
r. Iiwe
Oneepa
2418 +
Takaapa
r. Pugo
Tugumo
Ekaugi
Wagadimi
Apogo
Apuyai
Euwoudimi
Edegetadi
Etei
Ipoke
Wagaagabe
r. Dago
2610
Dago
L. Tigi
Puyai
Diyai
r. Dauwa
Scale 1 : 250000
0 1 2 3 4 5 10 15 20 25 km
2520
Kaitaka
Waiyai
Illegible Letters are represented by ~

PART 1 INTRODUCTION, by Anton Ploeg

In this monograph I present two ethnographic manuscripts that Sibbele Hylkema ofm left behind on his death in early 1998. Hylkema was a missionary who took up ethnography in the course of his work among the Ngalum, living in the eastern end of the central highlands of western New Guinea, and the Me, in their western end (see map 1). The two manuscripts published here have remained unfinished. They concern the Me; the first deals with their use of cowry shells, the second with the bride price. Hylkema remained unknown to most anthropologists, also in the Netherlands. Hence, in this introduction I present an overview of his life and work, set in the context of the colonial and post-colonial history of the highlands, and of the history of ethnographic research in the two areas where Hylkema has worked. Subsequently I present Hylkema's two manuscripts. Finally, in a conclusion I compare his discussions with work by other ethnographers who worked in Melanesia.

The use of the name 'Ekagi', instead of 'Me', in the title of the monograph is controversial. The name, also phoneticised 'Ekari', was made current by Dutch colonials shortly after they had contacted the people. An earlier used name 'Kapauku' or, in Dutch phonetisation, 'Kapaoekoe', was an exonym employed by Papuans living on the south coast (de Bruijn 1955: 325). Its pejorative connotations discredited the term, but Leopold Pospisil, the first and best known ethnographer of the Me, kept using it in his ethnographic work so it became widely known. Later, 'Ekagi' themselves argued that they were properly called 'Me', or 'Mee', their own word for 'people' (for instance Giay 1995: xviif). They opine that also the term Ekagi was an exonym, this one employed by their easterly neighbours, the Moni. Hylkema disagreed. He regarded the term 'Ekagi' as a local term and maintained that the term 'Me' was promoted especially by people educated at school and who often lived and worked outside Ekagi habitat. By their use of the term they wanted to emphasise that they still belonged to 'the people' (2002: 246f). Alfons (also: Bernard O.) van Nunen ofm, a colleague of Hylkema, supports this view (pers. comm. 2007). Van Nunen worked from the late 1950s among a group of Moni living at Kugapa in the valley of the Weya, a river flowing into lake Paniai from the east. They were then neighbours of groups of Me who inhabited the remainder of the valley. Van Nunen (pers. comm. 2003) finds it implausible that 'Ekagi' is a Moni word because in this language words for people and groups of people end with 'ni', as in the term Moni. The Moni term for the Me was in his view Isani. Carolyn Cook who worked among the Amungme, also called Hamungme and, by Cook, Amung, living on the southern slopes of the central highlands, east of the Moni, reports that they prefer the name 'Ekagi', since in their language too the term *me* means 'men' or 'people'. (1995: 62n). The Me and the Amungme languages are interrelated (Silzer & Heikkinen Clouse 1991: 24).[1] In this book I use 'Me', and not 'Mee', since Me is the spelling that Benny Giay, himself a Me, uses in his writings (e.g. 1995).

However, the medical officer K.W.J. Boelen who was posted to the Me from 1951 to 1954 (no date: 5, 216) pointed to further complexities in the terminology. He wrote that at the time the Me did not have and did not feel the need for a name for all the Me speakers together and referred to them as 'me', 'the people'. He added that the Me then 'readily' adapted to the names that Europeans used to refer to them, for instance the term 'Kapauku'. In contacts with Europeans the Moni used that same term to refer to the Me, although they had, and probably still have, the term 'Isani' to refer to them. Boelen continued:

> The Mapija people [Current spellings of their name are 'Mapia' or 'Mapiya'. They live in what is now regarded as the western part of Me habitat] call themselves Timorini or Simorini to distinguish themselves from the inhabitants of the Kamu and the [Paniai] lakes whom they call 'Ekagi' and from the inhabitants north and west of the Mapia whom they call 'Jabi''(1955: 1).

This information came from Auki, a very prominent Mapia Me man (Ploeg 1996: 218f), who, in Boelen's view, may out of politeness have provided answers to basically unanswerable questions. Boelen opined further that 'Ekagi' is 'most probably' a Moni word and 'Jabi' 'possibly' an 'Ekagi' [sic] one, or a term used on the north coast to refer to highlanders (1955: 1-2). In his publications he used both Kapauku and Ekagi.

These contrasting views put me into a quandary. Whatever the merits of either case, it is up to the people themselves by which name they want to be known. However, because I am concerned here with manuscripts written by Hylkema, I have reluctantly decided to retain the name Ekagi in what he has written, while using the name Me in my own introduction and conclusion. That I use more than one name for a single ethnic group may seem unsatisfactory. However, it is by no means the only group with which this is the case. In part 4, the Conclusion, I refer to another instance.

In my Introduction and Conclusion I use the 'ethnographic past'. That seems called for because cowry shells, featured prominently in both the Hylkema manuscripts, are no longer in use among the Me. I also use the past tense when discussing the history of the Me since their incorporation into, first, the Netherlands East Indies, later Netherlands New Guinea and, later again,

---

[1] Amung(me) and people called Damal, or Uhunduni, belong to a single ethnic group. The Damal live north of the main range. Silzer & Heikkinen Clouse refer to the language that they and the Amung(me) share as Damal, or Uhunduni (Ellenberger 1996: 21).

Indonesia. I include in that history the ethnographic record, so I refer to the writings of J. Victor de Bruijn[2], Pospisil, Giay and others in the past tense. But I make an exception for Hylkema's work that I introduce here, because that was not published before and is only now added to that record.

HYLKEMA'S EARLY LIFE AND ETHNOGRAPHIC WORK AMONG THE NGALUM

Hylkema's parents had a dairy farm near the town of Boalsert, in Dutch Bolsward, in the province of Fryslân in the north of the Netherlands. In that area Frisian was spoken, the first language that Hylkema learned. His parents were tenants, and with 30 to 40 cows they had a reasonable income. However, they had started farming during the depression years of the early 1930s. The economic hardships of that time had made a deep impression on them and also after World War II they continued living a sober life. They got fourteen children, of whom Sibbele was the fifth.

The area where Hylkema grew up was an enclave of Catholics in a province in which Protestants predominated. That mattered since in the Netherlands at that time socio-cultural divisions between Protestants and Catholics amounted to an ethnic division. Hylkema's parents were deeply religious. That adherents of another faith surrounded them, probably added to their religiosity. They educated their children to become practising Catholics. So Hylkema went to a Catholic primary school. He opted for the priesthood when he was about to leave school and, a few years later, he decided that he wanted to become a Franciscan priest.

He was ordained in 1959 and went to New Guinea in 1960. There, he was first posted to the Ngalum, in the eastern highlands close to the border with Papua New Guinea, in Apmisibil, an un-administered area.[3] He had to set up a new mission post and had to get an airstrip constructed. The Ngalum language was not known and, to learn the language, a *lingua franca* was unavailable. Hylkema received his first lessons while co-operating with Ngalum in the physical work on the airstrip to be. In late 1965 he wrote home that he was writing up his linguistic data for the benefit of his successors. It seems likely that these data contained ethnographic material. However, his letters do not say when he started working towards an ethnography. His training had not prepared him to be an ethnographer, but it is clear that by the late 1960s he aspired to become one. In mid 1967, when he was on leave in the Netherlands, he consulted Jan van Baal 'on the advice of his superiors' (van Baal 1974: vii), because he wanted to write

---

[2] In some publications this name is spelled 'de Bruyn'. I use here the spelling that de Bruijn himself used in his autobiography (1978).

[3] First, Hylkema used the phonetisation 'Nalum', but in his later writings he shifted to 'Ngalum', in accordance with the pre-nasalised 'g'.

an ethnography of the Ngalum and felt he needed anthropological training. At that time van Baal was a professor of anthropology in Utrecht and Amsterdam. Moreover, he was one of the most influential managers of Dutch social science research in the non-western world. Van Baal's description of their first meeting makes me think that Hylkema presented himself as a novice. When he asked what books to read to become an ethnographer, van Baal answered that reading books was not a prerequisite, but that his task consisted of 'looking, listening and writing down' (1974). From that date Hylkema had at most two years to collect further anthropological information among the Ngalum. He wrote to his family in August 1968 that he had been told that he will probably be re-posted, so he realised that his time in Apmisibil was now short. In mid 1969 he was in fact re-posted, to the Me.

While working among the Me, he continued drafting his Ngalum ethnography. His letters home do not say when he finished a first draft, but three years later, during his leave in the European summer of 1972, he discussed the second draft with van Baal, which led to the text as published. Van Baal's editorial efforts were, as he himself put it, 'intensive' (1974: vi). So the anthropological cast of the analysis in the book is likely in part due to van Baal's work. The result, entitled *Mannen in het Draagnet*, 'Men, Carried in the String Bag' (1974a), is a highly unconventional ethnography. Hylkema was aware of this, but he argues that the topics that he presents reflect his bias as a missionary. Hence his focus is on individuals, the gendered world in which they live, their network of relations and their positions in their social fields. This order of presentation entails that, for instance, the book opens with Ngalum conceptions about life and death, while clan organisation and initiation are discussed in the second half and pig husbandry in the penultimate chapter. Throughout Hylkema shows himself aware that he deals with a socio-cultural situation in flux.

Notwithstanding the unconventional organisation of the data, they are rich enough to allow their use in comparative studies of New Guinea highlands ways of life. That this has scarcely happened, is primarily because the text, against van Baal's wish, was not translated into English. While van Baal considered Hylkema to be an exemplary ethnographer, it is Kenneth Maddock who, in his review in *Oceania*, gave him the ultimate accolade by commenting:

> It seems certain that *Mannen in het Draagnet* will come to assume, at least for anthropologists who read Dutch, something of the Domesday Book quality that Leach attributes to Malinowski's Trobriand corpus (Maddock 1976: 167[4]

[4] Leach made this comment in his paper 'Concerning Trobriand clans and the kinship category 'tabu''. The first sentence of that paper reads: 'For social anthropologists Malinowski's accounts of Trobriand Island culture are a kind of Domesday Book.

Until 2002, the book remained Hylkema's only scholarly publication. Nevertheless, he continued his ethnographic work while he was posted among the Me. But before discussing this work, I want to deal first with the colonial history of the Me.

COLONIAL INCORPORATION OF THE ME

Europeans desultorily contacted groups of Me from 1910, but only in 1935 did they become aware that these people formed part of a sizeable population extending over a sizeable part of the highlands. In that year an exploration party, comprising Sjirk van der Goot, a colonial administrator, H. Tillemans msc, a catholic missionary, and H.J.T. Bijlmer, a physical anthropologist, reached the Mapia, in the west of the Me habitat. Soon afterwards, Frits J. Wissel, a navy pilot seconded to the NNGPM, the Netherlands New Guinea Oil Company, spotted the Paniai lakes, and the people living there, from the air on one of the last days of 1936 (Wissel n.d.; *pace* Galis 1953: 43). Wissel's observations prompted a spate of exploratory activities (similarly: van Baal, Galis and Koentjaraningrat 1984: 141). The Assistant Resident Commissioner J.W. Cator found an overland road to the lakes in late 1937. Less than one year later, a patrol post in the area was set up by Jan van Eechoud, then a police officer, at Enarotali on a spur on the eastern shore of Lake Paniai, the largest of the three lakes (Schumacher 1954: 93f). It was the first patrol post in the Central Highlands. That same year colonial interest in the highlands had heightened when members of the American-Dutch Archbold expedition had reached the Grand Valley of the Baliem in June, part of the area that the expedition was to explore (Klein 1938: 483f). From Paniai the junior administrative officer — *adspirant-controleur*— de Bruijn started from early 1939 an active programme of patrolling (de Bruijn 1978). The botanist P.J. Eyma researched the area during most of 1939 (Eyma 1940). A large-scale scholarly expedition organised by the KNAG, the Royal Dutch Geographical Society, and led by C.C.F.M. le Roux, then Keeper at the Leiden Anthropology Museum, made investigations during the second half of 1939 (le Roux 1948-50: 16). It was the most expensive expedition of the Society so far (Wentholt 2003: 95f).

De Bruijn wrote about his explorations in administrative reports, articles in journals and his autobiography (1978). Eyma's data have remained largely unpublished due to his early death in a Japanese concentration camp. At least some of his manuscripts have survived and are now in the library of the National Herbarium in Leiden, the Netherlands (Ploeg 1997). Le Roux's voluminous report of the KNAG expedition was published posthumously after World War II (1948-50). Le Roux had earlier been a member of the 1926 Stirling expedition that had entered the central highlands from the north, via the Tariku river,

---

Palpably incomplete, palpably imperfect, they yet transcend in some indefinable way everything of like kind' (1962: 120).

MAP 3 The extent of the Me habitat, as traced by Boelen in the early 1970's

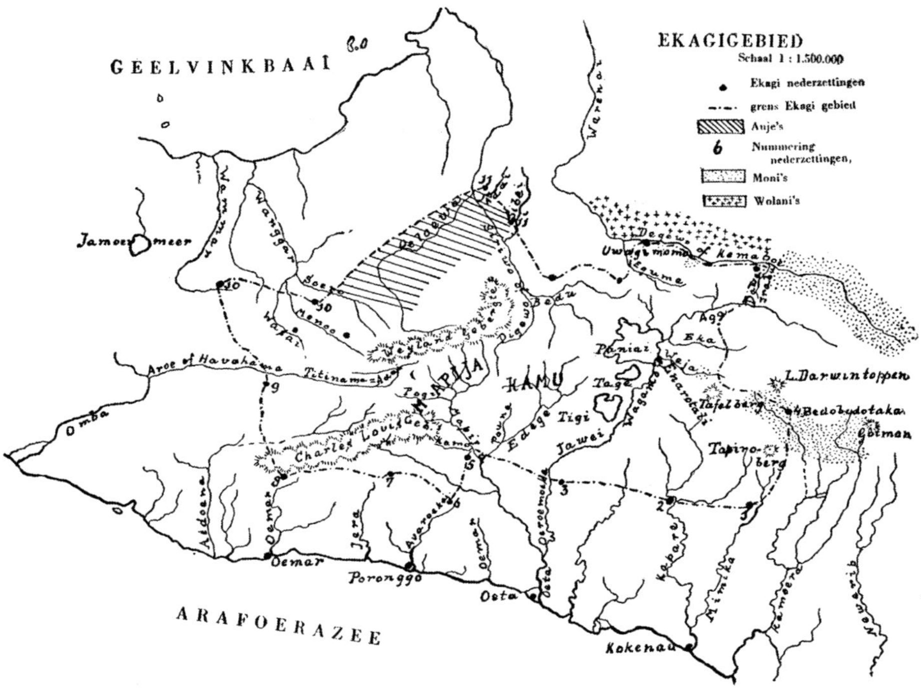

formerly the Rouffaer river, and his report incorporates data from that earlier expedition. His ethnography is not thorough, yet quite extensive given the relatively short period of time the expedition lasted and the current lack of knowledge about the people and the languages they spoke.[5] Le Roux's primary expertise was in topography which comes through in his mastery in covering the highlands landscape, both in writing and by photographs. Exploration was cut

[5] Van Baal's comment that le Roux's work did not amount to much (1989: 247) seems unjustifiably harsh.

LEGEND

Boelen made this sketch map on the basis of numerous patrols by himself and other officials in the colonial administration, and of reports by earlier explorers. I have retained the Dutch geographical words. *Gebergte,* abbreviated: *Geb.* means mountain range; *toppen* means summits. The dot – dash line shows the outer limits of the Me habitat as known at that time, while the numbers refer to villages reached by a series of expeditions and patrols (Boelen 1955: 4). Boelen mentioned the numbers 10 and 11 twice. The 'Auje' mentioned on the map are people whom the Me at Paniai include among the Me, although they speak a 'quite different' (Boelen 1955: 2) language.

The list of expeditions and patrols is as follows:

The first British South New Guinea expedition led by Goodfellow, 1910-1; the 1931 Bijlmer patrol
The 1934 patrol by H. Tillemans msc.
The 1937 patrols led by Assistant District Commissioner Cator.
The 1936 expedition by Colijn, Dozy and Wissel that reached the summit of Puncak Jaya; the 1950 patrol by Veurman and Mickelson.
A patrol by Tillemans.
The 1931 Bijlmer patrol.
The 1935 expedition by Bijlmer, van der Goot and Tillemans (see p. 5).
A 1932 patrol by Tillemans; patrol by Smits ofm.
A 1939 patrol by Tillemans.
1912 and 1913 parties of the military exploration of New Guinea led by ten Klooster and Binnendijk respectively.
The 1926 patrol by Assistant Resident Commissioner Kuik.
The 1938 patrol by van Eechoud.
Several other patrols in the late 1930s.
The 1953 patrol led by Cadet *Controleur,* cadet patrol officer, Peters.

---

short by the outbreak of World War II, but resumed shortly after the war. Enarotali then became the local headquarters of the colonial administration. The promise of large populations, also elsewhere in the highlands, brought missionaries of various denominations, including Catholic missionaries of the Franciscan order, to Paniai to proselytise among the Me and Moni, and to use the area as a base for explorations farther a field.

It soon became clear that the Paniai and its surroundings, the Kamu valley to the west and the Kema valley to the north and northeast, did indeed carry large populations. Farther west (Hylkema 2002) and north, the population was far less dense. Boelen traced the extent of their then habitat. Map 2 is a copy of the map that he produced in Boelen 1955. On the basis of numerous, wide-ranging patrols by members of the medical service, he estimated that at the time the total Me population was 44.700 (Boelen 1954). This figure tallies with the one arrived at by K. Groenewegen & D. J. van de Kaa, the leaders of the team that surveyed the demography of West New Guinea in 1959-62. They quote administrative reports putting the population in the Paniai area and surroundings at about 50,000 (1964: 1, 122). Contemporary figures for the wider area seem to be unavailable. The majority of the people belonged to a single ethnic group, in this introduction called the Me. Upstream in the Kema valley, to the east, lived Moni people and there were pockets of Moni living among the Me (van Nunen 1973: 8-9). Hylkema (2002: 247f) argues that, at the time of colonial incorporation, the Me were splitting into two ethnic groups, one living in the Paniai area and the Kamu valley, the other, much smaller, farther west. The colonial administration inadvertently arrested the process by recording names and habitats of ethnic groups. Since at least the late 1950s, the Me population has been on the increase. The 1991 language index of P.J. Silzer & H. Heikkinen Clouse gave an estimate of 100,000 Me speakers (1991: 19). For the late 1980s, Hylkema reports a 'population explosion' (2002: 232).[6]

The way of life of these newly contacted highlanders immediately intrigued the colonial arrivals. Although the van Overeem-Kremer expedition that had approached Mount Trikora from the north, had come across the densely populated Toli and North Baliem valleys in 1920-2, they had apparently not expected the occurrence of another densely populated highlands area. They were impressed by the agriculture practised by the Ekagi on the plains and the lower slopes of the valleys near the lakes (Boelaars 1995: 277f; Eyma, in Ploeg 2000b: 405f). The occurrence of expanses of ditched, mounded, composted and fenced gardens among the Me contradicted current notions of New Guinean industry. For Europeans noted their existence at the same time that two colonial officials, G. Kepper & L.H.W. van Sandick claimed that the inhabitants of New Guinea had to be taught how to practise agriculture (1938: 901).[7]

---

[6] Vriend (2003), however, views aids and other sexually transmitted diseases currently to be a grave threat to highlanders.

[7] It seems to matter that the two authors had formerly worked as colonial administrators. Kepper was a former labour inspector (Klein 1938: 900) and van Sandick had been responsible for the administration of west New Guinea as a Governor of the Moluccas (Klein 1938: 817). The compilation in which the quoted paper appeared, contained, however, a lengthy paper by van der Veer, an agricultural adviser of what was then called the Colonial Institute, that surveyed New Guinean

The members of the van Overeem-Kremer expedition had noticed how eager the local people – who later became known as the Western Dani, or Lani – were to acquire cowries. Paul Wirz, the anthropologist of the expedition, named the Toli valley the 'country of shell money' (Wirz 1932). Accordingly, Bijlmer, another participant of the 1920-2 expedition, took cowries along on the 1935-6 expedition to what turned out to be the western part of the Me habitat. Apparently he anticipated that they would be useful. In his book about the expedition he mentioned, without further comments, that he used cowries in his first transactions with the Me (Bijlmer no date: 170-1).

And in the report that van Eechoud wrote after he had founded the Enarotali patrol post, he pointed out that the economy of the Me was based on the cowry (1939: 170). He attributed a keen economic motivation to the people: 'nothing is gratis, everything has to be paid for' (ibidem: 133), with the cowry as a major means of payment (ibidem: 169-71; see also Eyma, no date). According to de Bruijn the cowry had even more importance for the Me: 'the cowry dominates the life of the [Me]' (1978: 62). He wrote in his autobiography that, in 1939, he requested his immediate superior, the Resident Commissioner in Ambon, in the Moluccas, to give the administrative officers a monopoly in importing cowries, because their inflation would be to the detriment of the Me. He added: 'I was sparing with them, almost stingy, rationing them severely, to the annoyance of quite a few mission workers and my own police' (ibidem). Le Roux and de Bruijn also noticed the subdivision of cowries into categories of different value (Le Roux 1948-50: 350f; de Bruijn 1955d: 534). Already van Eechoud noted that the Me transacted with *Cypraea moneta* and rejected *Cypraea annulus* (1939: 169). De Bruijn described the composition of the Me bride price of which cowries were an important part (1955b). It is noteworthy that in this paper he reported the inclusion of *Cypraea annulus* in one of the bride prices described. He also noted the commercial appearance of the *yuwo*, 'pig feasts', during which pigs were slaughtered and pork, and other commodities, were sold, for cowries. They were festive occasions attended by large numbers of people (de Bruijn 1978: 171f; Boelen no date: 163f). These early reports led for example van Baal, in an ethnographic survey written in the early 1950s, to characterise 'highlands ethnic groups as genuine trading peoples driven by an un-abating passion for shell money' (1954: 445). At the time van Baal wrote this, the warlike attitudes of the Dani, especially the Grand Valley Dani,[8] had not yet become apparent to outside observers.

---

agriculture, as far as was known at the time (1938: 457-523). The paper made it quite clear that New Guineans were most competent agriculturists.

[8] Yulia Sugandi (pers. comm. 2010) pointed out to me that Grand Valley Dani prefer to be called Hubula (Alua 2006). Since this name has not yet gained much outside recognition, I have not used it in this book.

Since the late 1930s, after Europeans such as administrators, missionaries, researchers and visitors had started interacting with the Me, they imported and used large numbers of cowries as a means of payment.[9] Dubbeldam (1964: 299) has attempted to calculate the numbers concerned, but did not arrive at even a tentative figure. However, inflation was less than might be expected because, in reaction, the Me started distinguishing between old and new shells, the new ones being the ones that the Europeans imported. They categorised old shells separately and held them to be more valuable than new ones (Dubbeldam 1964: 299f). Thus the old ones retained their value for several decades. In 1969, when Hylkema arrived among the Me, cowries were still in use. Consequently he was able to observe how they handled shell transactions.

POSPISIL'S ETHNOGRAPHY

As mentioned, the first trained anthropologist to carry out research among the Me was Leopold Pospisil. He worked in the Kamu Valley, west of Lake Paniai and separated from the lakes area by a single mountain range.[10] He started work there in the mid 1950s, at a time the Dutch colonial administration had not yet established a patrol post in the valley (1958: 4). In the 1960s and 1970s he made several return visits. Most of his data refer to the Kamu Me. A first monograph, published in 1958, included a discussion of the importance of cowries in their way of life. He also described the grading of cowries according to their physical properties (1958: 117f). The large number of shells satisfied what Pospisil termed the Me 'craving for counting': 'People count their wives, children, days, visitors at a feast and especially their shell money. Hours are spent by people squatting over strings of shells and counting them' (1958: 117).

At the time Pospisil started his field research in the Kamu, 'new' shells had penetrated there. Moreover, Pospisil himself introduced cylindrical blue beads (1958: 117) that enjoyed an apparently brief period of popularity as a means of payment (Hylkema, this vol. p. 144). At the time, the Kamu Valley Me distinguished the old shells into a number of categories, with sharply differing values. Pospisil lists six categories, with the most valuable ones worth as much as 150 times more than the least valuable ones (1958: 117f). For Pospisil, cowries functioned among the Me as 'the currency in a money economy' (*ibidem*). He regarded the various categories as denominations in a monetary system. In his second monograph, dealing with Me economy, he supported his conclusion that cowries functioned as money using a definition by the economists Umbreit, Hunt & Kinter: 'any commodity or token that serves as the common medium of exchange and the common measure of value' (Pospisil

---

[9] The Japanese did so during the war, but the numbers are not known (Dubbeldam 1964: 299).

[10] The 'Kamu Valley' is in fact a set of valleys located in the middle reaches of the Edege river (see map in Pospisil 1958: 65).

1963: 301). And the Me did use the cowry in these two ways. Also an author such as Giay, himself a Me, regarded cowries as 'true money' that people needed to be able to survive (1995: 20). Like Pospisil, de Bruijn and Dubbeldam (1964: 298) provided lists of categories of cowries of different value. Leo Dubbeldam was an official in the colonial administration posted in the Paniai area in the late 1950s. His list refers to that location and that time period. There are differences between his and Pospisil's lists: Dubbeldam mentioned five categories of cowries, including several precious ones not mentioned by Pospisil. One of the merits of Hylkema's discussion, presented in this monograph, is that he provides a reason for the differences.

As regards the kind of social relations that the Me established and fostered by means of their shell currency, in his later publications Pospisil portrayed them as running an individualistic, capitalist economy (1978: 18). Their individualism was such, he posited, that shared property did not occur (1958: 116). He was keen to emphasise the uniqueness of their way of life with a

> spectacular difference in their economy from the surrounding peoples – their use of true all-purpose money with shells of different but standardized denominations, their market economy in which the actual prices charged differ from customary prices because of the changes in supply and demand, and these in turn influence production. With this phenomenon went hand in hand the emphasis on individual wealth, entrepreneurship, profit motivation, and even well planned speculation (1989: 19).

Pospisil's empathy for the Me way of life permeates his writings. He seemed to delight in pointing out how they deviated from stereotypes about tribal peoples (1978: 3; 1989). His texts have become well known. Because he contributed a monograph to the *Case studies in cultural anthropology*, a series edited by George & Louise Spindler, a monograph that he, moreover, updated in a second edition (1964 and 1978 respectively), many students came to know about his views. Hence it is primarily through Pospisil's efforts that the Me way of life has become known to the outside world.

However, several of his conclusions have been questioned. His emphasis on the 'spectacular differences' with neighbouring peoples is, in my view, overdrawn. Also the Moni, westerly neighbours, and the Wodani, northerly neighbours of the Me, place a high value on cowries and spent much time examining them in order to grade them (for the Moni: van Nunen 1973: 18[11], van der Horst 1995; for the Wodani: Breton 2000: 561). Moni pig feasts resembled those of the Me (le Roux 1948-50: 586f). In passing le Roux mentioned that, in 1926, he witnessed among an ethnic group that he calls the Dèm a pig feast resembling a

---

[11] Van Nunen (pers. comm. 2003) opines that Moni were less pre-occupied, or, to use Hylkema's term, 'obsessed', by cowries than the Me were.

market for pork and other goods (1948-50: 327, 600-1). He located the Dèm north of the Nogolo, or lower Yamo valley (ibidem: 808). Pospisil's emphasis on the absence of joint rights to property also seems overdrawn. He stated that for instance parts of bridges and sections of drainage ditches were individually owned (1958: 116). But it is unlikely that the owners could unilaterally withdraw their parts of a bridge, or dam up their sections of a ditch, so it is doubtful to what extent their title conferred free disposal of what they owned. He also reported that the individual owner of a piece of land could freely dispose of his land. However, he also stated that the owner had to have the consent of his adult sons (1963: 132), and the members of the local lineage concerned had to grant access to the land (ibidem: 141). In Pospisil's terms, these were political rights that curtailed the economic rights of the individual owners. This categorisation does not seem convincing to me. What matters are, rather, the limitations imposed on reportedly exclusive rights to land.

Also Hylkema questioned Pospisil's conception that the Me were individual owners of land. At the 1990 conference '*The Mek and their Neighbours*'[12], he presented an unpublished paper dealing with Me land tenure. In this paper he argued, contra Pospisil, that after a tract of land had been sold, if the transaction can be so called, the seller nevertheless retained a right of option when the buyer left or died (1990b: 1). As regards 'the acquisition of territory' he added
It is remarkable that in a collection of 144 traditional folk tales there is constant talk of discovery, conquest from the enemy, uxorilocal marriage and inheriting, but a transaction in the sense of purchase and sale is never mentioned. In a collection of 58 clan-myths once in passing mention is made of an ancestor trying in several places to acquire a hunting-ground in exchange for shells ... but all his efforts fail (1990b: 4).

Pospisil's conclusions were sharply criticised by Christopher A. Gregory in his 1982 book *Gifts and Commodities.* In this book Gregory emphasised the prevalence of Maussian type gifts in Melanesian distribution systems. Pospisil's point that the Me transacted to maximise profits, and had set up a capitalist economy, was for Gregory a 'profound misunderstanding' (1982: 51). In Gregory's terms

> The gift transactor's motivation is precisely the opposite to the capitalist's: whereas the latter maximises net incomings, the former maximises net outgoings. The aim of the capitalist is to accumulate profit while the aim of the 'big-man' gift transactor is to acquire a large following of people (gift-debtors) who are obligated to him (ibidem).

---

12 The conference was organised by the German researchers who carried out field research among the Mek from the mid 1970s. They had invited Hylkema on account of his work among the Ngalum, whose habitat is to the east of that of the Mek. However, he chose to present a paper dealing with the Me.

On the basis of Pospisil's own data, he traced such gift transactions in the inter-clan relations among the Kamu Valley Me, thus contradicting Pospisil's conclusions. In anticipation of my comments in the Conclusion, I would like to point out, first, that also in Gregory's conceptualisation donors, gift transactors, attempt to get returns, and may attempt to maximise them, although the income can consist of social capital, rather than or in addition to either items of wealth or money. Moreover, in a paper published in 1994, Gregory distinguishes between 'the analysis of abstract principles of exchange and the analysis of exchange in concrete situations' (1994: 936). The above quotation seems to me to belong to the abstract principles rather than the concrete transactions.

Hylkema's ethnographic data are most pertinent in respect of the disagreement between Pospisil's and Gregory's analyses of Me transacting. Accordingly, I first introduce Hylkema's stay and his work among the Me, subsequently present the two manuscripts, to return in part 4, the concluding part of the monograph, to the scholarly discussion of the Me use of cowries.

HYLKEMA'S RESEARCH WORK AMONG THE ME

Hylkema was posted among the Me in 1969. He was loath to leave the Ngalum and hence did not welcome this new appointment. After World War II the Catholic church, by means of the Franciscan order, had resumed missionary work among the Me in 1949 (Verschueren 1953: 220). When Hylkema took op his work, the Franciscans had established a number of mission stations. Hence, while among the Ngalum he had been a single pioneer, among the Me he became part of a group of missionaries and other mission workers, among them Me catechists, who carried on work that their predecessors had started long before (Sierat 1999: 272). And while among the Ngalum he had had to rely on the local language in order to communicate with the people, and had had to learn that language without the help of a *lingua franca*, among the Me missionaries he could to some extent rely on Indonesian. But reliance on Indonesian led to an incomplete understanding of the Me language, which, Hylkema thought, aggravated the misunderstandings between missionaries and their parishioners.

Hylkema was first posted in the far west, among Mapia Me, in a sparsely populated, rugged mountain area (Sierat 1999: 102). He stayed there from 1970 until early 1972 when he went on leave. While still in Mapia, the mission gave him more time to do ethnographic work. For Hylkema that was a prerequisite for effective missionisation. After his return from leave, he was posted to Uwebuto, on the western shore of lake Tage, immediately south of lake Paniai. From early 1975 until the start of his next leave, in early 1977, he was posted in Epouto, across the lake. Back from leave, he first went to Mapia again, but soon had to move to Waghete, on the eastern shore of lake Tigi, the southernmost of the three lakes. He stayed there until mid-1984 when he moved to Obaano, on the western shore of lake Paniai. But in late 1986 he shifted again, this time back to Epouto. He stayed there until he left New Guinea altogether, in 1994.

Because of the numerous re-postings, he learned about the cultural variety among the Me. He finally distinguished three groups among them: the Paniai-Tage, the Kamu-Tigi and the Mapia Me, with the Mapia way of life the most divergent (Hylkema 2002). Pospisil's data refer primarily to the Kamu-Tigi Me and those of Boelen, De Bruijn and Dubbeldam to the people in Paniai-Tage. Hylkema has retained the tri-partition in the manuscripts published in this book. But in view of the scatter of the Me population reported by Boelen (see map 3), I doubt if it covers the cultural variety completely.

Several of Hylkema's re-postings came about because working among the Me was in several respects not agreeable to him. As mentioned, he felt that his superiors had forced him to work there. But in addition he developed less empathy for the Me than he had done for the Ngalum at Apmisibil. His colleague, Jos Donkers, told me that he had an ambivalent relationship with the Me. Given what he wrote to his family about his reactions to the Me, I gather that he felt disappointed that they seemed to keep him out of their affairs. Nevertheless, they wanted, in his perception, to benefit from his presence. Giay's account of the reactions of the Me towards Europeans and their New Guinean subordinates suggests that they were and remained suspicious of them, at times hostile. They had reason to be so. Europeans had settled among them and had started interfering in their affairs, although uninvited to do so. Soon afterwards, during World War II, the Me suffered under the Japanese who had come to capture the Europeans. A number of Me died, killed by the Japanese, but also in air raids by allied forces. After the war the Me revolted several times (Giay 1995: Ch 3). Best known became the 1956 revolt that started in Obaano (Giay 1995: 47f; van Baal 1989: 532f). After the Indonesian takeover, part of the hostility was transferred to representatives of the Indonesian administration.

In Hylkema's view missionisation entailed making people aware that, with the rise of colonial and post-colonial states, they had become members of a much wider social and cultural world that they shared with very many others. He felt frustrated that he could not convince the Me that this had become their life-situation. In his perception the Me had, instead, remained turned in on themselves, continuing their internal politicking in which they tried to pressure, outbid and outdo each other. In a hand-written comment on de Bruijn's 1970 [1955b] paper on Me land tenure, Hylkema writes that a Me man 'acquires prestige when he dares, and has effectively mastered, making others obliged to him by letting them share in his wealth'.[13] This orientation strained Hylkema's

---

13 Authentiek prestige verwerft men zich eerst als men het aandurft en de kunst beheerst anderen aan zich te verplichten, door hen in de rijkdom te laten delen.

relations with the Me, in part because it was contrary to the way in which he wanted to relate to others, and in part because he felt that they neglected to unite in so far as that was desirable for attempts to deal with the post-colonial authorities.

The ambivalence in his relations with the Me has, however, added depth to his ethnography. For example, an implicit theme that in my reading pervades much of the bride price manuscript is whether or not the institution, and the arrangements going with it, accords with marriage as conceived by the Catholic Church. And in several instances in the cowry manuscript he shows his concern about the ways in which Me men tend to manage, in Hylkema's view, mismanage, money.

But also his relations with his colleagues were not optimal. There is a revealing reference in a book in which the Dutch mountaineer Bart Vos writes about his climbing in the central highlands of West Papua. In the course of his travels, he meets with the Catholic missionaries in the Paniai area, presumably in the late 1980s (Vos 1992: 4, back cover). About this meeting he writes

> One priest does not join us. According to the others he works continuously. In the 1960s he lived as a missionary among a Papuan people about [whom] he has published a well-known anthropological book. Now he writes about the customs of the [Me around the Paniai lakes]. The other priests claim that he has shelves full of notes, but they doubt whether anything readable will come out of his room. 'He', one of them tells me suavely, 'he digs in deeper and deeper, until we can bury him in his own notes' (1992: 112).

Vos has fictionalised, if not mythologised, his travelogue. Yet the quotation reflects the social distance between Hylkema and his colleagues. It seems that he cherished high expectations of his interaction with both the Me and his colleagues and was deeply disappointed when these expectations did not come true. Both about the Me and about his colleagues he wrote home that they lived side by side, but not with each other.

Notwithstanding the tensions in his relations with others, he did not make use of the opportunity to become a lecturer at the theological college in Abepura, near Jayapura. He did teach there, but only occasionally. His preference, it seems, was for instructing in a small group. He did the same in Paniai. In the late 1980s the position of priest among the Ngalum became vacant and he wondered whether he might try to return there. But given his age he decided against it.

HYLKEMA'S ME ETHNOGRAPHY

Apparently soon after his posting to the Mapia, in 1969, Hylkema started making ethnographic inquiries. He was also intent upon learning the Me language. After the bishop had assigned him to do ethnographic research, in mid-1971, pastoral work became a minor duty. When he showed the pre-final draft of his Ngalum monograph to van Baal, in mid-1972, he had already drafted seventeen essays, 293 typewritten pages, about the Me people in Mapia (Hylkema 1971-2). In the decade that followed he drafted another eleven monographs, altogether over 3000 pages. They were all typewritten and I do not know how many copies were made. He collected his ethnographic data during his regular contacts with a range of Me, including mission workers, but, in addition, made use of key informants. In the preface to his 1996 Me dictionary he mentions Paulus Wakei in Timeepa, in Mapia (Sierat, pers. comm. 2003), Severinus Dou and Bede Mote in Waghete, in Tigi, Willem Boma in Obaano, in Paniai and he singles out Isaias Tekege in Epouto, in Tage (1996: 9).

I find it hard to account for Hylkema's outburst of creativity. His brother and sister perceive his talents to be the heritage of his mother's family several members of which had artistic leanings, to the detriment of their farming (pers. comm 2004). In addition, his professional training had directed him towards putting his perceptions and ideas into words. This second point, however, applies as well to his colleagues most of whom nevertheless did not write monographs. The appreciation that he received for his Ngalum monograph might well have impelled him to keep writing.[14] Another likely reason is his conviction that effective missionisation was only possible on the basis of knowledge and understanding of the Me way of life. He may have hoped that by writing about them he would be able either to overcome or to vindicate his in some respects critical views about them. Finally, he may have focused on compiling ethnographic data out of his frustration over the unsatisfactory relationships with his colleagues.

In late 1978 he was in correspondence with van Baal about his work on the Me. He wrote home that he was supposed to have the text of a monograph ready and should actually stay in the Netherlands to discuss the English translation. Two other monographs were then being edited for publication (see also van Baal, Galis & Koentjaraningrat 1984: 43). Yet, these publications have not materi-alised and Hylkema's letters do not tell why. His sister and brother opine that he was apprehensive about having his work translated into English because his incomplete knowledge of that language did not allow him to check the accuracy of the translation. Donkers agrees: in his opinion Hylkema was a 'perfectionist', afraid to be misunderstood. He was also averse to have editors make changes in what he had written. Hence he held on to his manuscripts. Much later, in October 1994, a letter that he wrote to the editors of the publication series of what was then called the Centre for Pacific Studies at Radboud University,

[14] W. Schiefenhövel told me (pers. comm. 2002) that Hylkema was most gratified when the members of the Eipo research team invited him to come to Seewiesen, Bavaria, in 1990 to take part in the conference '*The Mek and their neighbours*'.

Nijmegen, shows that, also at that time, he found these monographs suitable for publication. Significantly, he offered the Dutch versions for publication (Ploeg 2000).

For much of his time among the Me, Hylkema lived by himself, at times because he was posted to an isolated parish, at other times because of lack of rapport with his colleagues, whether Dutch or Indonesian. In his later years among them, he settled into a routine in which he interrupted his ethnographic work with long walks, especially in the afternoons. My impression is that he did so primarily because he loved nature and less because he wanted to gather additional ethnographic information. In his letters dating from this period he mentioned some of the books that he was reading. Among them were Norbert Elias' *Über den Prozeß der Zivilisation*, works of the French philosopher / theologian René Girard, and of the Dutch Protestant theologian H.M. Kuitert. He read also van Baal's later works, dealing with the anthropology of religion, and with the author's own struggle with his religiosity. Among the modest number of books in his possession were anthropological books and papers about New Guinea, often complimentary copies.

Hylkema left New Guinea in 1994. Back in the Netherlands he first lived in an institution for Franciscan missionaries, but, again, he preferred to live by himself. So he shifted to a retirement home, near the area where he had grown up and close to his family, in the province of Fryslân. This place was on the edge of Warkum, a small town, surrounded by open country. There he resumed the daily schedule that he had followed during his last years in Paniai. Again he went in for ethnographic work and for long walks in the country. But in Warkum he could also remain in close contact with his family.

Hylkema continued his ethnographic work until his death in early 1998. In the 1980s he had produced a grammar and a dictionary of the Me language. He kept correcting and adding to them. And he had prepared a compilation of some 140 tales, in the Me language, with Dutch translations, altogether about 600 pages. The first part of the introduction that he wrote for this compilation has been published separately (Hylkema 2002). He wrote also shorter papers on a variety of topics. And many writings have to do with missionary work. He translated sermons delivered by catechists, transcribed Me songs, and wrote papers about Catholic worship, as the Me might perceive it. But when he died, his work was unfinished.

THE TWO MANUSCRIPTS BY HYLKEMA

His family was amazed by the enormous mass of writings that he left behind (Ploeg 2000a). Since the copyrights of his works belong to the Franciscan order, they were transferred to its Dutch office, and stored in its archives where they have remained. They include a large number of unpublished writings (Ploeg

2000). The older, titled monographs are typewritten and in cardboard covers. The linguistic monographs, dictionaries and grammars of the Me and Ngalum languages are computer printed and hardbound. During his last years he had been at work on two monographs, one dealing with marriage payments, the other with wealth items, especially cowry shells, objects that, in Hylkema's term, in a hand-written comment on de Bruijn 1970, 'obsessed' the Me. The two subjects overlap because cowries were an important part of marriage payments. They are the two manuscripts that I introduce here. Hylkema had not named them and they were not bound. Hence the two names with which I present them in this book, are my own. Hylkema had written them, at least worked on them, using his own personal computer. However, after his death, the texts were not found on the hard disc or on insertable discs. Publications referred to in the cowry manuscript include Schoorl's *Besturen in Nederlands-Nieuw-Guinea*, published, and made available, in late August 1996, less than one and a half years before Hylkema's death. So it appears that this text is based on data gathered in the course of over 20 years residence among the Me and, moreover, represents a late stage in Hylkema's thought.

In an evaluation of his work from late 1988 to early 1994, Hylkema writes (1994) that his contacts with a number of anthropologists, among them Pospisil, Adrian Gerbrands and Peter Kloos, made him aware that the era of publishing ethnographic reports was over. Instead, ethnographic data have to be examined in anthropological analyses. In my view, he attempted to do precisely this in the two manuscripts published here.

Hylkema had not finished drafting. He set about drafting in part by expanding sections of the existing text. Hence he upgraded sections of separate chapters into new chapters. In addition, he added in the printed versions numerous glosses in his distinctive handwriting. For the bride price manuscript he used data presented in his earlier, 1974 monograph on the topic (1974b). As regards the cowry monograph, he apparently was planning a large expansion. The manuscript that he left behind consists of chapters 1-10, 12, 14, 18, 22 and 25. In this book I have retained these numbers. It is not clear what he had intended to discuss in the chapters in between. The latter part of chapter 10, and chapters 12, 14 and 18, incorporate parts of an earlier chapter 9; 25 of an earlier chapter 11. The original texts of chapters 22 and 25 referred to a yet earlier draft with section headings such as 1.26 and 1.27. In the course of these chapters, Hylkema widens the scope of the argument. He starts from the cowry as an artefact, its use, its anthropomorphism, the different varieties, and the regional variations. From chapter 7 he starts discussing issues of gender and the role of cowries in the careers of Me men. He contrasts the cultural orientations of the Me and the Grand Valley Dani in chapter 10.

The table of contents of the bride price manuscript lists six chapters. Given how Hylkema kept expanding the cowry monograph, it is doubtful whether this list would have been the final one. However, he did not finish the six planned chapters. In the first chapter, that I renumbered 26, he examines the character of the transactions attendant on a wedding. The second consists of a series of bride prices showing how their content differed according to region and era. As it seems, Hylkema was in the process of splitting up the third chapter. In a first draft of that chapter he discusses what happened when a marriage ended prematurely, by the early death of a spouse, or by divorce, and in a second he argues that a marriage without bride price -—by exchanging sisters, or by bride service— is unsatisfactory to the Me. In the equally unfinished fourth chapter he discusses who contribute to a bride price and who receive from it. Here, he approaches the terrain covered by the cowry monograph, because cowries, including cowry transactions, were part of the prestation. It seems possible to me that at some stage Hylkema planned to combine the two topics into a single monograph. I gained that impression since he writes, in chapter 22 of the cowry manuscript, section 2.2, that in the following he will discuss wedding ritual, a subject that seems to belong to the bride price manuscript.

The above makes it clear that I had to edit texts that Hylkema had printed and had subsequently worked on. I have inserted the hand-written glosses into the text as footnotes. In addition, there are footnotes that I have written myself. I introduce these notes with the phrase 'by editor'. I also added paragraphs, 'by editor', to the main text. Because the manuscripts were unfinished, I had to devise ways to round them off. I took out repetitions. As regards the cowry manuscript, I arranged especially its last chapter in sections and sub-sections. The bride price manuscript was in a more preliminary stage. I had to decide what was the major point emerging from Hylkema's incomplete discussion. That I took to be tri-partitions in the parties of bride price givers and of bride price takers, and a corresponding one in the bride price itself. I shifted references to this topic to the end of the manuscript. While editing, I started out indicating my own complements to Hylkema's texts in square brackets. However, my editing was in several passages more intensive than the use of square brackets suggests. Nevertheless, most of the text in the edited manuscripts was written by Hylkema; editing consisted predominantly of changing the order in which he wrote it and omitting repetitive passages.

Although the two manuscripts are incomplete, it seemed fitting to get them published. They contain many data not found in the earlier Me ethnography. They provide lively descriptions of the agonistic character of many cowry transactions. They document changes that took place among the Me, also before the arrival of Europeans. And, finally, they document the extreme importance that the Me, until recently, attached to cowries. It seemed warranted to combine the manuscript discussing the use of shells and the one dealing with the bride price because shells, especially cowries, were such an important part of the bride price. Moreover, in the cowry manuscript Hylkema discusses changes in cowry use, while in the bride price manuscript he documents these by tracing changes in bride price composition. In fact, in my reading, Hylkema argues that Me sought to amass cowries because they could be used in bride prices, in other words the pursuit of wealth objects and the accompanying pursuit of prestige, was at the same time part of social reproduction. In line with this argument, Pospisil writes that cowries were used in compensation payments (1958: 146f). In this monograph I treat the two drafts as separate documents, putting the cowry monograph first, given the role of cowries in social reproduction.

When Hylkema worked on his manuscripts in the early 1990s, he was faced with a difficult choice as regards the use of tenses. At the time, the Me no longer used cowries. But they had retained other elements of their way of life that Hylkema made part of his ethnography. While dealing with cowries, he often, but by no means always, uses the past tense; in contrast, while dealing with these other elements he tends to use the present tense. Because he makes it quite clear that Me discontinued their use of cowries and in fact describes the historical process that preceded their abandonment, I have only in a few cases changed his use of tenses. I did so primarily by changing the present tense into the past tense to achieve consistency within single paragraphs.

In part 4 of the monograph, a conclusion following the two manuscripts, I attempt to put Hylkema's data and conclusions into comparative perspective. The bibliography, at the end of the book, combines publications used for Hylkema's two manuscripts and for my introduction and conclusion.

PART 2 THE COWRY, by Sibbele Hylkema

CHAPTER 1 AN ALIEN ELEMENT, LOCKED INTO THE HEART

1.1 INTRODUCTORY REMARKS

1.1.1 The 'Grote Winkler Prins'

As introduction, I quote from a well-known encyclopaedia. Especially those who have been personally involved with the use of the cowry as money in the interior of Papua, will find the few lines which the Winkler Prins encyclopaedia mentions under the heading cowry interesting.[1] In its entry the cowry is first alluded to as a genus within a family, then, within this genus, several species are distinguished and, finally, in its function as a means of payment two species are mentioned separately.

> The cowries ... form the family *Cypraeidae*. The principal habitat of the numerous species is tropical coastal areas on muddy or firm sea beds and their main source of food is corals or sponges. Species pertaining to the genus *Monetaria*, especially the money cowry (*M. moneta*) and the ring cowry (*M. annulus*), found in the Indian and Pacific Oceans, were used as a means of payment (1992: 209).

Van Baal (1975: 50) recorded, in a footnote, that the circulation of cowries as currency was not restricted to the interior of New Guinea, but that this was also the custom in Africa, and that they had been found in the Grimaldi cave.[2] He then went on to say that in the first instance the shells functioned as a gift and only later for the minting of coins, for small sums with a fixed value. With the exception of precious metals, value objects were not easy to divide up into fixed amounts, but shells were the exception which proved the rule, especially small shells that were available in sufficient, but not over-generous quantities. Cowries are just such shells.

1.1.2 Link between pigs and women

At the time I carried out my research,[3] the cowry played such an essential role among the Ekagi that the very existence of a society without the cowry seemed inconceivable. When cowries were brought up in conversations which had prac-

[1] By editor. The 'Winkler Prins' is one of the best known Dutch encyclopaedias. It has appeared in many editions and in several formats.

[2] By editor. The Grimaldi cave is located in northwest Italy. It contains palaeolithic remains (Encyclopaedia Britannica 1992: 839).

[3] By editor. Probably Hylkema was referring here to the early 1970s, when he was preparing his first series of monographs about the Me.

tically petered out, these would then revive and could be continued endlessly: people never tired of talking about them. Both jokingly and seriously, it was often claimed that Ekagi men had only three topics of conversation: pigs, shells and women. In order to prevent any misunderstandings, not only outsiders formed this opinion of the conversations. The judgement was just as likely to be heard issuing from the mouth of the Ekagi themselves. Sometimes it was voiced by men, when they were criticising their present society, but above all it was said by women when they were criticising men.[4] There was a circular, consecutive connection between these three matters. Pig rearing resulted in the accumulation of shells, ownership of shells was the prerequisite for the acquisition of women, and women's cultivation of sweet potatoes enabled them to rear pigs. Then the circle began again. In its capacity as a means of exchange in inter- and intra-regional transactions, the cowry linked women and pigs in bride price, fulfilling a role analogous to money in modern trade.

Looking at this circulation in hindsight, it can be said that it can be historicised, that it was relevant in a specific period. Then, not only was the cowry assigned a dominant economic, social and political role among the Ekagi, its part in the antagonism between new competitors reached also a climax. When these events are put in historical perspective, the relatively recent character of the use of the cowry is the more noticeable. Referring to specific individuals, informants could identify the era during which the cowry was not a part of the bride price. Further inquiry suggests the beginning of the 20th century. While it was only very recently, in the mid 1980s, that the cowry was radically banned and superseded by money, earlier it had supplanted other items and assumed a predominant position. The historical character of its use colours beforehand how to question the role and significance that it was assigned. The inquiry does not turn around role and significance of the cowry in general, but instead around its culture-specific role and significance among the Ekagi during a period dominated by the cowry.

1.1.3 Terminological distinctions

In previous sections the terms ornaments, valuables and coins were used, to be superseded by the terms means of exchange and money. Because of the role which these and other, comparable terms have in this study, the way they are used needs further introduction.

---

[4] This was the complaint heard from [Zakheus Pakage (Giay 1995),] the founder of the syncretistic movement *Wegee Bagee*: 'If we keep living in the mire and keep quarrelling about pigs, shells and women, we shall not have time for the Creator, Ugatamee.' In passing I noted down from the lips of a woman speaking about her next-door neighbour: 'He struts around with his women, pigs and shells, but his wife and children covertly dig up sweet potatoes from the adjacent garden that belongs to our son.'

A. Object of Exchange and Means of Exchange. To begin with, a terminological distinction is usually made between an object of exchange and a means of exchange. Not every object of exchange actually functions as a means of exchange. It is only possible to use means of exchange in case a person wants to exchange this object for something else, while the owner of this something else is prepared to accept the object because he knows that he in his turn can exchange it for whatever he wishes. It must be a socially and economically acknowledged object which is commonly given in exchange for other objects. In case two objects of exchange are transacted, this is designated as direct exchange or barter; in case an object of exchange is transacted for a means of exchange, it is designated as indirect exchange.

B. Valuables. Among means of exchange, valuables form a separate category.
To the members of a society their special value is not based on economic, but on social or religious grounds: i.e., such goods have for the members of a society a "subjective exchange value", and no objective "value-in-use". They figure mainly in ceremonial exchange. In principle they are not used for economic purposes, unless there should be a compelling reason (Dubbeldam 1964: 293).

C. Money. Several authors have used the term money to clarify role and significance of the cowry among the Ekagi. In addition, however, they equated cowries with money given the extensive similarities in their characteristics and use. Consequently, I briefly enumerate at this point the characteristics which Dubbeldam argues are most conspicuous in the functional use of money.[5]
1) It is a "medium of exchange".
2) It serves as a measure of value and as a currency unit.
3) It is a means of payment and of transferring purchasing power, even where no exchange takes place. Money can be used for paying off debts not originating from exchange (fines) and for the making of gifts that do not impose any obligation upon the recipient.
4) It can be accumulated for the purpose of savings, for investment and as a liquidity-reserve.
5) The fact that a good may assume the function of money is not only attributable to its being an object of desire, but also to a certain scarcity, to the cost of production, and to the risk involved in transport.... (Dubbeldam 1964: 297).
After mentioning that opinions about the material requirements are divided, but that use is more important, Dubbeldam states that the cowry complies with the majority of these requirements. It is a means of exchange, a measure of value, a currency, and so on, even though practically no non-obligatory gifts are known and cowries are not to be hoarded. Nevertheless, the cowry can be used to buy

---

[5] Dubbeldam was a Dutch public servant, posted in Enarotali in the late 1950s.

anything, in indirect exchange.[6] Besides being used as money, the cowry is not put to any other use, such as ornamentation.[7] The cowry is easily portable. It is relatively indestructible, and homogeneous, yet divisible into categories, witness the attribution of differential values. Its value is relatively stable and is personal, that is to say it is not the shell, but its value that interests the owner. It is imbued with purchasing power. Finally, there is a community [of people] which recognises and acknowledges it as a universal means of exchange. In the above [I have presented] the author's [Dubbeldam's] opinion. Because these characteristics will be dealt with in this study where appropriate, this brief introduction should suffice.

D. Markets. Bearing in mind the variety of objects which are liable to be exchanged and which can actually be paid for with cowries, it is possible to distinguish just as many different sectors or markets. The shells could be exchanged either for consumer items or for durable goods, for instance either for meat or for a canoe. Services rendered or work performed could be recompensed with them, but, at the same time, cowries were a substantial part of the bride price. As in the case of money, shells could be exchanged for each other, both within a single currency system, and between currency systems. When in distinction to direct exchange, such as barter of objects or of wives, cowries are used as means of exchange or payment, I use, for the sake of brevity, the term market and I distinguish among others sweet potato market, meat market, pig market, marriage market, and, in case of direct exchange, shell market.

1.1.4 Functional distinctions

The Ekagi used cowries as a means of exchange comparable to money and practised a money economy. Because this usage is emphasised in the literature and [there] is presented as more or less exclusive, it should be mentioned that cowries are used for other purposes as well. For instance, sometimes a cowry is tied to a baby's wrist purely for the infant to have something to suck on. It is remarkable that Ekagi, in contrast to for instance Moni, virtually never use the cowry as a decoration. Nevertheless, they knew about such usage, witness for instance the title used to address an ancestor in a prayer for shells: *mee gope mege gope*, 'You with the neck lace of cowries adorning your neck', indicates that its use as bodily adornment has only recently become obsolete. Or perhaps this ancestor is sketched according to a Moni model. Research revealed that sometimes an individual cowry was in demand not for its objective use value,

---

[6] [edited version of a handwritten gloss] This presents a problem. If money is in fact not [consistently] interpreted as money, but as in the case of cowries is subjected to restrictions, for instance because it is forbidden to exchange shells, or money, for specific pigs, then these exchange items do not function as money, since not everything can be bought with it. Sacred objects are excluded.

[7] By editor. In subsection 1.1.4 Hylkema qualifies this statement.

but as a subjectively valued treasure. On occasion, endorsed by religion, the cowry also functioned as an essential accoutrement in a ritual and as an amulet in daily life. Because the cowry itself remained the same in all these various functions, the equation of the cowry with money among the Ekagi needs to be qualified. In the Ekagi experience, the profane and the religious merge into each other. It is striking that since the beginning of the 1950s, when the use of the cowry as a currency became controversial, this battle has been fought not so much with economic as with religious arguments. The profoundest sense and significance the Ekagi attribute to the cowry is shown by their reaction to the regular importation of cowries and in their ideas about its mythical origins.

In the framework of an ethnography focused on a single topic, a complete picture is not to be expected: its scope is restricted both in breadth and in depth. Because the cowry actually functioned optimally as a means of exchange in relation to pigs on the one hand and to women on the other, the first step should be to form a clear idea about the position of women and pigs in the social system and in the portrayal of people in the cosmology. In the present context, women and pigs are here brought up in their relation to the cowry. As soon as one gets to know the mythological explanation of origin and genesis of the cowry, one is confronted with a plethora of religious customs and ideas. All of them require extensive discussion, both separately and in context. The topic [of the present monograph] allows merely indirect approaches.

1.2 ANTHROPOMORPHIC NAMES

1.2.1 Analogous to a body

Taking the perception of the Ekagi as my point of departure, I shall now give a description of the cowry as expressed in the standard terms, in which they account for even the smallest detail. The cowry as a whole is designated with the original word *mege.* A more detailed description begins with the body, in a general sense, as it is manifested in the body of humans and of animals.[8] This is not a procedure reserved exclusively for shells. Even in a mountain, to mention just one example, people perceive a *dagi,* head, or a *puga,* tail. In its natural state, the cowry has a split on one side, and a hump on the other. The discussion below begins with the side with the split.

As with the body in general --as for example in the case of a slaughtered pig-- people distinguish first a top and a bottom half. In opposition, the top half is, *pars pro toto*, called *dagi*, head, and the bottom half *dada,* bum. As they do in

---

[8] I suggest tentatively that Ekagi are intrigued by the seeming morphological relationship of the words *mee*, people, and *mege*, cowry. Given the traditional combination of the two terms, in line with the *parallelismus membrorum* characteristic of maxims, the morphological correspondence enables them to conclude that an intrinsic relationship exists between the terms.

the case of an egg, people identify the tapering half with the head, and the double curved one with the buttocks. In the case of the cowry, people go beyond these two names. Actually, with both halves their attention focuses on the two ends. As well as being referred to as head, the pointed end is also called *yuma,* nose. And, in contrast to the nose, the double curved one at the bottom is accurately spoken of as *bubu*, buttocks. The word *mugu*, hole, in the sense of an opening to a passageway or tunnel, fits in with both the 'nose' and the 'buttocks'. Something can emerge from such a hole. It can also disappear into it. The image refers to a body without limbs, or arms and legs.

In contrast to an egg, a cowry has a clearly distinguishable upper and lower side. However, although an outsider --for instance van Baal in the mentioned footnote (1975: 50)-- tends to identify the flat side, characterised by a split with serrated edges with the top half, the Ekagi see this as the rear, evidenced by the name *matoka*, backbone, for the split which stretches from 'nose' to 'buttocks'. They use the word *ego* to refer to each individual tooth as well as to both serrated edges. In translation the word 'tooth' comes to mind. However, the term does not refer merely to a part of a set of teeth or to such a set as a whole, but, more widely, to a sharp protuberance. To adduce but one example, the barbs attached to arrow heads are also referred to as *ego.* Analogous to the hips in the human body, the transition from the upper to the lower half is accentuated by a slight thickening on either side, and this is called *kagima,* protuberance or knob. The body is reduced to a head and a trunk. The limbs are missing.

In its natural state, the other side of a cowry is formed by a semi-circular hump. As counterpart to the spine, on the back side, this hump is aptly called *modo,* belly, referring to both a swollen belly and to the front of the body in opposition to its back. Although both men and women have a belly which, when observed externally, can either swell up or shrink, generally speaking the word belly has a typically female connotation. Internal changes herald a pregnancy and the symptomatic swelling is referred to with the verb *modo tai*, to get a belly. Before a shell is brought into circulation as a means of payment, the hump is excised. After it has been taken away, and, accordingly, the term 'belly' is no longer applicable, a cavity with a round opening is left. Because the round aperture and the cavity actually absorb the attention, the distinction 'top' and 'bottom' has become irrelevant. Without any link to the above mentioned distinction between 'nose' and 'buttocks' the opening is called *ebe*, mouth, thus referring to the cavity. Because people place a cowry on its under side, the back literally functions as the rear side and the front as the top.

What can be seen in the inside is, first, an open and a closed part. The latter is called *ega,* snail. Notwithstanding the primarily mythically coloured origin of the cowry, the designation reveals the knowledge that the cowry provides a home for a snail, just like other indigenous shell species.

After removal of the closure, the interior no longer appears to consist of two parts. Instead it conforms well to the model of the bowl, pre-eminently exemplified by a plate or a dish. The people recognise this model in a leaf, in which they can safely put a bit of salt, but also in a canoe. The remaining low upright edge in the centre of this empty space is left intact. Just as is the serrated edge on the back side, this upright edge in the inside is referred to as *ego*. The cavity is called *dokoo*, kom, in accordance with the different parts of a dish in its various forms. In close relationship with the Dutch word *bergkom,* 'mountain bowl', *dokoo* can be used to refer to a valley, for instance *Tigi-dokoo*, Tigi valley. Essential parts of a plate or dish are its firm, unbroken underside, a closed, surrounding wall and a round opening above. The bottom is referred to as *age*, the usual word for bottom. At this point I should mention that people accept that the bottom is not completely closed off, although a leaf should have no *mugu*, holes, whatsoever, used as it is as a bowl both practically, in the kitchen, and symbolically, in ritual. In order to serve their purpose, the bottom and sides of a dish should be so to say waterproof. Nothing should be able to enter or exit through a hole. However, when one looks at the bottom of a cowry, it is inevitably dissected by the slit referred to as the *matoka*, backbone. The term *ebe,* mouth, used for the wide opening on top, suggests placing something in the dish. The fact that it can also be used to remove something from the dish, is normally not given attention. Things enter trough a *ebe*, mouth, and, in contrast, exit through a *mugu*, hole. The rim of the side is called *eiyo*, edge, as for instance, the rim of a string bag, or the board of a canoe.

1.2.2 Seen from the inside

As the word split already indicates, the back side displays a narrow passage. In fact, the designation backbone for this split on the rear or back side only makes sense if one does not see in this a representation of a spine as seen externally, but as people can imagine, from the outside, what it looks like on the inside. Likewise, the removal of the convex, belly-like exterior at the front or upper side does not conjure up the entrails, but allows a glance into the concave interior, shaped like a bowl. As is the case with reed or bamboo, the interconnected vertebrae enclose an elongated, hollow pipe, viewed as a sort of passageway for the marrow. While the details of a cowry are named after body parts, the shell is not a reflection of the body as it appears on the outside, but [instead] as it can be imagined to be on the inside. The cowry reveals phenomena which are normally hidden to human eyes.

1.2.3 The line and the circle

Viewed internally, in analogy to a hollow tube with an opening at either end, the backbone, anus and nose on the rear side embody together the abstract, fundamental model of a line with its two extremities. In opposition to the hollow tube, the dish in the front or upper side can be interpreted as a reservoir, [which is] the abstract, just as fundamental model of a circle. Viewed as functional opposites, expressed in upper and lower side, line and circle conjoin in the cowry. Abstractly, line and circle form two oppositionally related, original symbols, referring directly to the male and female genitals, reduced to their essence. While in themselves these are elementary manifestations of principles of life, the line, analogous to a hollow pipe, imagines dynamically the typically male function of passing on, the circle, analogous to a bowl, the typically female function of receiving and preserving.[9]

1.2.4 Designated with men's names

In the sporadic instances in which a cowry is personalised and provided with a name, it is, witness the ending of the name, seen as a person of the male sex, for instance: *Duwa-uwigi-pai,* He who has just left all alone on a trading trip.

---

[9] In the cowry, van Baal (1975: 50) sees the ultimate symbol of the *vagina dentata.* The Ekagi are aware of this image and express it in the songs that accompany dances in which a woman in the end chases a man with a stick. They also imagine, in stories, a kind of primeval woman with only two teeth the size of bananas, reminiscent of the fangs of a rodent (Hylkema 1990a: 200). Maybe the crest on the bottom of the bowl suggests this symbol, but this is not likely; the opening called *ebe*, mouth, remains open. More than this crest, the hole, implied by the split, in the bottom of the bowl should worry the Ekagi. The bowl refers to the womb and not to the vagina. For the Ekagi the phallus is just as essential as the *vagina dentata.* In their relation to each other the two symbols are indivisible. Not accidentally, in the story of the primeval mother with the banana sized teeth, a giant shows up immediately to save the hero from the hands of this voracious woman. Likewise, the presence, in the cowry, of a female symbol evokes, by necessity, the oppositional male symbol in the appropriate form of a phallus, manifested in the reverse side, called backbone.

CHAPTER 2 HISTORICAL IMPORT, MYTHICALLY INTERPRETED

2.1 HISTORY AND ORIGIN

2.1.1 Dependence on import

For their cowries, traditionally the various ethnic groups in the Central Highlands, including the Ekagi, were directly and indirectly dependent on their import from the lowlands, initially from the coast. Once this fact has been established, it gives rise to more interesting questions relating to the history of the cowry [in the Central Highlands]. It is well known that the termination of the import and use of the cowry by the Ekagi is recent. However, conversely, has the historical trajectory of the beginning of its import and use ever been traced? Unquestionably, cowries were used as a means of exchange in the inter-tribal trade throughout the whole of the Central Highlands. However, in the literature, I can find no answer to the question in which direction the flow [of cowries] took place: from west to east or from east to west; or at which point cowries entered the highlands and from which coast.

In one of his studies, Pospisil (1978: 19) postulates that in the matter of cowries, the Ekagi were the first link in a trading chain which ran from west to east, and that they obtained the shells from the inhabitants of the southern lowlands, on account of the description of the latter as head-hunters and cannibals. Nevertheless, in an earlier study (1958: 126) in which he specifies the commodities which were traded inland from the Mimika coast, he notes the *woti* shell (*Melo hunteri Perry* [ba(i)ler shell]), the *dedege* or nassa shell [dog whelk], iron axes and machetes, but not the cowry.[1] A mythically coloured folk tale[2]

---

[1] By editor. Pouwer (pers. comm. 2004), who worked among the Mimika, or Kamoro, in the early 1950s, denies that they had been head-hunters and cannibals in the recent past; this notwithstanding claims to the contrary made by the Swedish traveller Lundquist (1952). Also Sierat (1999: 142-5) writes that Tillemans had come across the remains of cannibalism practised by Kamoro or Me. It is unclear how Pospisil came to his conclusion. He does not quote Lundquist. Possibly, he was relying on information provided by the Kamu Valley Me.

[2] By editor. To substantiate his arguments, Hylkema refers throughout both the cowry and the bride price manuscripts to the huge collection of what he calls 'folk tales' that he collected among the Ekagi (1990a). Introducing the compilation Hylkema (1990a: xxxvi ff) states that he refers with the term 'folk tales' to a specific genre in the oral literature of the Me. There, he distinguishes it from myths, especially myths about the origin of clans, and 'histories', relating events that took place in the time following the era of the ancestors. By contrast, the 'folk tales' that he identifies and that he refers to repeatedly in the cowry and the bride price manuscripts, describe imagined events, in both the seen and the unseen worlds. They are cast in the current, varied corpus of ideas about humankind and about the world. For this reason Hylkema found them suitable to buttress his arguments. The tale he presents in this chapter contains

from the west Mapia region (Hylkema 1990a: 233-4), states that, if nassa shells were required, these had to come from the south coast, but such stories offer no reliable information about cowries. Even after Europeans had started exploring the inland, the Ekagi showed no interest in the south coast. Also the inhabitants of the Mapia did not, despite the trading and indeed marriage relations with the inhabitants of the south coast (Boelen n.d.: 2).

Given this state of affairs, the north coast seems a much more likely place. But militating against this supposition, and indicating that cowry use is recent, is the fact that people recalled persons from the northern Mapia area whose bride prices had not included cowries. In that area the use of cowries, including their use in the bride price, never developed to the extent it did in the Kamu, Tigi and Paniai regions (Hylkema 1971-2: 92; 2002). Bearing in mind the commercial contacts between the Moni and the Paniai Ekagi, and the role the cowry played in the latter region, I wonder whether the shell did not enter the Ekagi homeland through a north-eastern gateway.[3] With the goods they had received from the Mimika coast, the Ekagi had enough to offer their eastern neighbours. At least it is remarkable that Dubbeldam, who otherwise did not touch upon this question, in an attempt to reconstruct the quantity of imported shells mentions in connection with the north-eastern highlands that bird hunters preceded a number of expeditions: 'Birdhunters (after 1910?) in the North-eastern Highlands, unknown quantities' (1964: 299). Although the author doubtingly places a question mark after the year 1910, I wonder whether the origin of the shell should not be traced back to the bird hunter.[4]

The beginning of an episode of relatively unlimited direct import into the Ekagi area more or less coincided with the arrival and establishment of administrative and missionary bodies in 1938. As well as money, these bodies also used the shell to buy food and building materials and to pay workers. And mindful of this purpose, to cut a long story short, cowries were imported by the tin and bag full.[5] [6] In this process a distinction can be made between indigenous and

---

elements of both a historical tale, since it relates events of the past, and of a 'folk tale', since it adds imagined events.

3 North-eastern gateway here refers to the watershed between the valleys of the Degeuwo [or Kema] and the Aga rivers. The first flows north into Cenderawasih Bay, the second runs in a south-westerly direction and debouches into Lake Paniai. In myths the gateway is identified with the Topiyoi-mogo mountain ridge to the west of the upper reaches of the Aga, seen as counterpart of the peak of Mount Monibago lying to the east, which is referred to at the moment by the ethnic name Moni, in the Me language 'Mou', *Moni ka bagee*.

4 By editor. Hylkema is very brief on this issue. I return to it in the Conclusion, part 4 of this monograph.

5 Benny Giay reported that Weakebo Mote returned from a visit to Ambon in 1941 with a five-gallon oil drum full of cowries (1995: 39). [By editor] Weakebo was a

exogenous importers. When the external importers stopped the trade, a move closely associated with the administrative handing over of the Netherlands to Indonesia in 1963, the indigenous people had already embarked on this venture and they continued the import until the moment at which the cowry had been actually denuded of all its value. Enterprising Ekagi, designated as shell hunters, in analogy with the well-known figure of the bird hunter, undertook not only long journeys by foot to the east through the mountains; they even bought aeroplane tickets to transport themselves to the eastern half of the island [as far as the boundary with Papua New Guinea]. Their preferred destinations were the Keerom via Jayapura and the eastern highlands, the Baliem Valley and the Star Mountains. Recalling the question of the historical origin of the shell, it is remarkable that to do this, initially they had to set out in an easterly direction. And only later, when these areas just mentioned had been scoured, did they go northwards, to the north coast and to islands such as Biak. Apparently these journeys were so profitable that they were not afraid to purchase relatively expensive airline tickets and to buy goods for barter in Jayapura.[7]

There was a conspicuous difference between the outsider and the indigenous import in terms of the quality of the shells. Although foreigners imported both mature and young shells indiscriminately, local people chose only those examples which would represent a high value within the compass of their own world.

2.1.2 Diffusion of wealth

The simultaneous importation of both money and shells created a remarkable situation, in the sense that, on the one hand the monetary and the shell

---

famous leader in the early phase of the colonial era. See also Boelen (n.d.: 182 et seq.) and Giay 1999.

[6] By editor. But compare Introduction, p. 9.

[7] Speaking in general about these trading ventures the question to what extent people plunged themselves into a completely unfamiliar adventure. I have known two of these men extremely well. The first of them was Marius Bobii, [whom I got to know] when I was priest in the Apmisibil, 1961-9. In the strictest sense of the word, Marius had no relatives there. However, on account of his work for the Catholic mission as the agent of the AMA [the mission aviation service], he had made such a name for himself and had put so many people under an obligation that he could fall back on the local Ekagi teachers. Furthermore, there was also Tomas Tokogo, at Mogodagi, whom I knew when I was posted to Epouto. Tomas had a partner in the Apmisibil in the person of his brother, who was serving as a teacher there. They corresponded regularly with each other. His brother paid for his flight and also introduced him to his own local connections. Because he had involved nobody in Epouto in his trip, the home-front was remarkably reserved about his enterprise. The general opinion was that Tomas would not allow anybody to share in the fruits of his venture, but would use all the shells he had acquired exclusively for his own socio-political purposes.

economies functioned separately side by side, yet on the other the systems flourished interwoven with each other. Money circulated in a gradually expanding circuit consisting of outsiders and indigenous people. In contrast, although shells were used as payment by outsiders, they refused to accept them. They circulated only within the indigenous circuit. It is astonishing that, as had originally been feared, the shell economy did not collapse entirely as a consequence of this unrestricted import, but was still maintained for decades alongside an ever growing monetary economy.

Just as the shell economy had only been able to develop as a result of a significant import, it was likewise dependent on import for its survival. Cowries, and certainly in the way the Ekagi treated them, are very liable to damage. One of the top priorities demanded of a cowry was that it be externally unblemished. Although, despite stains and tears, our paper money retains its status as legal currency, the cowry cedes more of its status the more it appears less than perfect.[8] A shell which might have been called 'shabby' or displayed such defects as 'a torn-off nose' disappeared from circulation as a matter of course, because when it was all said and done, such an object could not be palmed off on anybody.

I suppose that, before the opening up of the area, the limited import on the one hand and wear and tear on the other, meant that the number of cowries remained more or less constant.[9] [10] It is a fact that after the opening up, proportionally the quantity of cowries imported far outweighed the loss. However, this did not sound the death knell of the shell system. On the contrary, the import initially intensified it and made it more complex than traditionally may have been the case among the Ekagi, in contrast to the situation in other ethnic groups. Simultaneously, it intensified the pre-existing social structure. Astonishingly, despite the distribution among all layers of society which accompanied the import, the antagonistic division into *yakaagaa*, the younger generation, and *meibaagaa*, the older generation, and within the older generation the split between the *ibo*, higher, and *daba*, lower, less prestigious, with at the top elite

---

[8] It can be remarked that after the introduction of paper money, grimy, crumpled or torn notes were also regularly refused.

[9] Also in the event of fire -- a happening, by the way, which was relatively rare despite the use of an open fire and combustible materials-- large numbers of cowries were lost. Recently, people almost routinely state after a fire that a relatively large sum of money has gone up in flames. While in the first case the charcoaled remains could be presented when making a claim, in the latter case people had to take the victims' word.

[10] By editor. The Dutch version of 'opening up' is the stock expression by which Hylkema refers to the initial incorporation of the Ekagi area into the colonial state.

figures referred to as *tonowi*, rich men, endured for a great many years in close relationship to the availability of the cowry.

Whereas in former times the older generation had been able to place the younger generation in its debt by loans, and in the case of the rich men, the less fortuned members of their own generation as well as the younger people, by the second half of the 1950s an unequivocal change had set in. As money was disseminated and gained in importance, in the indigenous society shell and money became more readily transferable. The upshot was that first of all the traditional rich man, whose wealth was founded on shells, had to cede ground to the new rich man, whose riches were counted in money, and secondly, the younger generation was in a position to act more independently of both types of wealthy men. No longer could a rich man bridle and manipulate his debtor by indicating his debt, because the debtor could pay off his dues. Or, as Cecilia Degei[11] remarked: now there is an abundance of shells and money is 'as abundant as the white crests on the waves on the lake'. Now everyone is a *tonowi* (1976b). How did people try to keep this situation under control?

2.1.3 Distinction between old and new shells

What this import did lead to was a division in the stock of shells. Ever since the commencement of this regular import, people had referred to shells from before the opening up as *tota mege*, indigenous cowry, with the connotation of being authentic, or as *meiba ka mege*, literally 'the cowry of the older generation', or, referring to where they were found, as *peku mege*, [from the] lake [originating] cowry. Generally speaking, the opposite to *tota*, local, already present, indigenous, is the term *meta*, come from somewhere else, exogenous. But this latter term is actually never used in combination with shells, probably because there are yet more distinctions made among the exogenous shells. In contrast, such designations as *tuani ka mege*, white people's own cowry, and *ogai ka mege*, stranger's own cowry, or with reference to the place where they are found *age mege*, lowland shells, and *Waris ka mege*, Waris shells,[12] or simply just as *waris* are employed.[13]

---

[11] By editor. Cecilia Degei is the mother of Isaias Tekege, Hylkema's key informant in the Paniai-Tage region.

[12] Waris is the name of a village with an airstrip in the Keerom area to which people used to have themselves transported via Jayapura. [By editor] Hylkema does not make it clear why Me men who wanted to obtain cowries went inland to Waris, rather than stay in coastal Jayapura.

[13] Here we come across a process which is also revealed in the change of name from Mou to Moni. Initially, in the Ekagi language area, the Mou were alternatively called *Moni ka bagee*, referring to the mountain peak Moni [see also note 2]. Gradually this term of reference fell into disuse and Moni simply began to function as the name of the ethnic group. Moreover, in the same fashion the inhabitants of Mapia were probably

In the literature, the indigenous shells are more precisely referred to as Maldive cowries belonging to the genus *Cypraea moneta* (Dubbeldam 1964: 294). In contrast it is tempting to lump all the exogenous shells together as Zanzibar cowries of the genus *Cypraea annulus*, the ring cowry (De Bruijn 1952: 10 [1955c: 534]).[14] This is incorrect. Given the fact that both types were current in the Grand Valley (Dubbeldam 1964: 294), it can be assumed that the shell hunters there and elsewhere selected the cowries meticulously.
The money cowry has a thick yellowish-white upper section; it is rectangular with an irregular protruding lip, and the serrations are very close together. The ring cowry varies from greyish white to mouse-grey, with an orange circle on its dorsum, it is oval or round in circumference; the lip does not protrude and exhibits no irregularities. The serrations are somewhat more widely spaced [Hylkema abstracted the passage above from Dubbeldam 1964: 294].
Among the Ekagi, the latter type rapidly lost all its value and was used only in trade with members of other ethnic groups.

The import of mature and young cowries introduced a new form of household industry. Men could keep themselves busy for hours altering the appearance of imported, new *iyaa* shells of the money cowry to look like older, *wei*, shells which had been in circulation a long time.[15] Generally speaking, older shells of this type can be distinguished by their white colour and a certain roughness, whereas new shells are covered with a yellow wax, *bitu yago,* and are smooth to the touch. Quite apart from this, as new shells were used they naturally aged

---

initially called *Simogi ka bagee,* referring to that particular mountain peak, and then later simply called Simogi.

[14] By editor. Hylkema's first reference is to a *Dienstnota*, an unpublished administrative report by de Bruijn. In the course of his discussion he refers a number of times to this document, a copy of which was among his papers. In the mid-1950s, the editors of the *Adatrechtbundel* 45 published the report in four separate papers: de Bruijn 1955a, b, c and d. The text as published in de Bruijn 1955a mentions that he collected the data in September/October 1952 when he had been temporarily charged with the administration of the Paniai area 'owing to special circumstances'(1955a: 324). De Bruijn does not elaborate. Nor does he mention the episode in his autobiography (1978).

[15] As a shell ages, the bottom of the inside darkens because of matter adhering to it. Eventually, even spider webs are spun on the inside (Jan Tebai, Timeepa, Mapia region). To achieve this effect probably various techniques were applied. People could dribble pig's blood on the bottom [of a shell] and let it soak in and dry in the sun or under the roof. The bottom could also be spread with honey-comb, on top of which the brown powder obtained from a mushroom which had crumbled to dust was sprinkled. It was then hoped that the dust, fluff and small feathers which are normally to be found in a trouser pocket or at the bottom of a shoulder bag, would strengthen the effect (Isaias Tekege). Usually the outside was rubbed at length with tufts of grass to get rid of the yellow wax. See further Pospisil (1958: 127) [and chapter 3, sub-section 3.1.1].

steadily, so that shells which had been imported around 1938 could also be classified as 'old' some twenty years later (Dubbeldam 1964: 295). This makes it all the more remarkable that shells that had been imported from elsewhere, for instance from Waris, continued to be nominally distinguished from shells that had been obtained by inheritance, also when they were of high quality and had been in use for a long time. This added yet another distinction to the already existing classification in named value categories and varieties.

2.2 *EPIC/MYTHICAL REVIEW*

2.2.1 *Reaction to the first aeroplane*

This aspect will be gone into in greater detail below, but in order to put the subject in its proper perspective, a short introduction will be given at this point. How people reacted to this fairly abrupt influx of shells can be heard in the reminiscences of Eduard Tatogo of Uwebutu, recorded in January 1974. He was the, recently married, grandson of one of the men involved. In the language of epic poetry, these recollections touch upon all sorts of representations and customs which are actually part and parcel of current culture and which therefore should be interpreted within its parameters.[16]

Traditionally, people were familiar with the image of a spirit which moved or flew over through the air. This image is recalled in one of the names by which the primeval man is referred to: *wadouga ka mee*, the being who passes by overhead. Now it is also the case that the, in this event 'heavenly', male being is no more than the other side of the 'earthly' or 'subterranean' female being. It so happens that if the one breaks adrift, it can be assumed the same fate has befallen the other. Corresponding to the apparition of the male being in the air is a manifestation of the female being in the water. His appearance can actually be interpreted ambiguously. He may presage disaster, but he may also be the harbinger of good fortune. The way the people react to him is equally ambivalent. Their first impulse is to shut him out, but then they want to keep him. On the basis of the place allotted to man in the general order of things, it is typically his task to transform imminent calamity into good fortune. Both these reactions are expressed in the sacrifice. Now, years later, people can be heard saying that when an amphibian plane, actually a Catalina flying-boat, flew overhead for the first time, people were thrown into a complete panic and as a reaction sacrificed pigs at the mouths of the rivers. From the temporal point of view, this can be understood in the sense of *kabo duwai*, setting a limit, and *iyeiye tai*, instilling good manners or bringing someone to their senses. But, after this, people began to interpret their own reaction by drawing an analogy with the sacrifice for the first-born in the concrete form of *yoka paga duwai*, preparing a

---

[16] For the underlying corpus of ideas see *Oorsprong en Leven [Origin and life]* chapter 6 'Geïnstitutionaliseerd in the *Wegee Bagee*, p. 223, pro manuscripto [Hylkema n.d.].

birth ceremony, in the dual sense of imbuing the initially extremely weak newborn child with strength and awakening those yet to be born.[17]

2.2.2 The report of the Club of Kotomoma

Just as ambivalent as the reaction had been at that time, is the report of this reaction given below. During the translation it appeared that various expressions were open to more than one interpretation. When asked to repeat what he had said, it became apparent that the informant had difficulty in reconciling generally accepted [cultural] conceptions and the fictionalised course of events.[18]

> Once, long ago, when my father was still a little boy, five men journeyed to a *yuwo*, a pig feast, in Kotomoma.

A village of the Boma clan, situated at the foot of the Ogiyaidimi Pass, over which runs a footpath which goes from the Obaano Vale to the Kamu Valley.[19] Although it had never attracted much attention, in the 1970s this valley still flourished as a centre of the syncretistic sect of the *Wegee Bagee* [analysed by Giay (1995)].

> On the way in Mogoya, they heard news that in the Puyai Valley … [The rest of the sentence is missing in Hylkema's manuscript].

Mogoya is a hamlet on the shore of Lake Paniai, a quarter of an hour's walk from the Obaano Valley. The Puyai Valley lies in an extension of Deyaatei, 'the anchorage place at the mouth of the Deya River',[20] in the north-easterly inlet of Lake Paniai. From the time of the first flight, the mountain pass between Puyai, which lies to the north of this, and the Vale of Deya which is situated to the south, was the normal entrance to the Paniai region on the flight route Nabire – Enarotali; whether this is relevant or not in connection with what follows, it should be added that the word *pudai* in the Mapia region is used in the sense of 'the women's quarters'.

---

[17] By editor. Hylkema's Dutch term for this ceremony is *kraammaal,* confinement meal. In this book I use instead 'birth ceremony', the term used by Pospisil (1978: 65). I prefere that term because it makes it clear that the event involves more than just a meal.

[18] By editor. To make the report easier readable, I have indented its text.

[19] By editor. The Obaano river flows into Lake Paniai from the west. The Puyai valley is located north of the Obaano valley.

[20] It should be remarked that as well as this hamlet of Deyaatei, there is another such hamlet of the same name with a mixed population of Ekagi, Moni and Dani, north of the north-easterly entrance [to the Ekagi area], situated on the banks of the Degeuwo river. [By editor. This river is mentioned in the north-eastern corner of map 2. It is the Me name for the Kema river. Le Roux phoneticised the name as Derewo (1948-50, map in the back of vol. 3)].

> They pursued their journey to Kotomoma and lodged there with the Boma. That night, without interruption, they told each other folk tales, stories about what had happened in the past.

Stereotypically, people refer to killing time at such gatherings as recounting *teeta*, folk tales, or *tika kei tita mana*, historical events; witness the sequel in which Eduard meant to say that people told each other about events, which had still to take place at the moment of the telling, in other words people were prophesying coming events.

> One person began by saying: 'Friends, later there will be a constant throbbing of boats sailing over there on Lake Paniai.' This refers to a motorboat. Then another said: 'Who among you still does not know that in time to come there will be a constant succession of *wuukoma*, roaring boats, aeroplanes?' After that yet another chimed in and said that the *manita* will also arrive.

Here they were talking about a water demon, supposed to live in the lake, which manifested itself in the form of a water snake, the 'mother' of fishes.

> Naturally she was already present, but she would come again a second time. This was a reference to the fish.[21] All of this did indeed come to pass, everything they had said, even before the strangers had ever set foot there. The people went on to recount that each of these strangers would also bring an abundance of Deiyai materials with them.

Here for the first time a distinction is being made between *dokii*, to bring a person a thing that belongs to him or her, and *makii*, sending someone something. *Deiyai kagaba*, [is] the standard name for a sort of red cloth, Ind. *kain merah*, which was universally used as a contact commodity during the opening up of the Highlands. As the name indicates, normally its origins were associated with the regional centre, the peak of Mount Deiyai.[22] One of the female spirits who dwelled there, *Deiyai ka abe*, was to present this to the people. Furthermore, this succinct report raises the question of whether this location is indeed the original one. Possibly the original name was *Deya kagaba*, referring to the mountain pass on the flight route.

> After this, yet other people spoke of an abundance of shells that would pour in; is there perhaps someone who still does not know about this?

When the text was transcribed, several crucial words were lost; on the basis of the main theme of the argument it is possible to insert the noun 'shells'. There is the more reason to do so, given the use of the verb 'come' in the following sentence.

---

[21] By editor. I suppose this remark refers to the fact that the Dutch colonial administration stocked the lakes with fish [Hylkema 2002: 236].

[22] By editor. Deiyai is the tallest mountain in the range separating the area of the three Paniai Lakes and the Kamu basin.

All these commodities will come exclusively with the intention of seeking us out

As is the Indonesian word *kejar*, *eubai*, to look for somebody, is an extremely ambivalent expression. On occasion it has to be translated as 'look for/hunt somebody' in the sense of 'to afflict with signs of disgrace', 'to go after somebody'. In that case, the second part of the sentence should be translated as 'Friends, what shall we do, because unless we take steps we will come to grief?' However, on other occasions *eubai* means to seek somebody in the sense of 'strive for', or 'to associate with', for instance in the standard phrase 'Love God with all one's heart, soul and mind' [Mark 12: 30]. In the first use calamity is presaged, in the second good fortune. Because below *eubai*, to seek someone, is exchanged for 'to take someone with one, in a house, boat, etcetera', in the sense of 'to save someone from the brink of death, to bring to safety', as God shall one day take to Himself everybody who seeks for Him, the balance is finally tipped towards this latter meaning. Not only had the arrival of all these goods been prophesised earlier, there was also no real reason to be surprised or thrown into a panic when motorboats, aeroplanes, fish, red cloth and shells appeared with the whites. It had been foretold that all these commodities were intended for the people, de *mee*: the Ekagi, in other words they were not for the whites.

At this point attention is drawn to the fact that all which does not participate in human life, -- especially spirits, but to no lesser extent and in close association with these spirits, the various clan territories -- strives to recruit a particular partner chosen personally in the world of humankind in order to form an alliance. Generally this prophesy is put forward as corroboration of the idea that the means of transport mentioned, and in this case the fish as well, were set aside for [Dutch: *bestemd voor*] the Ekagi, or were endowed on the Ekagi,[23] and that the strangers were accorded no more than a subsidiary role in this bestowal. Their task was limited to supplying and distributing the goods to the local population. After they had acquitted themselves of this task, they should have withdrawn. In search of a pretext, not simply to extend their stay indefinitely, but moreover to be able to maintain a dominant position, they kept on post-poning this transference. On the one hand, in the original the *ogai*, strangers, are presented in the guise of importers; on the other, the goods arrive as it were without any agency.

The appeal to prophecies is general. The particular aspect of this version is that these prophecies are localised in Kotomoma. By situating the prophecies locally, it seems that the Boma of Kotomoma wanted to distinguish themselves in competition with other clans and locations. The Tatogo of Uwebutu could

---

[23] By editor. Here, Hylkema had written '*toegeschikt*', a word resembling the German *zugeschickt*, 'sent to'. I take it he meant, in Dutch, *bestemd voor*, in accordance with the meaning of the verb in the next clause.

agree with this because they belonged to the same phratry of seven clans as the Boma.[24]

> 'This, friends, is the reason we have to do something to prevent their purpose failing in the future, but what?' said the men that night. Then yet another took over the story and said: 'Friends, on the day on which the aeroplane flies over, we must slaughter adult pigs at the mouths of the various rivers'. Indeed, because an aeroplane suddenly flew over, people slaughtered adult pigs valued at twenty shells a beast at the mouths of the rivers,

Although no longer understood in a literal sense for a very long time, still a common designation for a fully grown pig.

> precisely as people had already agreed beforehand. One of the series of pronouncements then made in advance said: 'If the aeroplanes fly and then the motorboats drive about, their single, solitary goal is to save us, *ebukai*'. Then it was already being said that the aeroplane would return, because everywhere people had exchanged pigs for shells, at all the mouths of the rivers. People continued these conversations day in and day out, night in and night out, and in the process uttered all sorts of prophecies.

> Thereafter they clubbed a pig to death, at night. 'Friends', people said, 'let us seek out a place where the river flows into Lake Paniai to slaughter it, because motorboats, aeroplanes and shells are already on their way.' In order to distribute, *wudii*, the shells which had already come in via the Pudai Valley to various places, people slaughtered, after the arrival of the first specimens, a pig valued at twenty shells in exchange for a bunch [of shells] bound together with a grass stalk. In this fashion, using these shells, during a quick trip around the Paniai, Kamu and Tigi Valleys, people slaughtered pigs at the mouths of various rivers. This was done so that the shells would gain in strength.

In other words, at the moment the shells appeared, they were as limp as a newborn babe; however, according to another interpretation, people wanted 'to build dams' at the mouths of the rivers, *tai kabo duw ai*, in order to keep *madou*, the water demon of the Underworld, under control, to ensure that the fertility of the gardens would not be destroyed by the waters of the lake.

> When this had been done, they distributed, in every direction, the shells which had come up through the Pudai Valley. As they returned to Uwebutu, bringing with them these shells from the pig feast at Kotomoma, they visited pig feasts during the journey and distributed the

---

[24] By editor: None the less, Uwebuto is located at the western tip of Lake Tage, at some distance from Kotomoma.

shells for these people. With the shells they had brought with them they paid for a pig worth twenty shells and at the foot of the mountain

Mount Minou, in the Uwe Valley

they clubbed the animal to death. Having killed it, they purified the shells of any dirt or blood which was adhering to them during a communal meal.

The meal was to promote the sturdiness of the shells, just as the birth ceremony, that includes a sacrificial meal, is to promote the sturdiness of the newly born child.

When the shells had been cleaned, they were immediately put into circulation.[25] Directly after their return from the pig feast, the Tatogo bought two pigs with the shells. A prediction made there [at Kotomoma] said: 'Friends, whether the aeroplane and the motorboat will come depends on if we, our older and younger brothers and our children, treat the shells in the same manner. For, long ago people already possessed shells from the lake; these were *kawane*. Because people had always used the *kawane* as payment for meat, now they spread the shells in this same manner.

[The *kawane* is] a type of cowry, in the meantime devalued to virtually nothing in the Paniai region. As a variation on the division into *tota mege* and *meta mege*, original and imported cowries, here a distinction is made between *peku mege*, [from the] lake [originating] shells, and shells which have come from elsewhere (via a mountain pass as entry gateway), in analogy with the mythically supported division of the clans into autochthonous clans, that had appeared from the lake, and allochthonous clans, that had come from outside the area. Generally speaking, a characteristic of this clan-centrism is that the devaluation of this primordial type [of cowry] does not prevent those concerned from claiming its origin.

Another prediction which was raised at [that] night said: 'Friends, there will come a time when houses will be built on the bed of the lake, because one day Lake Paniai will dry up.' But this prophecy has not yet come to pass.

This pronouncement may perhaps refer to the competition between the various regions to have the future capital established within their area; in view of the fact that at this moment (1997) there are once again serious plans afoot to build this in the eastern part of the Paniai Valley, it seems as if the prediction will be satisfactorily fulfilled (compare Giay 1995: 158).

Yet another prophecy foretold: 'Dear Friends, one day in the future there will be a famine, where will we have to go to obtain food, sweet potatoes?' This was interrupted by another speaker who said: Dear friend,

---

[25] In this epic-mythical representation, the principle is that the quality of a shell can no longer reasonably be called into doubt as long as it has passed the test in the framework of the transaction of the pork.

> we shall have no other option but to die, because in the end it is death which conquers all.' Yet another broke in to say: 'Friends, don't worry, after all the others have died one after the other, once the famine is over, the last person to survive will once again have a son to continue humanity.'

The central idea of the cult of the syncretistic *Wegee Bagee* which has its centre in the Pugo Valley is that at least one sweet potato and one human being will survive, so that once the famine has passed, the thread can be picked up again; in his heart everybody hopes that this honour of being the only person to survive will fall to him.

> After they had taken part in the discussions for days on end, and after they had distributed the shells in every direction, they built separate houses for the shells at various spots. My grandfather, Yawaiyaawii Tatogo, did that here. He built a special house in which to keep the shells. Every time he was sent new Deiyai materials, he was also sent shells, *makii*. He did not spend one single one of those shells for his own benefit, *mapugai*.[26] After the death of my grandfather, gradually all the shells which were sent to him disappeared into the water, one after the other.

This expression was often used with reference to the payment of fines; to which the following bears witness. It can be understood here in the context of the holding of sacrificial meals.

> Gradually the shells got beyond reach, as these shells were constantly being distributed ever farther a field. People have sacrificed all the shells that originally had come in via the Puyai Valley, in order to pay for the pigs killed to hold the sacrificial meal.

The following answer was given to the question, 'Who sent these shells?'

> Somebody from Nabire, my grandfather did tell me the name, but I have forgotten it.

Possibly he was thinking of a personage in the Jou myth of origin, who was said to have gone to Nabire many generations ago; but after consultation with others he continued in a purely mythical vein:

> *Deyai kagaba abe*, the Deyai cloth spirit woman, visited him repeatedly to deliver shells. Every time he had spent a shell to pay for pork, he had received a new one, and every time that the spirit woman had brought him a new delivery, every three to five months, and a pile had built up in the four corners of the house he had built, she would disappear once again. Nobody else was allowed to enter the house; only he and that only during

[26] In this report, three expressions are introduced in succession, all characteristically used in the framework of the bride price: on the one hand *mege makii*, send shells to somebody and on the other *mege wudii*, parcel out the shells, distribute them, with as the unworthy, uneconomic alternative *mege mapugai*, to spend the shells, squander them.

> the day. It was a warehouse, a repository of shells. If he had ever spent those shells for something else, he would have fallen ill. This is why he kept the shells in that house. Whenever he caught any game, he invariably first left this in that house for a night. Then he prepared it; either in that house or in his own home.

These sorts of buildings were to be found dispersed throughout the whole of the Ekagi area, for instance both at Potigouda, south of Lake Paniai and at Abaimaida in the Mapia region. Generally they were said to be used as a birth house by a snake, which was closely associated with an *abe*, a female spirit. In her manifestation as a snake, the female spirit gave birth to these shells (compare Giay 1995: 145 [and see also chapter 25, section 25.5]).[27]

The ideas, usages and rituals mentioned here are ripe for focused, thematic research and description. However, the available material is too extensive to make it part of a study of the bride price. The above report, time- and place-determined as it is, refers prosaically to a corpus of ideas that several tales elaborate and play upon, as in a fairy tale. When these tales refer to the *abe,* the female spirit, they often do so in the most charming manner. Below we return to the points which are relevant to the position of the cowry in Ekagi society.

---

[27] By editor. Below Hylkema repeatedly refers to this story as 'the report of the "Club of Kotomoma"'. This seems to be an allusion to report of the Club of Rome, which was also concerned with the future. If this is so, it is also likely that Hylkema heard the story shortly after the latter report was published in the mid-1970s.

CHAPTER 3 CHARACTERISTICS, CATEGORIES AND VALUES

3.1 COMMONLY USED ADJECTIVAL MODIFIERS

3.1.1 Qualitative dichotomies

[As mentioned above] the Ekagi divide their stock of cowries into two groups, using the past participles *tota* and *meta* of the verbs *tou,* to be, and *mei*, to come, used as adjectives. Moreover, dichotomies are made within the entire stock, or within a specific category, by using several pairs of adjectives.

A. *wei* – *iyaa*. Closely linked to the distinction between indigeneity and extraneity, shells are first contrasted using the terms *wei*, already dry, and *iyaa*, still completely fresh, wet. *Wei* can be specified more precisely in either direction by using the terms *poko*, mature, hard, worn-out, and *weike*, gradually drying out. *Iyaa* can be defined more specifically by adding the contrasting set of adjectives *bune* and *dege*. Whereas the qualification *iyaa bune* indicates that the shell is part of a group which is still fairly fresh, *iyaa dege* indicates that it is still classified in the group completely fresh. The terms *bune* and *dege* will be discussed below. The words chosen call to mind an organism that was once alive and is either not yet or already quite petrified. In practice, all these qualifications were [also] used for wood. Although in the case of a cowry, it is the shell which most readily springs to mind, in one of the folk tales there is an explicit reference to the snail which made its home in the shell.[1]

B. *ibo* – *weneka* / *yoka*. Sometimes shells are distinguished by employing the adjective *ibo*. The standard opposites are *weneka* and *yoka*. Literally *ibo* means large, and it is tempting to translate *ibo mege* as large shells. However, often certain shells are designated as *ibo* which are certainly no larger and may even be smaller in comparison to others. As regards dichotomising shells, both pairs of words *ibo* and *weneka* and *ibo* and *yoka* are used metaphorically. In analogy to the use of both terms in the case of shells, people distinguish within a group of two or more brothers, purely on the basis of seniority and regardless of length, between *ibo*, Ind. *kakak*, elder brother, and *weneka*, Ind. *adik*, younger brother, or, on the basis of generation, within two lineages between *ibo*, parent, and *yoka*, child. Whereas qualifiers on the grounds of a difference in age or family imply a hierarchical ordering, when these are used in conjunction with the shells this is explicit. Consequently *ibo mege* can only be translated adequately as 'shells of high value.' The terms *weneka* and *yoka* are used less in this case. Although in translation the expression 'low value' can be used, it seems that people are not referring to the really worthless shells, but only those which are mediocre or ordinary.[2] On the basis of the unilateral use of *ibo*, it is

---

[1] By editor. Hylkema refers here to a passage in his collection of folk tales, 1990a: 233-4, where, however, there is no mention of a snail.

[2] By editor. Compare the word use in Hylkema's dictionary 1990a: 393.

possible to draw the conclusion that certain highly valued categories are differentiated among the stock of cowries.

C. *etike – aka*. Especially among the shells to which a high value is attributed, is it possible to make a division using the opposite pair of adjectives *etike* and *ake*. Both terms are primarily used in the sense of 'left' and 'right', for instance in combination with hands. Just as in Dutch, both qualifications contain a connotation of better and worse. This sense comes into full play when evaluating high quality shells, rather similar to our expressions of first and second class.

D. *buna – dege*. Finally, usually in connection with the sorts of shells with a mediocre value, the pair of adjectives *buna* and *dege* was used. Although, with reference to colour, these two adjectives can be translated as dark and light, it seems that colour actually plays no role at all in the classification of shells. Often, a shell qualified as *buna* was actually whiter than one qualified as *dege*. As in the definition *ibo*, highly valued, *buna* and *dege* were used separately, but here the one just as much as the other. In this instance too, the metaphorical significance can be gauged by the way they are used to denote the relative age of brothers. The vocabulary provides only four terms by which to relate brothers to each other, for example *mabii*, the second youngest brother, and *amooye*, youngest brother. If there are five or six sons, the terms *mabii* and *amooye* can be distinguished by the use of the adjectives *buna* and *dege*. Irrespective of whether the one is lighter or darker coloured than the other, the *mabii* or *amooye* [who is] born earlier than the other is specified by the used of *buna*, and the one born later by *dege*. The idea of a hierarchical order embodied in seniority is made explicit when the adjectives *buna* and *dege* are combined with shells. The most important implicit message in the expression *buna bodiya* is that this sort of *bodiya* occupied a place approximately halfway in the recognised hierarchical ladder among the cowries. Furthermore, it implies that qualitatively this particular specimen is a first class *bodiya*.

E. *ida* - … .[3] In yet another approach the shells can be described as *ida* and … in the sense of substantial and void, according to whether they in fact do or do not function [as a means of exchange], despite all [their] good or bad characteristics.

In the above, the adjectives in front of the nouns define an individual specimen of the category concerned, for instance *buna bodiya* means a higher quality *bodiya*. When the definition is placed after the noun, for instance *bodiya buna*, the shell concerned was being identified as belonging to the higher quality group within the category *bodiya*. In fact, to be correct people should say *bodiya buna bodiya*, but this is seldom heard.

---

[3] By editor. The word contrasting with *ida* was not mentioned in the manuscript.

3.1.2 Purely formal adjectives

In addition to the typically contrasting pairs of adjectives used to refer to the qualitative categorisation of the shells, on other occasions other terms were used attributively with the general name *mege*, but usually in combination with the name of a category, such as *yoo* or *bodiya*. Some, such as *nau*, *deke* and *katagita* or *mukata*, referred to the specific shape. A cowry was said to be *nau* if the sides displayed no cracks, which meant that they appeared more oval and less rhomboid. *Deke* was applied if the sides of the rhomboid shape were unusually long, so that the *yuma*, nose, appeared more pointed than usual and also the *ebe*, mouth, tended to appear more elongated than rounded. *Katagita* or *mukata* indicated that the shell looked unusually flat.

3.1.3 Geographical adjectives

Sometimes, shells were defined by a geographical name, for example *Tage-bodiya*. Nominally this shell is being accorded a nexus with the Tage Valley, but this connection was not further elaborated. To interpret this usage, a place of origin springs to mind, but it is possible the reference was to a regional preference.

3.1.4 Specific adjectives

Sometimes, the noun was defined with the help of another noun functioning as a generic name. For instance, a distinction was made between *kubawi-yoo*, *muka-yoo, nono-yoo* and *munidagi-yoo*. This combination leads to the supposition that, as well as being divided up according to their general shape, cowries were also separated on the basis of their individual value. Category and value did not coincide. Although identified as *kubawi*, shells of this category could be given different values, according to their specific characteristics.

Especially when the term *bodiya* was used, this could easily lead to confusion. With *bodiya* shells, category and value frequently coincided, but sometimes it appeared that a shell categorised as *bodiya* was equivalent in value to the categorically more highly rated *yoodagi*.

3.2 REGIONALLY VALUED CATEGORIES AND CATEGORIES

3.2.1 Names

Besides the generic name *mege*, cowry, there was a host of other special names used to specify all of the shells according to type or category. As is often the case with designations, these special names can also be linked to existing words. For instance, the basic meaning of the noun *bodiya* is fire, of *yuu* shouting, cheering, while *mitouyautuuya* can be parsed and translated as 'in between two bones', meaning the *radius* and the *ulna*. The connection is purely extrinsic. Closer investigation using these nominal specifications produces interesting results.

Superficial contacts do justify the conclusion that the cowry was used as a means of payment throughout the whole of the Ekagi area. However, more detailed research has revealed that the manner of their use was anything but uniform; consequently generalisations formed on the basis of region- and period-determined research are somewhat premature. Synchronically, cowry use was strongly determined by region. Moreover, also within regions diachronic shifts were taking place.

3.2.2 Data from the Mapia region

During the time I spent at Timeepa in the Mapia region in the 1970s, it was more or less by chance that I was confronted with the names *bodiya*, *katage* and *kawane,* used as names of shells inspired by their size and shape. For instance, on occasion a series of shells threaded onto a string was referred to as *bodiya* and *katage*. This prompts the conclusion that both types of shells were regarded as of high value in the region. In order to make manifest how poor seven brothers were, a folk tale relates (Hylkema 1990a: 11) about the six older brothers that they did not have any shells with them; and about the youngest that he owned only one *kawane*. This was actually a *kawane* which was no longer valid, in other words was not worth a cent. This seems to sum up the local value adequately.

3.2.3 Data from the Kamu region

Broadly speaking, the data given below are also relevant to the situation in Tigi, making it possible to speak of the Kamu-Tigi region. On the basis of research carried out in the Kamu region in the 1950s, Pospisil distinguished a number of denominations among the cowries. Having first (1958: 117) given the value of each in the type of beads which were then being used, later (1978: 18f) he expressed this in terms of their exchange value among each other. The first he mentioned was the cheapest, elliptically shaped, fairly smooth *kawane* (two to three beads). Five *kawane* were given the equivalent value of one *tuanika mege*, a shell 'originating from the whites', that is: a recently imported shell (two to eight beads). Only its newness distinguished a *tuanika mege* from the rectangular, fairly uneven, but qualitatively much more valuable *bomoye* only by its newness. Among the *bomoye* a distinction was made between the *dege bomoye* (approximately thirty-five beads) with a general value of fifteen *kawane* and *buna bomoye* (approximately forty beads) with a general value of twenty *kawane*.[4] Two other sorts of shells of high value mentioned by Pospisil were the

---

[4] As mentioned, although with reference to colour they should be translated with 'light' and 'dark', this combination has nothing to do with colour; it merely indicates a difference in value.

epaa mege[5] (approximately sixty beads) and the *bodiya* (sixty to 360 beads). In value the *epaa mege* was equivalent to two *bomoye*, but even though the *bodiya* invariably surpassed the *epaa mege* in value, it was said that its value, based on the size of the shell, could vary, so that when exchanged the rate was sometimes one *bodiya* to ten to twelve *bomoye*.[6]

Discussing the market value of the various shells, Pospisil notes that a piece of pork weighing about two kilos normally sold for one *bomoye*. This observation gives us a point of comparison in connection with the systems current in the Kamu-Tigi and the Paniai-Tage regions. Strangely enough, the *bomoye*, which Pospisil had earlier generalised as 'the most frequent type of native money encountered in the Papuan trade' (1978: 19) was nominally recognised as a specific category in the Paniai-Tage region. There, however, it was seen as a category typical of the Kamu-Tigi region. Hence, it was held in so little regard that it could not be exchanged for meat and, where possible, was excluded from intra-regional barter.

The data can be conveniently summarised as follows:
bodiya (sixty to 360 beads; ten to twelve *bomoye*)
epaa mege (sixty beads; one *bomoye)*
bomoye (thirty-five to forty beads; fifteen to twenty *kawane*)
tuani ka mege (two to eight beads; five *kawane*)
kawane (two to three beads).

3.2.4 Data from the Paniai Region

In this instance the designation Paniai region is thought of in combination as the Paniai-Tage region.

A. De Bruijn

Describing the situation current at the beginning of the 1950s, in his official report de Bruijn makes a distinction between *tota mege*, indigenous, and *tuanika mege*, *oge mege*, imported shells. Among the indigenous cowries he makes a passing reference to a distinction between 'large and small sorts of cowries',

---

[5] This expression can be literally translated as 'cerulean cowry' and 'basic cowry'. Probably the latter is meant. Given the fact that the designation diverges from the usual names of types, even though it is referring to a shell of high value, and it is not found anywhere else in the data, it seems to me that the informant did not intend to specify the category with this expression, but wanted to give its position in the hierarchical scale of values: a shell which belonged in the lower part of a string.

[6] Just as in what was said earlier, Pospisil erroneously tried to recognise actual colours in the terms *buna* and *dege;* it is possible the same sort of misunderstanding was made in his indication of size. As mentioned, in combination with other shells *ibo* was not normally used in the meaning of 'large', but in that of 'valuable'.

evidently meaning those of high value alongside the ordinary varieties. Under the heading high value, he mentions the varieties *yoo*, *kobawi* and *bodiya* – we shall come across these three below -; under the heading inferior, the *megepo*. Under the heading imported shells, he lists *deba-po*[7] and *ogai-pode* (De Bruijn 1955d).

B. Dubbeldam
Writing of the situation as it was in the middle of the 1950s, Dubbeldam (1964: 298) distinguishes between shells of various values expressed in New Guinea guilders (1957), as follows:
1. The *yoo*, the biggest shell, an obligatory part of the bride price, with a value equivalent to one full-grown pig, in Enarotali (1957) amounted to about fl. 60 (sixty guilders). This was the recognised monetary equivalent of one *yoo*, and a few shells were actually sold for that price.
2. The *yoodagi* or *munidagi*, roughly about fl. 25.-.
3. *Kubawi*, a smaller shell, fl. 7.- to fl. 8.-.
4. *Bodiya*, fl. 6.- to fl. 8.-
5. *Bomoye*, fl. 5.- (a full-grown pig would fetch about 10 to 15 shells of the last two kinds combined).
Ed. Note: the Dutch New Guinea guilder, fl. 1 equalled US $ 0.28.[8]

In this survey, relevant to the second half of the 1950s, first of all we again come across the *bomoye*, said by Pospisil to be the commonest sort, and not mentioned by De Bruijn, but here it is at the bottom of the ladder. Remarkably, however, the *bodiya*, which is given as the equivalent of ten to twelve *bomoye* by Pospisil and is also classified as valuable by de Bruijn, is here usually considered the equivalent of only one and a half *bomoye*. One innovation in this survey is the presence of the relatively highly valued *yoodagi* and *munidagi*.

C. Hylkema
In contrast to the authors just mentioned, first I make a distinction between types and values. On the basis of my data, relevant to the situation in the Tage region at the beginning of the 1970s, in use as an adjective to modify *yoo*, a whole series of generic names was mentioned above [sub-section 3.1.4]: *muka*, *kubawi*, *nono* and *munidagi*, for example, *kubawi-yoo*. These compounds are based on the assumption of a distinction between types and values: the first part indicates

---

[7] At the beginning of the 1970s, the name *deba-po*, literally laurel berry, was in use regionally, especially in songs, in the sense of a synonym for cowries in general, with the connotation of an unrestricted quantity, but without an indication of import, as well as a name such as *aiayi po*, myrtle berry.

[8] By editor. The editor referred to in this sentence is James B. Watson, the editor of the volume in which Dubbeldam's paper appeared. The exchange rate was the one current at that time.

the formal type and the second the intrinsic value. In other words, although shells of the *kubawi* type were generally assigned to the category *yoodagi* on the basis of their value, the value of some of them could be detracted from because of their shape.
Broadly speaking, the *muka* was seen as a shell which was characteristic of the neighbouring Moni. It was said that if at his death it transpired that a Moni man was in possession of a *muka*, his wife should be killed. This should be understood in the context that a widow was usually remarried to and possessed by another man. This prompts the conclusion that the Moni attributed an extremely high value to the *muka*. Looking at the context in which the *kubawi* (Hylkema 1990a: 6) and *nono* (Hylkema 1990a: 392) are treated in the folk tales, it is possible to postulate that they both belonged to a category of highly valued shells, comparable to the *yoodagi* which is still to be discussed.

During my research in the Tage region in the 1970s, money had become so popular that shells and money were regularly exchanged for each other. Besides the traditional, more or less standardised rate of exchange used for the shells, to which Pospisil refers, here I came across the use of a to some extent standardised rate of exchange for the exchange of shells for money, similar to that used by Dubbeldam (1964: 302). But as what follows shows, I simultaneously stumbled across such remarkably specific internal differences that the figures can be taken as no more than a rough guide.

While I was researching the cowry in the Tage region, I chose the bride price as my point of departure. On this basis, we can begin by distinguishing four categories of values. Characteristic of a current classification model was that the three higher values were indicated separately, each with its own name: *yoo*, *yoodagi* and *bodiya*. The remaining lowest values were, in the first instance, lumped together under the general name *mege*, cowry.[9] As do de Bruijn and Dubbeldam, I take, in the discussion below, the highest category as my point of departure.

1. *Yoo*

The highest category was specified by *yoo*, shine, lustre. Certainly, the shells in this category were conspicuous for their size, but this was not the decisive factor in how they were ordered in value within the category. To give an illustration of the complexity of the shell money system attributable to the striking differences in value, I note the customary differences and distinctions in the recognised

---

9 The same model is reflected in the classification of reptiles. Under the general designation *yina*, meaning reptiles, initially a distinction between them is made by giving the larger species its own noun, such as *eguwai*, *kigei*, *tebe* and so on. Whereas the remainder, fairly insignificant smaller species, are put together under the general name *yina*.

hierarchy within this single value category. The category *yoo* was subdivided into four sub-categories. At the top was the sub-category *yoo-tapo*, external *yoo*, while *yoo-tugo*, internal *yoo*, was at the bottom. Possibly as a synonym for *yoo-tapo*, but perhaps on the basis of a formal division within the category itself, people mentioned the names *yoo-aidaiga-uwinaa*, going along the mountain ridge, and *yoo-edi-kepu*, soaked by the rain.

Between the *yoo-tapu* at the top and the *yoo-tugo* at the bottom were the sub-categories *yoo-owaa-yato*, in the direction of the house, and *yoo-wuguwugu*, fluttering. On the basis of quality, the shells in this class could be more precisely distinguished attributively into *yoo-etike-yoo*, right, and *yoo-aka-yoo*, left, in the sense of 'top quality' and 'second best'; generically into such groups *bodiya-yoo, kubawi- yoo* or *muka-yoo*; characteristically into shapes which have already been explained, such as *nau-yoo*, *deke*-yoo and *katagita* or *mukata-yoo*.

The close connection between the cowry and the bride price is clearly demonstrated in the use of the *yoo*. In fact, shells belonging to the *yoo* category were used only for bride price and traded or exchanged for future use in the bride price.

A *yoo* could be exchanged for a fully grown pig; or possibly for a piglet, should the buyer be given to right to raise it to maturity. Or it could be exchanged for shells from a lesser category. The traditional standard was that one *yoo* equalled twelve *bodiya.* I leave aside the question of whether the term *bodiya* here is an indication of value or of a category [of cowry]. More or less implicit in this standardisation is that fact that *yoo* could be exchanged only for *bodiya*, and not for *yoodagi* which are just below it [i.e. the *yoo*] in value; even though there was a standard rate of exchange of one to two between the *yoodagi* and the *bodiya.*

From the time shells could be exchanged for money, the sub-categorical values could be registered in figures. One *yoo* was the standard equivalent of Rp 20,000, or IB 1000.[10] At the time this research was done, Ambrosius Gobai of Epouto, bought a *yoo* from Wodeiwii Tekege of Mogodagi. Initially the latter insisted on Rp 30,000, but eventually Ambrosius actually paid Rp. 20,000. He

---

[10] After the transfer of sovereignty to Indonesia in 1963, until 1969 [the year of the Act of Free Choice], there was a specific unit of currency known as Rupiah Irian Barat, the IB; when the change was made to the Indonesian Rupiah, for practical reasons an exchange rate of one to twenty was maintained. Consequently, initially such round numbers as 1000 or 100 were lost. Although the IB has long since disappeared from circulation, even in the 1990s Rupiah coins and bank notes were regularly referred to using the IB system, for instance a Rp 100 note was called *idibi*, five.

paid only Rp 14,000 for a *yoo* of Willem Tekege of Epouto; this particular shell belonged to the lowest sub-category of *yoo-tugo*.

2. *Yoodagi*
Although the name still betrays the fact that the *yoodagi*, *yoo*-head, or *yoo* pertaining to the sub-category 'head', was originally seen as a sub-category of *yoo*, the *yoodagi* was seen as an independent category of highly valued cowries, *ibo mege*. On the one hand, this idea was expressed in the way that a *yoodagi* was seen as the equivalent of the rounded figure of IB 100, on the other hand this rounding off also possibly contributed to its independence. At one time the expression *puga duwata*, with a cropped tail, did the rounds as a synonym. In a folk tale the *yoodagi* is in passing divided up into *ibo kapee*, attributed a high value, and, by contrast, *yoka kapee*, attributed a low value (Hylkema 1990a: 393).

Within the category *yoodagi*, several named sub-categories were distinguished, such as *kubawi*, *muka*, *nono*, *yoodagi* and *munidagi*. In general, people gave the *kubawi* a slightly higher and the *munidagi* a slightly lower value than the actual *yoodagi*. Just as in the case of the *yoo*, they applied the entire range of adjectives to specify this category in greater detail.

Besides its role in the bride price, the *yoodagi* category was also used as payment for canoes, piglets and for pork. Although the number of *yoodagi* required to pay for a canoe or a piglet could vary according to the size of the purchases, in the meat market in the Paniai-Tage region one yoodagi was asked as a standard price for a *kado,* a portion of pork weighing approximately two kilos. In the Kamu a similar portion was paid for with one *bomoye.*

In the Paniai-Tage region in the second half of the 1950s the *bomoye* was attributed the lowest value (cf. Dubbeldam). By the beginning of the 1970s it was considered alien currency and was only to be found on the collection plate. Consequently it can be deduced that proportionally the *bomoye* and *yoodagi* were two coins of more or less equal value, so as the Dutch guilder and the German mark.

On the money market there was a standard exchange rate of one *yoodagi* for IB 100, or Rp 2000. But there were occasions on which in exchange for one *yoodagi*, people insisted on and received one *kado* of meat, in one exceptional instance as much as three kilos. Taking supply and demand and the quality of the individual shells into consideration, the rate fluctuated between IB 300, or Rp 6000, and IB 60 or Rp 1200.

3. *Bodiya*
Following the *yoodagi* in value was the *bodiya*, fire. As with the name *yoodagi*, in the Paniai-Tage region the term *bodiya* seems to have indicated both a special type of cowry and a particular value. On occasion, a portion of meat could be paid for with a *bodiya,* which had the value of one *yoodagi*. Again in the case of this cowry, a number of the various previously mentioned adjectives could be appended. Generally speaking, the *bodiya* was used for the purchase of bows, string bags, bundles of rope-making materials, or beds with sweet potatoes still growing in them. On the shell market, the standard exchange rate was two *bodiya* for one *yoodagi.* Accordingly, on the money market one *bodiya* was exchanged for IB 50, or Rp 1000.

It is remarkable that, besides the *kawane*, the *bodiya* was in vogue in all the regions. But it is difficult to make sense of all the data about the *bodiya*. With reference to its position in the Tage region, it is said that normally one *yoo* was exchanged for twelve *bodiya*. In view of the monetary value of both of them, this would mean that either the *yoo* had recently been strongly re-evaluated or that the *bodiya* had been devalued. As the *yoodagi* and the *bodiya* had a standard relationship of one to two, generally speaking the *bodiya* was not as highly esteemed as the *yoodagi*, even though a kilo of meat valued at one *yoodagi* was sometimes handed over for one *bodiya*. However, Dubbeldam says that normally the proportional relationship of the *yoodagi* and *bodiya* was one to three or one to four. Speaking of the position of the *bodiya* in the Kamu region, Pospisil reports that categorically the *bodiya* was put higher than the *bomoye*, sometimes it could even be exchanged for as many as ten to twelve *bomoye*, while one *bomoye* was the standard price of a portion of meat at the market, as was the *yoodagi* in the Paniai-Tage region.

In this case, in the Kamu region the *bodiya* should have been the equivalent to the *yoo* in the Paniai-Tage region. However, especially as the *bodiya* was included in a string in all the areas, this seems unlikely. Although in the Paniai the *bomoye* was still universally attributed the lowest value in the 1950s and by the 1970s was considered to be alien to the area, on the basis of what has been said above, the conclusion has to be drawn that in the Paniai-Tage region the *bodiya* had recently substantially weakened.

4. Shells of little value
During the transfer of a bride price in the Paniai region, the attendants put down not only highly valued shells, as it were the large denominations, but also what seemed to be a jumble of separate shells under the particular designation of *mege*, in the sense of unclassifiable shells or those not worth mentioning, in the sense of small change. Seemingly perhaps a jumble of single shells, they were immediately valued by one or two men and sorted. After having been initially divided up into two halves, within each half they were again sorted out into

separate smaller piles. One half was composed of higher value shells of the *yoodagi* and *bodiya* categories; the other half contained inescapably low value specimens. The separate piles of shells of negligible value once again demonstrated that these specimens did seem to be named. Among them were to be found such shells as the already noted *kawane* and the *mitouyautuuya*, between two bones, as well as the *yuu*, din. These shells were used to pay for such ordinary goods as penis gourds, rattan bow strings and the *kebouye* leaves used as tobacco wrapper. Translated into money their value varied from IB 20, Rp 400, to IB 1, Rp 20.

Keeping to the relevant data this produces the following outline:
yoo, divided up according to value into *–tapo*, *-owaa yato*, *-wuguwugu*, *-tugo*; and according to generic shapes into such groups as *bodiya-*, *kubawi-* and *muka yoo*; IB 1000
munidagi, approx. IB 100+
yoodagi, approx. IB 100
kubawi, approx. IB 100-
bodiya, approx. IB 50
mitouyatuuya, *yuu*, approx IB 10
bomoye, kawane, approx. IB 1

3.2.5 The data compared
By editor. Redrafting his manuscript, Hylkema moved this sub-section to chapter 5 in which he planned to make a preliminary assessment. There, he subdivided the sub-section into three parts: 5.2.5, 5.2.6 and 5.2.7.

CHAPTER 4 KNOTTING AND COUNTING

4.1 BUNDLES AND STRINGS

4.1.1 Bundles

To ensure that a number of shells remained together temporarily as a group, it was possible to bind them on a grass stalk or something similar, as is done with a bunch of keys on a key-ring. Having threaded the shells one by one, in no particular order, on the stalk via the anterior, the 'nose' end of the shell through the split on the ventral side, the two ends were finally tied together to make a closed ring, *uko*.

4.1.2 Strings

When cowries were to be offered in payment for the purchase of a pig or for handing over bride price, the bulk of the shells were threaded beforehand into one or more strings on a piece of cord; and the resultant string was used in the sense of an extended cord or ribbon. Speaking of the number of shells the words *muto*, complete, or if the emphasis was on its elongated shape, *one*, rattan, or in emphasising its length, *bado*, were used to indicate the string.[1]

As expressed by the word *muto* and, given the context, probably also by the word *bado,* in principle such a string was composed of sixty shells. In the Mapia region, where the bride price involved only one string, this was indeed supposed to be complete, in the sense of containing sixty shells. If the string was accepted by the bride giver, the bride taker removed one shell before it was handed over, so that in fact the number was reduced to fifty-nine.[2] In the Paniai-Tage region, where the bride price involved more than one string, in the 1950s a string would often contain fewer than sixty shells (de Bruijn 1955d; Dubbeldam 1964: 303); by the 1970s the number was fifty at the most, sometimes even no more than thirty shells. Only high quality shells of the categories *yoodagi* and *bodiya*, were suitable for inclusion in such a string.[3] Observing the order in which the shells were strung, it is possible to discern the ranking assigned by the stringer to each shell in relation to the one before it and the one which followed.

---

[1] The word *bado* has multiple meanings: 1. foot, leg; 2. end of a descending line, for instance the 'foot' (tendril) of a hanging liana swaying above the ground: *buda bado,* or the mouth of a river: *uwo/one bado*; 3. sixty.

[2] In analogy to similar practices in other areas, this gesture probably signified that the bride taker, due to hubris, accepted either the risks inherent in the shells, given their mythical origin, or the risks entailed by the number sixty.

[3] In this context, de Bruijn (1955d: 534) mentions: *yoo*, *kobawi*, *bodiya*. Possibly here *yoo* should be understood as a variation of *yoodagi*. The genuine *yoo* was transacted exclusively individually.

Taking into account the designation *one*,[4] the string was not perceived to be a circle but a tendril and, given the naming of each end, as an ascending straight line. As was the case with rattan, the base end was called *epa*, basis, and its pole was *imo*, top. In contrast to our conception of a hierarchical ladder, the most valuable shell embellished the base and the least valuable was at the top. Corresponding to the spatially ascending, hierarchically descending line, the *bubu*, the buttocks, of the lowest cowry formed the actual base, and because the shell above it was directly attached by its anterior to the posterior end (nose to the buttocks), the shell at the top of the string formed the *yuma*, the nose. Hence the string was heaviest or densest at the base, lightest or puniest at the top.

For the string there was a preference for a piece of string, *gaa*, spun from the bark of the *oba* tree or – given the proverbial *parallelismus membrorum* – of the *mapo* tree. After having fastened the string to the connecting piece between the 'buttocks', it was then led through the slit on the ventral side and threaded through the 'nose'. Because the string was wound around both these fragile connecting pieces, they were subject to wear and tear with the danger that the anus or nose could at some time be completely broken off. The string used was a single, thin piece of unknotted cord. Consequently during the stringing separate stretches of string were not to be tied together. If it were necessary, the string could be lengthened by spinning and splicing an extra piece onto it. If it happened to be noticed during or after the stringing that a shell was not in its proper place in the ranking order, or had been included in the string when it should not have been, it was impossible simply to cut through the cord at that spot, take out the shell and then join the ends together again. If a shell needed to be removed, it was necessary to unstring all the other shells which had been added later one by one. Even should the shell concerned be near the basal end, the shell could not be unstrung from the bottom; if this were done there was a risk that all the shells would display their shabby side. Moreover, during the threading of a string, people should not have allowed themselves to have been influenced by others, if so they would grow emaciated.[5] When unstringing, teeth

[4] On its own, *one* indicates an ascending or descending line in the form of a string; depending on the context it usually meant concretely 'rattan' or 'umbilical cord'; in both senses the implicit connotation of a stream is made explicit in the compound *uwe one*, running water or river, in contrast to *uwo peku,* still water or pool; and following on from this *one bado*, river mouth. In view of the fact that in this compound the word *bado* is probably not used in the sense of sixty, but as *pars pro toto* in the sense of string, tendril.

[5] Moreover, it was advisable not to change one's mind during the stringing and not to be distracted by the playful remarks made by others: 'A person who replaces shells on the recommendation of somebody else, will grow thin.' Sometimes others would say: 'That one is called *Duwaawigipai,* 'A person who undertakes trading trips alone', in other words: 'He doesn't join in as one of the party, he has to operate on his own, consequently you should replace it with another.' But when that one in its turn was

were not to be used, on pain of the punishment that these would be broken. As the word *one* already suggested, and the way the string was treated, confirmed that an unhindered, flowing line was just as essential as the fact that a series of distinctive shells was bound together nose to anus.[6]

Each string was composed of shells of both categories, in a fairly balanced proportion. Broadly speaking, in a string of fifty shells, it could have been expected to find ten *yoodagi* alongside forty *bodiya*. The usual division maintained in the most highly valued category into good, *etike*, on the right, and less good, *aka*, on the left, was also used in the string. Although numerically the lesser one, a string of only thirty shells could be worth more than one of fifty in value.

4.2 DENARY SYSTEM

4.2.1 Combination of ten and sixty

The Ekagi use a combination of a denary and a sexagesimal system. First of all, they have terms which enable them to count from one to ten, *gaati*. As in our system, they possess terms with which to indicate the multiples of ten: twenty, *mepiina* , thirty, *yoka gaati* or *amonaato*, forty, *mepiiya*, fifty, *gaati beu muto,* and so on. And finally, just as in our own system, they have the possibility to combine the multiples of ten with the units: *ena ma mepiina*, twenty plus one, *wiya ma mepiina*, twenty plus two, and so forth. Instead of going on to one hundred the system stops at sixty, *muto* or *bado*, and from there, just as with a hundred and one, counting is resumed with the combination of 'one over sixty', *ena* (*miyo*) *daimee* /*daimita muto*. Just as with our number 200, sixty can be multiplied: *muto wiya*, two times sixty, *muto wido*, three times sixty. Multiplication also forms the basis for the terms for twenty, *mepi-ena*, one time *mepi*, and forty, *mepi-iya*, two times *mepi*. Terminologically fifty is derived from sixty: *gaati beu muto*, sixty minus ten. There are two terms current for thirty. The usual term in the western language area[7] *amoonaato*, literally the (one) half is clearly related to sixty. The common term in the eastern language area, *yoka gaati*, is less easy to explain. Literally it is a compound of

---

called *Uwagapai*, 'Someone whom others allow to be killed', in other words: 'He doesn't fit in the group and is like the proverbial rotten apple in a basket', then, to ensure that it does not lead others astray, you should stick to your own choice.

[6] By editor. In a handwritten gloss Hylkema has added: 'In the Mapia region, people identified the string of shells that formed part of the bride price, with the spine of the as yet unborn son. The string of cowries is construed as the nerve bundle, the seven strings of nassa shells as the ribs.' Hylkema touched upon this topic above, in chapter 1, p. 25f.

[7] By editor. I assume that Hylkema refers here to the Mapia region, the lightly populated, rugged mountain area, to the west of the Kamu basin. The eastern language area then includes both the Kamu-Tigi and the Paniai-Tage areas.

'child/small – ten'. Terminologically the system used throughout the whole language area is characterised by a great uniformity. Only a few terms are regionally restricted. Although in other places the term *ena* designates one, in the Paniai region the term for this is *kato*. And although [as mentioned] elsewhere, thirty is indicated by *yoka gaati*, the term *amoonaato* is used in the Mapia region. In the eastern language area sixty is *muto,* complete/whole, in the western language area this is called *bado*, foot.

4.2.2 Heterogeneous composition

In comparison to the other ethnic groups in the Highlands, the Ekagi stand out through their use of an exceptionally highly developed system of counting. In contrast to the systems current in other places, they not only employ original terms for the numbers from one to four, in principle they can count on in an unlimited fashion without pointing to particular parts of the body, such as fingers, arms and the like. However, investigation has revealed that their system is of heterogeneous composition. Naturally to begin with the words for one: *ena* and *kato*. It causes a surprise that different terms are used in different regions; I can offer no explanation for this. Moreover, it appears that the terms *wiya*, two, *wido*, three, and *wii*, four, are firmly anchored in the [Ekagi] language. These are compound words. The constant factor can be traced back to the sound ≤ *wi* ≥. The variations *-iya*, *-ido* and *-i* are generally used – in a chameleon fashion – as a suffix: *-iya* in the function of twofold, for instance in *badouya*, both feet, and of an encompassing plural; *-ido*, in the function of a previously mentioned plural, for instance in *badoudo*, the already mentioned feet (three or more); and *i*, in the function of an absolutely unrestricted plural, for instance, *badoo*, feet (an undetermined large quantity).

This use of suffixes betrays an original general distinction into two, into a specific number larger than two, and into an undetermined large quantity. In this respect there is a close connection with undeveloped systems that are current elsewhere. While these numbers are anchored so firmly in the language, the remaining terms for the numbers five to ten are very foreign. A comparison shows that according to their sound and meaning they are virtually identical to the names of the numerals used in the various islands to the west of Irian [see also Pospisil 1989: 20f].

4.2.3. Quantitative and qualitative orientation

Taking into account their knowledge and use of a highly developed system of counting, Pospisil[8] (1978: 3) postulates that the Ekagi are generally more

[8] This research result does not seem incomprehensible in view of the method applied. When reading his publications, the reader forms the opinion that he was personally continually busy counting, weighing and measuring. Apart from the fact that, when he indulged in this, the researcher was making his presence emphatically felt, he also

quantitatively than qualitatively oriented. This observation does not do them any justice. Although the Ekagi do have such a system of reckoning and although the young people are initiated into it through play – as an alternative to the Indonesian terms used in the current school education system –, practically speaking numbers higher than twenty are seldom used. It offers the Ekagi the opportunity to extend beyond the kinship terminology that spans five generations and to enumerate the preceding forebears to the tenth or twelfth generation. Remarkable is, however, that when calculating the origins of [a clan genealogy ??], the Ekagi do not set the figures horizontally next to each other but in vertical order.

The numbers above twenty are universally used when collecting fencing posts, since fences built of upright poles have become more popular than those built with horizontal poles. In the context of the assembling of various building materials for a house, it turned out that an elderly man in the Mapia region knew the precise figures by heart, as well as the particular place and function of each piece of material in the house. To initiate the work, four long, thin, forked poles were required to support the ridge-pole. Then for a big house forty, for a smaller thirty, split planks of roughly the same size for constructing the front, back, and both side walls; 120 split planks to make a front and back room and 180 split planks for the central space. Forty stakes were needed for the rafters of a large house, thirty for a smaller one. Finally forty rattan canes were required for the bindings.

Nevertheless, this quantitative approach did not eclipse the qualitative considerations. At least as important as the quantity of split planks needed for a side or interior wall, or the number of stakes required for an average roof con-struction, were such characteristics as hardness and durability, in other words the quality as based on the different species of wood. Ideal for the four long, ridge-pole support poles with forks at the ends were the long, thin but none the less durable trunks of the hardwoods *akago* and *duwogo* (*Aquivoliaceae ilex)* trees; types of such hardwoods as *amo*, the myrtle, and *digi*, the beech, were considered ideal for the split planks used as an upright fence or a wall. Prerequisite for the roof were light, flexible woods such as that obtained from the willow-like *onage*. When admiring a fence or a house, people were not impressed by the quantity, but by the sturdiness and above all the quality of the materials used. It was not the number of planks as such which distinguished the house of a well-to-do man from that of a man with fewer means, nor indeed the way it was divided up in

---

expressed such a remarkable, highly unusual interest in quantitative aspects that the informants would have found difficulty in not going along with it.

9 By editor. Hylkema had written the following gloss on this page of his manuscript: The Ekagi distinguishes mass, then shape/order by means of lines next to each other; then number; then hierarchical order; a string [of cowries?] is not the same as a handful.

rooms or the construction as such; size did exert an influence, but the decisive factor was the species of wood used. Consequently, the community found itself in a quandary, having to reassess his identity, when a person generally taken to be inconsequential, above all still relatively youthful, was found to have built a small but none-the-less extremely sturdy house, using the best materials. Once people do have access to a highly developed system of counting, this is of enormous assistance when the planks are cut, often far from the place where they will be used; this is the more so since these activities are often farmed out to others to do.

CHAPTER 5 PROVISIONAL ASSESSMENT[1]

The cowry has been successively introduced in the previous chapters as an object which originates in the ocean and is accorded a dominant role in the societies of the Central Highlands of Irian/Papua by way of money. Following this, the subject of its direct and indirect import was raised, as well as the mythological interpretation. After mentioning the various adjectives which were current in standard language use for each individual specimen, I have subdivided the shells, into categories and values, while referring to the work of four different authors. Finally, a distinction was made between the use of individual shells, which might be tied together into a bundle, and the use of shells strung together to form a string. The time has now come for a provisional assessment, in which two matters will be taken into consideration. Naturally, both the correspondences and the differences between the four authors mentioned will be conspicuous. Instead of marking time with a comparison between them, we shall expand our scope by investigating their data in the light of the criteria that objects have to meet before they can be designated as money. I shall add a list of [such] criteria which are not all of equal importance, but which have to be understood in relation to and harmonised with each other.

5.1 FOUR DIFFERENT AUTHORS

5.1.1 Quality of the various data

The authors have worked independently of each other. Dubbeldam has used Pospisil's data. Personally I have aimed at independent, unbiased research. I have the impression that no single author can claim to have made a lengthy, significant investigation. Had de Bruijn, for instance, made a profound study, he would not have been able to have overlooked the existence of the *bomoye*. The data are the result of short, local, incidental pieces of research. In fact, people were more interested in gaining a general total impression than in a specific, detailed study. On the basis of my own experience, I suspect that none of the authors tackled this matter of detail in his research. This casts doubts on the nature and the depth of the research that each of them carried out, as well as on the quality of their data.

---

[1] By editor. For several reasons it is clear that this chapter is a late addition to the text and that it has remained unfinished. First, in a handwritten gloss, Hylkema changed the number of the following chapter from five to six. But its sections and sub-sections were still numbered as if they belonged to a chapter 5. Moreover, several sub-sections in the new chapter 5 seem to be incomplete. .Sub-section 5.2.2 consists of a single sentence and, in contrast to Hylkema's usual style of writing, the bulk of sub-section 5.2.3. is composed of short sentences, sometimes even in telegraph style. It ends with an incomplete sentence. Sub-section 5.2.5 is composed of just a few, sketching their topics. The end of the chapter repeats conclusions reached at the end of chapter 4.

My lack of data about the use [of cowries] in the Mapia region shows that I did not focus on the topic. I just happened to pick up my data and I have not verified them. In my Tage period [from 1972 to 1977], the shells did capture my interest in the context of an investigation of the bride price. When engaged in this project, I was aware that an Ekagi seldom allowed another to see the contents of his wallet, but that his reticence about the secret of how cowries were actually used was at the least as great as his openness about the secret of the mythical origins of the shell. Whenever anyone was allowed to listen to an anecdote about how and where a snake or a lizard laid cowries[2], the person so favoured had to realise that thereafter he still did not know how the story-teller actually obtained his shells. I methodically followed in the fortunes of my key informant as he assembled his bride price. Moreover, at the beginning of the 1970s, I was in the fortunate position that, as a representative of a foreign institution, I was no longer involved in the shell economy as an interested party and was consequently from their point of view no longer seen as a real or phantom rival. But I have also taken the liberty to use the knowledge so acquired to cast light on and interpreting the data of other authors.

5.1.2 Regionally and temporally relevant data

The researches of the three authors, whose results I have used above, were carried out in the 1950s;[3] one in the Kamu region. The Kamu is more or less relevant to Tigi; the other two worked in the Paniai region. I personally worked in Mapia and in Tage, relevant to Tage-Paniai.

5.2 TESTED AGAINST THE CRITERIA FOR MONEY

5.2.1 Scarce and not easily reproducible

People used various items of value, for instance, nassa shell, beads and large sea shells. They made a choice. The shell was suitable because it was available in sufficient but limited quantities. Traditionally the shell was not easily procurable. This situation changed abruptly because of importation. To a certain extent this was obviated by making a distinction between money shells and ring shells, and among the money shells into new and old. [This led to] two sorts of forgeries. [The] ring shell [was] good as an export commodity, [the] money shell [was] distinguished in value on the basis of age.

5.2.2 Easily portable and indestructible

Of themselves, cowries fulfil the requirement of being portable and durable.

5.2.3 Homogeneous and divisible

After an initial moment of doubt, the ring shells were rejected, thereby honouring the demand for homogeneity. But, for instance, people did not choose

---

[2] By editor. Hylkema presents several such stories in chapter 25.

[3] By editor. As regards de Bruijn's inquiries, see chapter 2, note 14.

the bead or nassa shell instead. These lacked individuality. In order to serve as money, something has to be divisible. In the case of precious metals, a distinction has been made according to sort: gold, silver, copper and nickel; should people opt for silver, coins can be made in larger or smaller sizes, with lesser or greater weight. In fact, the shell is divisible. To do so, on the one hand the category and on the other the value of the individual shell plays a role. Category and individual value do no coincide. Theoretically it is possible to construct a hierarchy of values, as each author shows. However, it is not immediately clear on what grounds [they had to do this]. People distinguish categories; ideally from these emerges a general hierarchy of values. But it is simultaneously obvious that the value does not follow automatically from category. Besides these people use a value ..[Here Hylkema's manuscript has a break].

5.2.4 Regional restriction

Remarkably, even though each author attempts to reconstruct the hierarchy of values, each arrives at a different conclusion. Comparing the various data reveals that, first and foremost, throughout the whole area, the cowry species, *mege*, is divided up into categories. In view of the fact that various names for the categories are found throughout the region, there is no reason to suppose that certain categories were confused with each other regionally or were called by different names. The Winkler Prins [Encyclopaedia] says that species of the *Monetaria* genus are used as a means of payment, but in particular the money cowry and the ring cowry. The fact that the Ekagi make further distinctions in each of the scientifically defined species, above all in the money shell, and especially because they have named the categories distinguished,[4] raises an interesting question: whether both species are scientifically divided up any further and – should the answer be in the affirmative – whether and how far these scientific and folk divisions correspond to each other. I have not investigated this in any greater depth.

5.2.5 Simultaneous regional differences

A comparison of the data shows that, within the same period in these regions, the same categories were in circulation but that their values diverged according to the region. In Paniai, alongside those which were quite clearly devalued, other highly valued categories circulated, which did not occur in the data pertaining to the Kamu.

---

[4] In itself this is not unusual. A recent investigation into the sub-species which the Ekagi recognise in the species crayfish, *udi*, resulted in twenty-two different names of types; although this was not based on focused research, seventeen of them are to be found in my Ekagi-Dutch-Indonesian dictionary (with thanks to Piet Bots ofm).

5.2.6 Historical fluctuations

This fact favours the hypotheses that, in the course of history, one category was supplanted by another and also that the cowries entered from the east via the Paniai region and from there passed on to the west. This premise is corroborated by the fates of the *kawane*, *bomoye* and *bodiya*. Although in fact the *kawane* is no longer a desired means of payment anywhere, in the report of Kotomoma [chapter 2] it was referred to in passing as a *peku mege*, a shell from the lake, indicating its proto-typicality. In an account of the time in which shells in the Paniai- Tage region were still 'secreted', *pai*, by reptiles,[5] the shells so acquired were designated as *kawane* and *bodiya*. Various data suggest that in the distant past the *kawane* occupied a position comparable to that of the *bomoye* in the Kamu region in the 1950s, and to that of the *yoodagi* in the Paniai-Tage region in the 1950s and the 1970s, but that it later lost value so that in all three regions it finally counted as a negligible quantity. Whereas the *bomoye* was regarded as the bottom category in Paniai in the 1950s, and by the 1970s had in fact been eliminated from the list of currency still in circulation, in Kamu it was still the category most in use. On the basis of the data available, it can be postulated that the *bodiya* would have been subjected to the same process in its geographical progress from east to west had the system of shell currency been maintained.

5.2.7 New better than Old

It seems that when faced with a choice between old and new, unaware of the gap between their thoughts and their actions, people generally begin from the assumption that originality and age lend a certain value. By and large, [this is] the product of an ambivalent socialisation. In fact, old, *wei*, 'dry' shells were more highly valued than new, *iyaa*, 'wet' shells and therefore people expended a great deal of time and energy on making new shells seem old. But the historical devaluation shows that, in spite of themselves, in practice people did actually prefer the new to the old.

[5] By editor. See also Chapter 25.

CHAPTER 6 EXTRINSIC FACTORS

6.1 EXTRINSIC SURPLUS VALUE

6.1.1 Derived from use in the pig market

Any self-respecting person could not and did not indeed expect that a single shell or string of shells would simply be palmed off on him. Unquestionably a string which consisted of haphazardly collected shells, gathered here, there and everywhere from a number of people – for instance, when a number of heads of families wished to buy a pig for a communal meal during the celebration of Christmas –, was sure to have been looked upon askance. The upshot was that in any transaction a shell, and in a particular string each separate shell, had to be and was actually continually subjected to critical appraisal. Starting from the assumption that the shells display their own value and that good wares need no praise, it was permitted that a silent appraisal be completed. However, should this produce other than the desired results, a shell could indeed be the centre of an oral appraisal. Instead of placing the quality of the shell itself at the centre of the debate, frequently an extrinsic argument recounted how the shell was obtained. [However,] Not every previous transaction had to be accorded the same importance. Such an argument was adjudged to be sound, if a pig or pork featured in an earlier transaction. Subsequently, on the basis of this transaction, all the shells concerned could be qualified as *idaa-po*. This classification contains a play on words based on the dual meaning of *idaa*, 'full of content' and 'meat'. While every shell had to prove that it was not a loose entity, but that [on the contrary] it had substance, because it had served in the meat trade, a *po,* because it was a round object or berry, had proven itself to be a fleshy one, full of substance. People had reason to feel offended if someone later actually continued to dispute its already proven value.

Here we come across a remarkable interaction. On the one hand, the raising of pigs reached its completion and apotheosis in the exchange for shells.[1] On the other hand, the shells only acquired meaning if they were accepted in exchange for pork. Having been born of blood – as noted in the previously mentioned report[2] - the dirt and blood, *paga*, still adhering had to be cleansed with pork, so that it could begin to 'acquire sturdiness and strength', just as a ball which is pumped up.[3] Furthermore, people did not hesitate to sing the praises of a whole string, using the qualification *idaa-po*, even though only twenty of the fifty shells had indeed been acquired through the purchase of meat.

---

[1] Because of various mythically coloured, 'unnatural' characteristics, pigs were often no longer to be exchanged for shells.

[2] By editor. The report of the Club of Kotomoma, see pages 36f.

[3] As a mother, if her toddler is by chance smeared with her menstrual blood, wipes off that blood with meat which she then consumes herself to prevent him weakening, since a baby comes into the world limp and crumpled.

6.1.2 Abstracted from use on the marriage market

Just as it can be presumed that individual shells had to be accorded extra value because they had been used in a transaction for the purchase of pork, a complete string could be recommended because it had been accepted in the framework of the bride price. In practice, strings sometimes served in a number of successive bride prices, without any or a substantial change in composition.

6.2 CONDITIONAL EXCHANGE POSSIBILITIES

In what has been said above, the value of each category or sort of shell is given an exemplary parity in relation to commodities, to other categories of shells and to money. But the possibilities for exchange this parity gave were actually limited. The commodities, shell and money markets did not interact freely and each market worked according to its own laws. Should someone offer a string bag worth one *bodiya* on the commodities market, he would usually have not been satisfied with a number of *mitouyautuuya* which might perhaps have been exchanged on the shell market for one *bodiya*. Or should a person have had a portion of pork on offer at a pig feast, he would have expected to receive one *yoodagi*, and would not have been happy with two *bodiya*, even though together they may have been worth one *yoodagi* on the shell market. Should one *yoo* have been demanded in the bride price, people would not have been able to have presented twelve *bodiya* or a pig as a substitute. Payment should be made with the proper coin. From this point of view, on the commodity market, one guilder was clearly of more value than four 25 cent coins. In the case of shells, quality outstripped quantity; a trend which had been transferred to the money economy.[4]

The upshot was that a person should first trade his shells on the shell market for the exact type of money, although there was every chance that there one had to have five 25 cent coins handy in order to secure one guilder. In contrast, if a person wanted to sell a pig, he did not expect one *yoo* in exchange, but a string composed of *yoodagi* and *bodiya*. Only in case a person necessarily required a *yoo* for a bride price, could he offer a pig in return for a *yoo*. Its owner would be prepared to accept the pig, to help this person, or, more aptly, to put him under an obligation. Normally in a transaction concerning a pig, the freedom of trade of the buyer was limited by certain conditions. But in such a situation, the buyer found himself in a position in which he could state conditions. He could, for instance, demand the right to raise the animal, in order to be able to ask the full price on the market at a better moment.

---

[4] When older women offered me precisely five eggs for Rp 200 per egg, they did not expect ten Rp 100 notes or four Rp 250 notes, but one Rp 1000 note from me; after that, from all sorts of nets, bags and purses they would conjure up small bundles of Rp 100 or Rp 250 notes tied up with string or with grass stalks – the profits of trading with others – in the expectation that I would change this for larger currency, or else run the risk of being punished by having to do without their commodities for a long time.

6.3 NEED FOR AN OBJECTIVE STANDARD

6.3.1 Shell and meat adjusted to each other

At first glance, the division of the cowry into categories and sorts reveals at least a general correspondence to our customary monetary system, ranging from one cent to ten guilders. All these distinctive categories or sorts seem to be adjusted to the *bomoye* in the Kamu, or the *yoodagi* in the Paniai region, as a unit of currency, like our guilder. Whereas thereafter, instead of precious metal, a portion of meat figures as a purely commercial yardstick, setting the standard as it were. As legal tender the guilder is an impersonal and simultaneously a purely commercial fact. In itself it embodies a certain, objective value; whether or not it corresponds to the commodity on offer, it is completely detached from the person who offers the coin.

From the standard expressions for indicating the size of a pig, it is still possible to infer that traditionally people accorded the relation of shell and pork a certain standardisation (VI, p. 89). For instance the expression *mepiinaage* evoked in fact the image of a full-grown pig; that of *wiyamagataage* a half-grown animal. In the meantime, people are scarcely any longer aware that traditionally the expressions, in the literal sense of 'worth twenty (*yoodagi*)' or 'worth twelve (*yoodagi*)', did in fact indicate the number of shells which could be fetched for them on the meat market and consequently the number of portions into which the animal could be divided up after it had been slaughtered. The literal sense was already obsolete. Everyone knew that that a pig described according to size as *mepiinaage*, worth twenty, could actually be divided up into twenty-two or twenty-four portions and would therefore fetch twenty-two or twenty-four *yoodagi*.

Although there was clearly a need for an absolute yardstick, and although, by making a *yoodagi* and a portion of meat equivalents, an objective standardisation was within grasp, this was frustrated. Because just as the value of the shell was not bound to the category itself, the portion could also be manipulated. On the one hand, it was laid down that one portion, *kado*, *mitoo* or *dedo*, should be composed respectively of meat with fat, *kado*, meat on the bone, *mitoo*, and of pure meat, *muge*, there were no rules about either the corresponding proportions or the joint weight.

6.3.2 Commercial substitutions in an interpersonal competition

Illustrative of the purely objective pragmatism that people felt worthy to pursue was the transaction between two men, members of the same men's house, at a pig feast. From the way the arrangement was set up, it was obvious that in principle the customer wished to banish every personal element from the exchange, in order to make a purely businesslike deal. After the slaughter, while seated, the seller made up the portions in front of him. When he had finished, his customer approached him from behind and silently offered him a cowry over his shoulder. Without ascertaining the identity of the buyer, the seller took the offered shell and began to assess it. Apparently the shell did not answer to the portions laid out ready. At this point the seller should have handed the shell back over his shoulder in silence, leaving it up to the customer whether or not he wished to offer another shell. However, exemplifying the prevailing spirit of enterprise, the seller began to rearrange his portions, until he had composed a portion of equal value to the proffered shell. Not content with this offer, once again the customer silently stretched his hand out over the shoulder, his fingers pointing to the shell which the seller had put down in front of him. When the man withdrew, thinking that he had been swallowed up in the crowd, the seller looked around. Over his generally stony countenance appeared the glimmer of a smile. I had the impression that in the pecking order in the local men's house, the seller was one step above the customer. Without having spoken a single word, the two rivals had tested their power. However, it was really not quite clear which of the two had actually won any victory.[5]

Without a fixed standard, every exchange degenerates into a competition. Because he stalled his commodities out in front of him, the seller was throwing down a challenge; by offering him a shell, the customer revealed himself as the person who accepted the challenge and went on the attack. However, within this arrangement, the trial of strength contained in the exchange was in principle transposed to two matters. By offering a cowry while remaining out of sight, in the eyes of the customer his behaviour assumed the character of a gamble. By taking this gamble, on the one hand, he kept himself out of range, but simultaneously he trusted his fate to the shell. Not the customer but the shell accepted the challenge. When the gamble failed and the shell lost, the customer decided that his shell lacked value or, even more seriously, that he had not found favour with the supernatural being involved in the gamble, but he was at least spared loss of face in relation to the seller. Indeed this would have been so had the seller abided by the code of conduct and had not looked around. Generally speaking, if there is an amazingly close bond between the owner and what he possesses, this bond between people and shell evolves into a distinct

[5] By editor. In a handwritten gloss Hylkema suggests a kin relationship between buyer and seller which would have complicated their interaction even more. Hylkema wrote: 'What an amazing business. It was important for wife's brother to show his face because he was receiving more for less, [because he was a] privileged exchange partner.' Hylkema refers to van Baal's discussion of the contrast between exchange and trade (1975: 43). While in the case described, Hylkema opines exchange, between partners, to be the expected mode of transacting, instead the two men behaved as parties in a trade relationship.

identity,[6] revealed in the almost but not quite identical terms *mee*, person, and *mege*, cowry.

6.4 LIMITED POSSIBILITIES FOR EXPANSION

6.4.1 Regional shell systems

Compared with the exchange of goods in kind, a shell system developed in analogy to the monetary system offers the opportunity to expand the choice of utensils and food, commercial contacts and partners tremendously, both in time and in space. Nowadays, when someone hews out a canoe to sell, he can accept shells *in* payment in order to transform these later, at a time suitable to himself into, for instance, meat for a birth ceremony. Undoubtedly, the shell system also had an enormous impact on the development of various other cultural institutions. But given the potential it offered, it is all the more remarkable that these were not fully exploited, but tended instead to be curbed by place, time and person. If people had been stimulated by commercial, socio-economic motives, the system would have been developed in a different direction to the one it took. Apparently other interests carried more weight.

As shown by what has just been said, throughout its history the shell system was constantly evolving, but it is also obvious that this development did not proceed apace at the same time in each region. Consequently, instead of one common monetary system, regionally differentiated shell systems held sway. Although this did not exclude inter-regional trade, it can be argued *a priori* that it hindered inter-regional contacts, but probably simultaneously stimulated those contacts which were intra-regional. Far from everybody would have been served by an unrestricted trading sphere; in fact the opposite was far more likely. This limitation can be illustrated by the pig or meat market and the close relationship this had to the marriage market.

6.4.2 Regionally limited meat market

On the one hand, in their capacity as sellers men did cross regional boundaries in their quest to purchase pigs for planned pig feasts. On the other hand, in their capacity as buyers, men frequently cautioned each other that the radius within which -- at the instigation of the female half of the population -- pig feasts should be attended and meat should be accepted, was to be curtailed rather than expanded. Conscious of his wife ['s wishes], a man had to be careful not to be left behind by other local men, but at the same time many lamented the expenditure to which this obliged them. Instead of allowing themselves to be tempted into reciprocal competition by the women, in this undertaking men should have made clear agreements and consequently formed a common front.

---

[6] A variable often resorted to in the giving of names in the clan myths, for instance Myths p. 72, 1; p. 85, 8. [Not found].

6.4.3 Regionally limited marriage market

Although in principle the shell system made everybody a trading partner, in fact also in this system trading took place with relatives via mother, sister and wife. Even though a common shell system and a uniform bride price should have expanded the choice of a partner to the whole ethnic group, in principle a regionally determined bride price, in the wake of a regionally particular shell system, limited this choice. In the Mapia region people were aware that the bride price was relatively cheap and that this made it attractive for men from outside the region to seek a bride there. Their response was not to screw the bride price up, but to prevent this happening, men from outside were warned off the marriage market by the ingenious use of various conditions preventing marriage. The Ekagi limited the choice of partner on the grounds of patri- and matrilineal[7] relationships between clans or sub-clans. Insofar as it is possible to speak of preferred marriages, it was not kinship but spatial proximity which was the determining factor, notwithstanding Boelen's (1955: 6) ideas about this.[8] On the marriage market people were clearly inclined towards a segmentation of the area. Instead of seeking a distant bride, people did prefer to look around in their own environment.[9] Although people saw the area as an entity, witness the term *Tage dokoo*, Tage valley, the areas Epouto and Uwebutu on either side of Lake Tage stood out as two segments. While it was not a necessity that the water formed a barrier, given the availability of canoes, the number of intra-segment marriages was considerably larger than that of inter-segment marriages. That shells were a component in the bride price, did not prevent the network of trading partners being in a process of restriction rather than expansion.

---

[7] By editor. I suppose that Hylkema, here and elsewhere in the manuscript, uses the term 'matrilineal' to refer to relatives via the mother, instead of relatives in the female line.

[8] By editor. In the paper quoted, Boelen had mentioned several Me expressions referring to the existence of marriage ties between clans or sub-clans, or, in contrast, their being prohibited or preferred. In a footnote which I elaborate on here, Hylkema first corrects Boelen's use of the Me language which had led him to an erroneous interpretation of the existence of preferential marriage ties between clans. While he criticises Boelen's argument that kin relations are paramount in guiding the choice of a marriage partner, he had, however, two sentences earlier given that impression himself. Moreover, Boelen had added that the Me were apt to manipulate kin relations and to change marriage preferences. Hence I do not exclude that kin relations do play a role.

[9] The expression *gebe bage* (de Bruijn 1952: 9) is incorrectly noted and translated. First of all the expression is really *gebo bagee*, in which *gebo* does not mean 'faraway', but can be adequately translated as 'immediate vicinity': 'people from the immediate vicinity'.

CHAPTER 7 MALE AND FEMALE ROLES

7.1 TYPICALLY MALE MATTERS

7.1.1 A fluctuating assortment of valuables

Besides the cowry, a number of other valuable items could function as a means of payment. However, enumerating them raises the difficulty of where the lines should be drawn between means of payment, adornment, ritual accoutrements and amulets. As van Baal (1975: 50n8) remarked only small items of value which are in short supply are suitable to be used as money. Foremost among these was the nassa shell, *dedege, Nassarius sp.*. Regionally people used, at least until recently, these shells, specially polished and bored for the purpose. Unlike the cowry, the nassa shell was not divided up into separate categories. Competing with it and used as substitutes for various sorts of indigenous grey, dark red and shiny black seeds such as Job's tears, were several kinds of imported glass beads, *dau*; most prominent among them the large, cerulean blue type, *epaa dau*, followed by a small, polychrome bead, *paga dau*.

As well as being a means of payment, these nassa shells, seeds and beads, when strung into strands, were used as a bodily adornment, most usually in the form of necklaces. During the time I was a priest in Timeepa [in the Mapia region], the body of a woman had to be exhumed because the nassa shells which had been attached to the short apron which covered her pubic area had not been removed.[1] Every Sunday, without fail, one of the parishioners wore a multi-coloured penis gourd band around his waist, made from string wrapped in orchid bark and decorated with strings of small beads. In former times, other different sorts of shells, among them the dazzlingly white, oval *woti*, *Melo hunteri perry*, and the brownish-yellow, dish-shaped *pakooba, Cymbicum diadema,* also served as gifts or money. Pospisil (1978: 24) says that people speculated with these shells on the exchange market. Although the *woti* was admirably suited for making a pendant to be worn around the neck or attached to the bottom of a carrying-net, the *pakooba* was too large for this and, if people wanted to use it for bodily adornment, ritual accoutrement or amulet, they had to make do with just a shard.[2]

Throughout the course of history, in the bride price and comparable institutions, as well as shells both large and small, seeds and beads, feather head ornaments

---

[1] By editor. I presume that Hylkema is referring to his first posting among the Me, in 1970-1972, when his main task was pastoral care.

[2] By editor. A handwritten gloss by Hylkema reads: In this context, items which could be included in the category of decorations included pig's teeth as ornaments to be worn or placed on a carrying net; dog's teeth or those of marsupials and rodents which were worn as a fringe around the edge of a collar, and also the conspicuous *wupi*, [a small cushion serving as lumbar rest]. All were heavily subject to fashion.

in a huge variety of plumes and crowns have also served as a means of exchange, as have such stone and iron tools as chisels, knives and axes. Into the 1990s cowries and nassa shells were used in combination in the bride price in the Mapia region. [In contrast], in the Paniai region the nassa shell had already disappeared more than a generation ago, not only from the bride price, but also from the exchanges, and indeed even from the assortment of bodily adornments. In the meantime, money had gained such a position and influence there that people had already made room for it in the margins of the bride price.

7.1.2 Quantitative and qualitative distinctions between the nassa and the cowry
In view of their relatively highly developed system of counting, the question inevitably rises whether or not the Ekagi were more inclined to think in terms of quantity rather than quality. This question bears re-examination in the context of the nassa and cowry shells. Nassa shells and beads were invariably strung into strands. Although it was asserted that there was a standard length for these strings, sometimes the ell, called *pekaana*, literally one eye, was mentioned, in analogy to a segment of the stem of a bamboo, [but] sometimes it was the distance from hand to hand with the arms stretched out to the sides, or sometimes the distance from the crown of the head to the toes. The last was the requisite length of strands used in the bride price in the Mapia region. Probably this indicated that this strand was composed of a number of 'eyes'. When it was worn as a necklace, such a strand was wound around the neck a number of times so that at times the breasts was almost completely bedecked with a forest of shells or beads.

In contrast, cowries were used individually in the food and utensil markets, and only in the pig and marriage markets were strings of them used as a means of payment. Consequently, apart from the type of bead, when nassa shells and beads were used, the quantitative element was of overriding importance, not in the sense that people counted them individually as component parts, but in the length of the string. When cowries were at stake, it was not the length of the string which mattered but, in view of the target number of sixty, apparently what weighed most heavily in the first instance was also the quantity. Although people in the Mapia region in the 1970s still adhered to this [quantitative criterion], there also the quality of the shells were decisive factors in composing [the string] and in its evaluation. In view of the numerical reduction introduced there from fifty or even fewer shells, a strand in the Paniai region was valued not on the basis of the quantity of the component shells but on their quality. As the different ways of threading of nassa and cowry shells into strings clearly reveal, the Ekagi did make a distinction between measuring, counting and evaluating.

7.1.3 The male aspiration to acquire a cowry monopoly
Beads and nassa shells were used by both men and women as currency and as decoration, without the distinctive entitlements of men and women being

questioned in principle.[3] However, the men did clearly strive to exclude the women from the shell economy. In the 1970s, many, mainly young, men displayed an unequivocal tendency to deny women both use and property rights. More pragmatically, their older counterparts were not prepared to go to such an extreme. Adult men were well aware that, in their capacity as husbands, they shared their relationships with women with other men, in their capacity as brothers. In this society, 'brother' is an elastic concept, and the man so designated might be no more than one of a whole range of relatives. Moreover, had the man wanted to claim the whole shell economy for himself, and had he with [the payment of] bride price indeed obtained exclusive rights [over his wife] and accepted the responsibility of taking care of her needs, he could not forbid a brother to give his sister some small token by way of a gift, and he could not prevent her from accepting a present from her brother. Generally, this sort of gift was interpreted as a complaint that the man had not fulfilled his responsibilities in providing for her. If the present was in kind, in the form of game or pork, any self-respecting spouse regarded this as a debt of honour which would have to be reciprocated. Hence, he added this to the list of his debts to the brother, promising that it would be repaid on a later occasion. Because food was involved, the situation was clear-cut. But what should be done if the woman was carrying her brother's shells around? Perhaps she was simply taking care of them for him as a good sister should. Furthermore, the woman could hedge around the situation using the argument that the shells had not been given into her possession, but only to pass them on to her son.

Adult men were inclined not to argue with their wives about the entitlements of their brothers or sons. However, paying the distinction between small and big money all due respect, they claimed the right to sift through their shells and to offer their wives advice about how they should go about taking care of the big money. In this, they did not venture as far as a father's brother who had the right to control and use the shells of an orphaned nephew without any further consultation. Moreover, there was an even greater number of adult men who were not ashamed to stimulate [their wives] in their desire to acquire property and their spirit of enterprise and, on the grounds of this encouragement, derived the right to demand that they pay for their own expenses. In fact, this was more than simply a matter of principle. When a man deprived his wife of the property rights and the rights of use to the highly valuable cowries only, he also effectively excluded her from all transactions in which large money was involved. They included the purchase of the imported string needed for making pubic skirts/aprons, of canoes, of meat and such like. Conversely, should his wife prove to be headstrong, he could then leave it to her whether or not she bought the canoe which she desperately needed for catching crayfish.

---

[3] By editor. I assume that Hylkema is referring to the difference in use and property rights held by men and women in relation to cowries.

Although shell transactions, certainly the larger transactions such as during pig feasts or in legal actions pertaining to fines or bride price, were carried out in public and [although] it was repeatedly affirmed that in fact each transaction should take place in public, enormous preparations in the framework of the characteristic *mege kitigi*, the shell whispering, actually took place covertly beforehand, behind closed doors in the men's house, or in the scrub at the sides of the house. During the public sessions there were at least as many women as men present, but the silent message conveyed by the locality chosen and by their [the men's] behaviour sent signals that they were expected to keep a certain distance. In a sense, they literally remained on the sidelines, assuming the role of silent witnesses. If they did feel the need to express their criticism of the behaviour of the men, this was usually delivered in a subdued murmur. Nevertheless, the volume was loud enough that it could be understood by the men. Any woman who wished to raise a strident voice in this situation was really asking for a public punishment and was generally promptly served. However, if those present were requested to take a really deep look in their purses and empty these out over a mat, this applied equally to the women and many a man was shocked to behold the quality of the shells which the women apparently possessed. In response, a few women displayed no discomfiture about entering the centre of the circle and putting down their contribution personally. Generally speaking though, a woman usually had her contribution laid down by a male relative. During the time-consuming preparations, the women and children were well aware that they had to make themselves scarce or be punished by a snarled order to keep quiet. This was a typically male event.

7.1.4 Based on the difference in powers of judgement/discernment

The distinct actions of measuring, counting and evaluating clearly test the human powers of judgement to a varying degree. In close association with the fact that a person grows not only physically, *mee*, but also mentally, *dimi*, each of these actions by and large corresponds to a certain stage of development. Although from this perspective it is assumed that from their birth all children are initially each other's equals, a girl never transcends the quantitative stage. However, it is hoped that, for his own sake and that of his closest female relatives, a boy successfully passes through this quantitative stage to reach the qualitative stage beyond.

As a justification of the monopoly as regards cowries to which men aspired, the stereotypical argument adduced was that women had been passed over where intelligence, *dimi*, was concerned or, in a slightly more nuanced version: the intellect of women was less evolved than that of men. Consequently, they lacked such typically male attributes as resoluteness, judgement and rhetoric, which were presumed to be essential to successful participation in the intricacies of the shell market.

On the one hand, this argument did not prevent many a woman from rebelling openly or covertly and, albeit from the sidelines, taking action in what was typically a male domain. On the other hand, it also reveals the flexibility in the ideas of a husband who, convinced of the intelligence of his wife, did not stand in her way, but was able to exploit this indirectly to his own advantage. Remarkably, although the average man has found it difficult to rid himself of his scepticism and distrust of money, the majority of women have eagerly seized the chance to participate in the money economy. Albeit on a modest scale, by selling sweet potatoes, fish, vegetables and eggs to the foreigners, it is apparently a frequent enough occurrence to have ensured that nassa shells and beads have massively disappeared from the social stage. For a long period of time, money was simply referred to as small money/cash. Correctly, of course, as only small sums changed hands in the market in foodstuffs. Only those people with a permanent salary had large sums at their disposal, however, for this very reason, they had placed themselves more or less beyond the boundaries of the society. In the 1970s, in the family of a primary school teacher in Uwebuto, where the wife still confined herself to the traditional horticultural tasks and the husband was paid a monthly salary, it appears that they had reached a workable joint compromise: he left the money economy to her and he handed her his monthly salary, while he continued to participate in the much more exciting shell market.

7.2 USED AS INTERMEDIARY AND SAFE

7.2.1 The woman as intermediary and safe

Even when men claimed a monopoly, this did not signify that a woman had to remain in total ignorance of what her husband was up to. Certainly, by law a wife was accorded a role subordinate to that of her husband in the circulation and storage of shells but, in a harmonious marriage, the wife occasionally assumed the task of acting as intermediary between her husband and his trading partners, the majority of whom were her consanguineal relatives, ferrying shells between them if, for tactical reasons, the men wanted to avoid meeting them personally or considered such a confrontation undesirable. Many women welcomed this task. Not only did this confidential position flatter their self-esteem in respect to the other women, it simultaneously offered them the opportunity to give their opinion, solicited or unsolicited, diplomatically. Perhaps even more important was the role assigned to them in the cultural male-female relationship of functioning as their husbands purses, in the sense that they took care, in the literal sense of the words, of their husbands shells. In a polygynous marriage ideally this role should have been divided up among the wives so that each had the right to take care of the shells which her husband had acquired for her son by her own labour, especially by her efforts in pig-breeding. Of course, what is sketched above presents an ideal cultural pattern. Actually, as the result of envy and friction between the wives and consequently between the wives and the husband, in practice he very seldom or only partially honoured this.

In a modern society, people do not throw their money around but allow only a very limited number of people a glimpse inside their wallet. This was exactly what happened in the shell trade. In order to boost his personal prestige, a man was always expected to carry at least a few shells with him. A person who was stony broke suffered, and not just mentally, as is betrayed by the standard saying: 'If a man does not have a shell with him in his carrying net, he grows enervated and thin.'[4] Those men who did carry their shells with them, wrapped these in a *wediye*, a sort of reddish-brown piece of cloth from natural fibre, Ind. *kain sutera*, in a *pugeuka,* a caterpillar cocoon, or in a looped imitation cocoon ending in a long ribbon, which was used as a purse. This cocoon, either tied or rolled up, was carried with them in a string bag or in a *ute*, a specially looped, smallish shoulder bag.[5] Sometimes a short, decorated bamboo cylinder was used instead of a cocoon. Though my informant was unsure whether men had worn shells on their bodies in their penis gourds, which they now do with rolled up paper money, he did incidentally confirm that shells were sometimes hidden in the roof stuffed into a penis gourd.

In certain situations, for instance when he had to defecate or wanted to visit his wife to make love, a man was expected to set aside his carrying net, on the grounds, for instance, that if he did not the shells in the net would be adversely affected, both externally and internally, and would pay for this in loss of radiance and power. Consequently, it would be left unattended or in unknown company. For this reason he preferred to store the bulk somewhere safe so that it was protected from thieves and just as much from him personally, because he could no longer, in the heat of the moment, impulsively spend more than his intelligence permitted him.

Generally speaking, in such instances a *kugo* was used, a special, exceptionally large string bag without a carrying strap, made not as was an *agiya*, an ordinary

---

[4] *Agiyaida nipoona ma beu kitouyogoko, yame ko mee taka beu epoo na beu.*

[5] The importation of shells was preceded by the import of red material, *Deiyai ka kagaba*, Ind. *kain merah*. Despite the superficial likeness of this textile to the naturally formed *wediye*, it was said that even in former times it was not used to transport shells. Men carried this material unwrapped with them in the string bag, as a sort of amulet or magic talisman, which could summon shells to appear. In the mythological context, it was presented to people by *abe*, the female spirit of Mount Deiyai [see p. 37], preferably in a dream. On the basis of its colour, it was associated with blood, while, referring to sacrificial observances, shells, as were people, according to the formula: *emouda to ewaa kiyaa, emo tagiida ewaa kiyaa*, 'can only come to light on ground on which blood has been poured' [see chapter 25, section 2].

string bag, to transport articles but instead for the storage of valuables. In the houses in the Mapia region which had more than one room, this bag was locked away in a narrow room, behind the door which led to the women's quarters. This meant that at night a man would have to step over a woman to reach this door. In the Paniai-type dwelling which had only one room, the woman was even more closely involved. A mother had the right to request her son, and a wife to request her husband, to hand their shells over into her keeping. If the relationship was harmonious, this was indeed what they did. Possibly she was expected to put them away in the *kugo*, the string bag which was hung up on an inside wall [of her house] behind the place where she sat. However, as it was known that in an unguarded moment every boy would take a peek in that net, despite the prohibition which had been instilled in him from a very early age, this seems unlikely to me. In fact the place was never discussed. It was her secret.

This custom was actually not based purely on safety reasons, just as the husband held on to receiving and disbursing, not merely because of the safety precautions. The one had to do with the woman's femaleness, the other with being a man. The fact that they were kept in this way was good for the shells; in some way or other this improved them. The custom honoured the mythical origin of the shells. One very interesting piece of information was given to me incidentally by my key informant, Isaias Tekege, about his mother's father, Yogebedo Degei, of Badauwo. It was said that when he had placed the corpse of his mother on the death platform, he excised her *kagi*, her rectum, and kept this as an amulet. When this amulet felt dry, he suffered from a lack of shells; when it felt moist, he had them in abundance (Hylkema n.d.: 200).

7.2.2 Safely stored in a rock crevice

If a man had evidence, or might even just have nurtured a suspicion, that his shells were not safe with his wife, that she was using them for her own purposes or, what was more likely, had passed them on to others, initially her brother in the wider sense, and later her son, none of his male relatives could accuse him of not having respected her rights. In view of the frequency of such triangular relationships, it comes as no surprise that many a man had a hiding place of which both mother and son were ignorant. Shells were supposed to be kept in a dry spot, beyond the reach of either the groundwater or the rain, heavenly water. In connection with what has just been said above in this context about women, it was certainly not by chance that stereotypically caves or grottoes were used as storage places. Women, and caves or grottoes were extensions of one another. Nevertheless, it was also averred that wealthy men made use of such storage spaces in order to protect themselves from any eventually aggressive tendencies in their sons. On the other hand, the sons stated that they wanted at any cost to be present at the death of their father, as they were worried that their father would carry his secret with him to the grave. Both sayings illustrate the relationships between the two.

CHAPTER 8 ENTREPRENEUR

8.1 IDEAL PICTURE OF A SUCCESSFUL LIFE

8.1.1 Pessimistic and optimistic views of life

According to a specific view of life, human existence, all the glamour notwithstanding, is so insecure, plagued by so many uncertainties, that it makes little sense to make a proper effort to strive for and to worry about goods and chattels. The only definite fact in life is that nobody escapes death. Consequently, death is the only thing which matters. If a person espouses this point of view, there is no point in risking life and limb in the quest for land or pigs. Essentially, in terms of a territory, traditionally a person can make do with the possession of a tree, later with a piece of ground large enough to dig a grave. Notwithstanding all temptations, his requirements, reduced to their very essence, consist of a one single need, sweet potatoes. Despite all his impulses, a man is still earth-bound in his dual needs of food and sex. Needs to which women too are thought to hone down their concerns, because of their lack of *dimi*, intelligence. Caught up in a mood of euphoria, a man might well claim that he can escape these commonplace needs and the responsibilities to which they give rise, without having to labour. Like a marsupial, he can pluck the fruits the tree provides him in safety among the foliage. Or perhaps, chattering like a flock of parrots, carefree and insouciant, he can eat up all the fruit on the tree, before flying on to the next fully laden tree.

Alas, a human being is not a marsupial nor is he a parrot. He is tied to the earth by his pedestrian requirements and he continually has to come down into the valley from the mountain range; and to claim food and sex he has to doff his crown of bird-of-paradise skins in the presence of his wife. Even if a person has humbly acquitted himself of his duties to his wife and the earth, he still cannot be certain of having these needs fulfilled. In the wake of a prolonged dry or wet period, a time of famine lurks just beyond the horizon. It is no accident that famine and death are proclaimed in conjunction with each other in the report of the Club of Kotomoma, as a direct response to the prophecy of the arrival of aeroplanes and motor boats as portents of a flood of shells. This prediction held up a period humming with activity and a lust for life before the eyes of the people.

In Ekagi society, both visions are just as militantly and inextricably linked to each other as the *ibo* or *tonowi* and the *daba*. Interestingly, although *ibo* and *daba* are original Ekagi words, *tonowi* or *tonawi* sounds rather alien, as borrowed from somewhere else. In this context, *ibo*, great, high, refers to entrepreneurs, and as the next step on the ladder, *tonowi* to those entrepreneurs who have really made their name. In contrast to this, *daba*, small, lowly, designates people who in their own opinion because of a lack of opportunities and means, [but] according to that of others because of a lack of vision or enterprise, have never applied themselves to anything and consequently have never made a success of anything. From this point of view, the [biblical] Parable of the Talents could have been written for the Ekagi.

8.1.2 Selecting a type of enterprise that brings in returns

It is clear what should be understood about being a success in life and therefore what should be embraced as an ideal for which to strive. The Ekagi see both before them in the real-life figure of the *tonowi.* As long as a person is not in a position in which he has a chance to succeed at his own risk, he can work for a third party. Later this can be even more lucrative, providing that he makes full use of the position he has gained. A marriage tie is an essential condition for success while working at one's own risk. In a moment of honesty with himself and his partner, an Ekagi will dare to admit that when push comes to shove, whether he remains *daba*, small, or becomes *ibo*, big, depends on his wife: 'the wife makes the husband big.' From this point of view, marriage itself is already a form of enterprise. Traditionally it is expected that a man will apply himself simultaneously to various sorts of work in his attempts to be enterprising. In a nutshell, this can be summed up as: crafts, horticulture, hunting, pig-breeding, the marriage market and the begetting of descendants. When it is all said and done, the last is the most important, the crown on all his work. Without a 'replacement' in the sense of an heir, the fame which a man has gathered far and wide turns into a name which is painstakingly avoided or mentioned only with vicarious shame, if not with outright horror.

It stands to reason that men have to carry out these above-mentioned tasks in order to participate in pig-breeding. This participation is what offers them the possibility to prove themselves in the other spheres. Traditionally, this was probably the only path which was open to them. As a consequence of the regular importation of cowries, and at a later stage of money, the figure of the *tonowi* became undermined. Recently it was repeatedly confirmed both in the men's house and in the church: now everyone owns shells, everyone is a *tonowi.* It remained unclear however whether or not one should be happy with this state of affairs. In view of the importation of shells, people actually tended to adopt a completely different strategy towards each other. This context arouses the surmise that, despite the changing times, people still wanted to keep the number of independent pig-breeders restricted, because of the inherent renown attached to their undertaking. Having tried his hand in various branches of enterprise and having tested his luck, while he endeavours not to neglect his other duties, a man has to specialise in what he appears to be good at.

Finding where a person's talents lie does not depend on the results he has managed to produce, but on the fact that he can sell them to others for shells. If a person in vain inspects the pigs that he has agisted, while never succeeding to collect the shells he is due, he should have tried his luck in some other branch of business. If a person was paid by his customers in shells for the string bags he had looped, he had beaten out his own path to future success. Although it was a much less prestigious route, the opportunity had presented itself for him to participate in the shell market and hence to achieve the status of an *ibo*, with the perspective of advancing even farther to become a *tonowi*.

8.2 PRODUCTION FOR SALE

8.2.1 Three possible opportunities for selling

Generally speaking, the gains from work and enterprise could be spent in three ways. Firstly, they could be expended on a person's own family; they could be exchanged, traditionally especially for food in kind or for *nassa*, more recently for money; finally they could be exchanged for cowries. Irrespective of their gender, individuals who lacked a spirit of enterprise were contented with the first possibility. If by chance there was a happily married couple who both had a keen head for business, both of them would divide their income between their family, and besides this the wife would also endeavour to exchange what she had left over for food and money, but the man would devote what he had left over to shells.

However, especially in polygynous marriages, in practice this ideal easily crumbled because the relationships were fraught. In this case the husband might have considered the part which was his so important that he not only tended to leave responsibility for the income for the family to the wife; he might even continually try to skimp on it. Even though they [the members of his family] might have really needed it, in times when a threat of a shortage loured, he stuck twigs in their sweet potato beds as a sign that these were up for sale, for shells. Instead of generously reserving a few good pieces of meat from a pig his wife has reared for his family, as well as the head and the intestines [to which they were entitled], he put all the portions up for sale. Although his wife could complain about this, the husband did not need to feel in the least guilty that he had neglected his children or had disadvantaged her children in respect to those of his other wives. On the basis of the difference in *dimi*, intelligence, by nature the woman lacked foresight, whereas he was able to take a longer perspective. Consequently, because she was not blessed with a spirit of enterprise, she was condemned to be *daba* and he by his very nature was destined to achieve the status of *ibo*. Instead of disadvantaging his children, he was actually doing his utmost to secure their future. If she were reasonable, a wife should have noticed that by opting to do this he too was actually economising on food.

8.2.2 Set aside to be spent on shells

The man gave the impression as if [everything] which was contributed to the family, [including] items bartered for other goods, did not reach the goal for which it was made, planted or bred. Just as the crayfish in the lake or the game in the forest only achieved their natural goal if they were outsmarted by human beings, or as the sweet potatoes used as fodder for the pigs were eaten as meat, they thought that the work and energy invested in enterprise by humans only achieved real completion if it was transformed into shells. At least this is what a man felt.

However, from the time the wife has the opportunity to turn the fruits of her own toil into money, it seems that she also has readily adopted this trend. When a girl takes the first yield from the garden which she has worked herself to market, and there are not enough buyers, she should be prevented from bartering her wares for foodstuffs which another woman has not sold. In fact, an older woman should buy her wares from her in exchange for money, even though it had not been her intention to purchase that particular produce. This is because the way in which a girl sells her first yield is decisive for the way she will sell it in future. Exchange in kind sets in motion a whole chain of exchanges in kind; selling for money engenders selling for money. Although a girl has to experiment to discover where her strengths and weaknesses lie, it is expected that her more senior relations will see it as their duty to set her feet on the right path. Since the women have been participating in the money economy, they have gained insight into the laws traditionally maintained by men. The upshot is that the women have no problem with dishing up sweet potato leaves to their housemates, while she takes her fish, eggs and vegetables to the market.

8.3 USE TO WHICH THE SHELLS ACQUIRED WERE PUT

8.3.1 Strictly private property

Shells were strictly private property. Even members of the same family kept their property to themselves.[1]

8.3.2 Dictated by the manner of acquisition

Nevertheless, a man was not free to spend his income as he wanted. What a man did with his shells after he had acquired them was partially determined by the way in which he had actually got hold of them. In certain cases, a man could not use them but was forced to keep them as a sort of capital. For example, the shells which people received for the first *kamu-tai*.[2] In fact, this actually made distribution inevitable. In the report of the Club of Kotomoma it is stressed that people did not keep the shells acquired for themselves but distributed them. This

---

[1] By editor. Hylkema had added a handwritten gloss:

Everybody prepares and works his or her own garden, even if he employs people [providing them] with lunch or a wage. Each person builds his own house; even in the Mapia region where several brothers build [one] house together, the house is the property of the brother who takes the initiative, and the others can hope that they will be allowed to use it.

[2] By editor. *Kamu-tai*: 'a religious ceremony to drive out a spirit being that brought in sickness or to bring in rain' (Giay 1995: xix).

aspect can only be satisfactorily discussed in the framework of the non-empirical origin [in chapter 25].

8.3.3 Besieged by consanguineal and affinal relatives
Everyone who was known to own shells harboured the fear that his property was threatened. On the one hand, this threat emanated from his wife, as the mother of a family or as intermediary in the relationship with her consanguineal relatives; on the other hand it loured from the side of his own male, patrilineal relatives. When responding to direct or indirect requests, a man had the tendency to excuse himself by referring to the multitude of debts which he had to settle in various places. Instead of actually doing this, in the first instance he tended to hoard his shells, telling himself by way of apology that he was waiting for the right moment to re-invest them in something else when prospects were at their brightest. [For instance,] In a marriage to a second or third wife, seemingly perhaps for his own benefit, but, at least in the long term, for the benefit of his children and grandchildren. In response to this tendency the society also has a number of standard maxims. Hoarding was harmful both to the man and to his shells: the condition of both of them would deteriorate as a consequence. If they were retained or if they were thwarted, shells would scorch deep into the hand. After they had been kept captive, the shells wanted to be released again as quickly as possible. Because circulation came as naturally to shells as it does to stink beetles which scuttle from tree to tree.

8.3.4 Squander or gamble
Remarkably, although people were keen to obtain shells, they often dispensed with the shells again with little or no deliberation. Remarkably, this happened among the women. Proof of this lies in what they consequently bought with the money, really just for the kick and the reputation which the conversion of her labour into money brought her. Anyone not participating in this soon felt left behind. As a sort of justification for her lack of entrepreneurial spirit, she described herself as *daba*. Generally speaking, a man had three possibilities at his disposal. Usually, in the first instance, succumbing to pressure exerted by his wife, he could use his shells for food, clothes, utensils or wages, generally referred to as *mapugai*, to spend, implying squandering. Although they were mentioned in the same breath, there was a big difference between a man who used his shells to buy food and clothes and one who allocated his for utensils and wages. The first man benefited only very fleetingly from them. Invariably, there was the pressure exerted by wife and family to use the shells for meat and other foodstuffs. This was no less a dangerous pressure because, when driven by physical needs, a husband too always remains a child. In the second case, in the course of time the shells did produce profit. By purchasing a new canoe, a man gave his wife the opportunity to participate in the traditional catching of crayfish, more recently in fishing, with the prospect of being able to sell the catch.

Generally speaking, in response to pressure exerted by patrilineal kin, two possibilities presented themselves. If a community was faced with the task of collecting a heavy fine, the whole gamut of standard arguments was run through to convince the members to contribute, to postpone their own interests until the acutely threatening danger had been averted. However, contributing to a fine was the equivalent of tossing shells into the water. Even though, at that moment the community was prepared to sing lofty praises to honour its saviour in a time of need, the average man still realised that [contributing shells to a fine] was just the same as throwing them away. On the one hand, they would continue to nag him, as the *tene*, the outer shell, of a drowned person would haunt a place and plague passers-by, especially its *ipuwe*, closest relatives, as long as its *aya*, its hard core or soul, remained imprisoned in its body, until the corpse was recovered and laid out on dry land or was buried in the earth, after which the soul could make its journey to the abode of souls. Closely associated with the payment of a fine was using of shells for a sacrifice. Strictly speaking, in both cases, people never saw their money again. In both cases it was consumed. If a man was really determined to make a full profit from his shells in order to realise his ambitious goals in life, his best choice was to invest them in bride price. Just as the final goal of labour and enterprise was the shell, the proper and definitive destination of the shell was in bride price.[3]

8.3.5 Bound by allocation

As long as a person had not allocated his shells for some purpose, he had very little defence if an appeal was made to his sense of responsibility. However, as soon as they had been allocated, he was more or less bound to honour this, which limited his freedom to trade, but also offered him a respectable excuse for not acquiescing in a request from another. If a man took a shell with him for the purchase of the raw materials for making a rope, he had to use that shell, and only that one for this particular purpose. If a person had allocated shells to buy meat for a birth ceremony, but as a consequence of unforeseen circumstances had not used them for this purpose, he was expected to keep them until the next such feast. If a person had made an allocation, he was not to deviate from this, on pain of the visible deterioration of the condition of both the person and his shells.

---

[3] By editor. On the page which contained the last paragraph of sub-section 8.3.4, Hylkema had added a handwritten gloss without indicating where he wanted to insert it. I opted for the end of the sub-section.
Swindle [??] was a form of income for the group. His own group was not bothered about how a man had obtained what he has, unless this would cause trouble for the group and it would be forced to pay a fine. Morally [four illegible words]. In order to win himself a reputation a man had to contribute: not just sit there with his mouth open, waiting until someone put something into it. In order to trade, a person has to have something put by, something he could lay his hand on.

8.4 NO DISTRIBUTIVE TRADE

8.4.1 Exchange between producer and consumer

Had, for instance, a person discovered that he was skilled in the making of string bags, in the sense that he was able to make money by doing this, theoretically he could use the shells so procured to plough back into his business by buying string bags and reselling them for profit somewhere else. Remarkably this almost never happened. Almost invariably, the traffic was between the producer and the consumer. People did not give their products to another to sell, even if either the producer or the consumer had to walk for hours, if not days, to do this (van Baal 1975: 42). During a pig feast people could expect that all sorts of utensils, such as paddles, would be offered for sale. Even after the church service there were people standing ready to do business. However, strangely enough this almost always concerned items which a person had made personally or had brought from somewhere else. In the latter instance, it was the strangers/outsiders, for example secondary school teachers, who had their pupils sell wares. Since the Ekagi have been able to sell goods at the market, people throng there in droves, even those who have only a few bundles of *idaya* [an edible leaf vegetable] or beans with them. Carrying a string bag full of peanuts, people walked to the market in Waghete or even Enarotali to sell them. If there were purchasers there who were planning to resell the goods they had bought elsewhere, for instance in Nabire, they were almost without exception not Ekagi. People did employ others to help them with the carrying, but these had to be paid to do this. Hence, a person who is adept in looping nets can sometimes, if so inclined, buy the essential raw materials at the market, instead of having to go into the field and collect the tree bark himself.

8.4.2 Middlemen

Because a trade route from the south coast passed through the Ekagi area on its way to the east and vice versa, it might be assumed that middlemen, who had more or less made this their profession, would appear. Pospisil also confirmed that people went personally to the brine pools in the Moni area to produce their own salt and then sold only a tiny proportion on to outsiders (1978: 23). Even though he makes no comment on this, there is reason to question if the trade in carrying bags and tobacco to the south coast was conducted by middlemen (1978: 23). There was certainly some distributive trade in connection with *yuwo*, in as much as people purchased the animals elsewhere, sold the meat at the *yuwo*, after which they paid the sellers. Nevertheless, even in this instance the buyer's freedom to trade was restricted. The seller could send his wife to fetch the head and so forth, but actually this was also a check on whether he had actually slaughtered the animal or whether he did not covertly use it to breed from. People could sell off parts, for instance by taking a leg and then reselling it later.

8.4.3 No trader in the strict sense of the word

Simply because the Ekagi stood out on account of his trading journeys, his *duwa uwii*, it might have been expected that he would have been just the person to plunge into petty trading by buying and selling, just as a peddler or a grocer does. The Ekagi was not a trader in the usual sense of the word: buying goods up to sell them again at a profit. This was exposed to the light of day when projects and small shops were established [as a part] of the development plan. Within a longer or shorter period, nearly every project or shop had failed, because the capital had disappeared. Many a project received a death-blow because the appointed leader, who had demanded control over all trading rights, had squandered the capital in his rivalry with the other top-ranking people and with undisguised scorn for the ordinary person. He could not prevail against his own people and he could not resist the prestige which would accrue from splashing his riches around, thereby benefiting his relatives and friends. Only if the leader was directly under the thumb of the priest did the business flourish. But, even then, only with all sorts of receipts and losses which could not be checked and which were recouped from others. If a person contributed to a ticket, he was an entrepreneur, but this did not apply to somebody who weighed up his chances beforehand.[4]

8.5 GAMBLER

He gambled, he rushed into it blindly. Just as later a person staked his money if any Tom, Dick or Harry claimed that he could multiply the sum. He would have been game for a pyramid scheme (Cf van Baal (1975: 37) on gambling as a form of negative reciprocity).

---

[4] By editor. It is unclear to me what kind of 'ticket' Hylkema refers to in this sentence. Possibly it is an airline ticket for a business trip to the coast that the traveller could not pay for by himself. In case the trip was a success, the contributor might get his contribution back and a share of the yield as well.

CHAPTER 9 IDENTIFICATION AND VALUATION

9.1 SELECTIVELY DEVELOPED CAPACITY FOR IDENTIFICATION

9.1.1 Learning by looking

The question of which characteristics were decisive while identifying a shell by sort, category and quality has, after all this, become only more pressing. However, I do not have any satisfactory answer.

In the literature this is said to be the secret of the Ekagi, one which they did not readily disclose. Therefore I need not feel ashamed [for my lack of knowledge] insofar as intelligent younger people also appeared to be confronted with an insoluble problem. Even though older primary school teachers played an active role in the shell market, there were many younger men who could boast of a higher school education or a permanent position [in the civil service?] who lived and worked locally and who mixed daily with their relatives. Generally speaking, their job did not absorb all of their day. Nevertheless, it seemed to provide them with a status, with which learning a skill that the older generation had mastered, but that in principle was already out of date, would have been inconsistent.

In theory it would have seemed likely that a person would have sought information by making enquiries of an acknowledged expert, or that he would have subjected himself to an initial training at the hands of a relative from an older generation. However, at a very early age, men find it below their manly dignity to allow themselves to be instructed. The word *tedemai*, to have one-self instructed, has pejorative overtones, synonymous with being told what to do, obey. Stereotypically, this is the behaviour expected of women. Men do not enquire because they do not wish to be instructed. Conversely, men also do not appreciate being asked. This is rapidly interpreted as having someone breathing down one's neck, being called to account, or with the threatening of a certain monopoly position in relation to a laboriously acquired specialty.

When, in the framework of our investigation, my key informant Isaias Tekege made so bold as to ask his father [, Imoudakebo,] outright how he was able to distinguish whether a shell was good or not, the latter answered with a terse: '*Dou*'. In this context, *dou* can best be translated in the first instance with 'you look'. In the eyes of the Ekagi, the central position in any learning process is taken by 'looking'. In order to learn how to build a good fence, a person should 'observe' while others are busy doing this in order to see how they do this. However, it is much more likely to be the case that a person, later, takes a covert 'look' at what others have constructed. When a person is its object, 'looking' is the equivalent to 'learning to know a person'. Initially, this is in the superficial sense of learning to distinguish a person physically, so that in the future one will recognise him again. Every stranger in their society will have personally experienced how literally this advice was taken. Children especially were in the habit of calmly and quietly, but unabashedly, assessing a stranger objectively from a safe distance. Then, on a deeper level, it occurs in the sense of diagnosing a person's character or disposition. Actually, these two levels are inseparable. In a nutshell, looking is the equivalent to personally acquiring knowledge or gaining knowledge and insight of someone or something.

9.1.2 Recognising

When shells were the object [of examination] the technical term was *mege dou*, to look at shells, as a synonym for becoming acquainted with them, indirectly to identify and appraise them. Participation in the shell trade was out of the question, when a man was unable to identify a shell. Whenever a number of people contributed shells, as during the assembling of a bride price, and the offer was not accepted [by the bride givers], so everybody could reclaim his contribution, it was apparent that each person could unerringly recognise the shells he had contributed from the large pile displayed. As if everybody, as a consequence of repeatedly looking at them for a long period, had acquired a photographic memory of his own shells. Generally, this included also those who were unable to appraise the value of any shell.

If a person was able to recognise a particular shell among a great pile of them, he had undoubtedly made a considerable achievement. Presuming that the ability to identify is a protracted process, which is attested to by every baby in the world, it is simultaneously selective. The complaint that people of other races, above all races of a different colour, are extremely difficult to tell apart is universal. The Papuan has precisely the same experience. Even after I had lived among them for years, the older people repeatedly confused me with a white colleague, despite what were great differences in our eyes. Although they would never confuse two shells, in their confrontation with us, their ability to identify left them in the lurch. The first question this raises is on the basis of which characteristics do we in fact identify somebody ourselves. Next is the question which of these characteristics we use to describe this person so that a third party will be able to form an adequate picture of him or her.[1] These do not have to be the same characteristics everywhere. All the more so since in one society people are accustomed, from their youth, to seeing their fellow human beings wearing clothes, and in another society people who are undressed. According to their own standard expression, the Ekagi recognise, within their own society. a person in the distance by their gait and closer by, not as is usual among us also by his face, *ebe peka*, literally: mouth-eyes, but by his nose, *yuma*. Consequently, it is

---

1 As illustration, I give a quotation from a novel chosen at random: 'In his imagination, he saw his striking young face: the large blue eyes, the long, pronounced nose, the somewhat mocking mouth and the black locks which hung down to his collar.'

no accident that they also possess an extensive, standardised vocabulary to characterise a person's nose.

9.1.3 Active and passive participation in the shell market

When shells had to be appraised, Isaias' father could compete with other men self-confidently and decisively as someone who knew the ropes. And, as he advised Isaias, his skill was entirely self-taught, acquired by making his own mistakes. As he said, he had never been close to his father, Bobeukebo, even though he was his eldest son. When Bobeukebo had taken a second wife, Imoudakebo had sided with his mother and had distanced himself from his father. Isaias' mother, who had heard both Isaias' question and Imoudakebo's answer, advised Isaias to pay particular attention to those shells which recognised experts had adjudged to be 'good'. She was shrewd enough to take part in shell transactions on her own account, albeit in the margins of the male society. However, for their appraisal she was dependent on an expert. Generally, she sought advice from her husband in this department, but in view of the fact that she was loath to be belittled, I do not discount the possibility that on occasion she went to a cousin in Enarotali, with whom she had a warm relationship, for counsel. One of Isaias' more practical friends, who had been trained in the cattle-raising business in Epouto, had resigned himself to the fact that he was beyond understanding the fine points of the skill. He thought that people in the same position as he was would have to be the first to have cash ready, when a shell met with the approval of experts.

9.2 APPRAISAL AND APPRAISERS

9.2.1 Meeting an expert

Once Isaias had mentioned to me in passing that people in Tigi exhibited more interest in the *makota*, the serrated edged aperture on the underside, whereas in Tage it was the *ebe*, the mouth or front of the shell which was important. An attempt to verify this did indeed reveal that Tage people did study the front of the shell more often and longer than the underside. However, far from satisfied with Imoudakebo's terse answer to Isaias, we questioned him together on another occasion, asking to which aspects he paid particular attention when appraising a shell. In response, he began by taking three separate shells out of his *ute*, his shoulder bag, a *yoodagi* and two *bodiya*, followed by the beginnings of a string of shells. As the shells lay on the table in front of us, he first drew our attention to the rim, *eiyo*, around the mouth, *ebe*. Here, closely linked to type and age, all the colours of the rainbow were visible. Accordingly, this phenomenon is called *wayamo*, rainbow, or *bui*, referring to a multicoloured cordyline. The rainbow was clearly visible in the *yoodagi*, but in both *bodiya*, it was somewhat blurred, *bagugiye*. It surrounded the whole rim of the *yoodagi*, *wayamao bodidaa tita*, but was only partially present in the *bodiya*. When I laid a shell which I had happened to pick up from the road alongside his shells, he began by categorising and appraising this as a *yuu*, [literally] cheering, shouting, a shell of little merit. He continued by demonstrating the difference between the serrated edges of the aperture in his shells and mine. The *ego*, teeth or barbs, on the underside of his *yoodagi* were all equally large, clearly separated from each other and set at regular intervals. Those on my *yuu* turned out to be fused with each other and some of them were skewed rather than straight. His explanation also revealed that a shell was classified as *ibo*, big, not on the basis of size but of its value. Although they were of lesser value, both his *bodiya* were larger than the *yoodagi*. Again in the string, size was not really a factor in the order in which the shells were strung from greater to lesser value. Later, during the presentation of a bride price, I saw shells as big as a naturally big *yoo* lying on the mat among the small change in the category of my *yuu*.

Although at first glance he had labelled my *yuu* as low-quality, Imoudakebo could not resist picking this shell up from the table time and again and examining it. The shell was new to him. He was not yet 'acquainted with' it. As he did this, he explained that the more a shell 'dried out', in the sense of ageing, the more chance it had of being successfully introduced into a higher category, but that this particular one would never be placed in the higher category of the *yoodagi*. The irregular nature of the indentations could never be corrected. What he told us was clearly visible in the shells: all you had to do was to 'look at' the shells. But in order to see what he told us, it was not necessary to peer at a shell for such a long time as was the normal practice. Just as with the identification of a face, his eyes probably registered many more details than he was able to express in words.

9.2.2 Blind appraisers

Isaias' father was not alone locally in his ability to judge shells. Although members of the younger generation acknowledge their lack of skill either openly or diffidently, members of the adult generation were inclined to exhibit their mutual competition by giving themselves airs about being experts in the art of appraisal. Despite this undeniable competition, there were also men who had won themselves such a name that they were generally recognised as experts. Because Imoudakebo's advice depended on keeping one's eyes peeled, two partially sighted or blind people deserve a special mention.

When talking about this topic, people used to drop the name of a certain Dimikebo Pekei. His eyes suppurated constantly. He saw so badly that when he moved around, other people had to lead him by the hand. Despite this, he enjoyed some fame as an appraiser. He managed to do this by rubbing the shells backwards and forwards between his fingers. In Timeepa, in the Mapia, on various occasions I had seen an elderly but still extremely vital blind man passing by at a remarkably high speed, tapping right and left with a stick. When I asked my local key informant, Paulus Wakei, who the man was, he told me he was a Mote who lived in Kamu, but who was generally travelling around.

Unable to undertake other activities, he had specialised so deeply in the appraisal of shells that in the wider area he was a renowned, respected appraiser. In the role of an itinerant trader, he had made the appraisal of shells his profession. In his case too, his eyes were in his fingers. Undoubtedly various characteristics can be established using the sense of touch. Among those mentioned is the difference between a smooth and a rough, or between a smooth and a rather bumpy surface. Given time to think about it, a great many other possibilities would become apparent. Nevertheless, these blind men puzzled also my informants.[2]

[2] Leafing through a Reader's Digest, I once read a Chinese anecdote which I quote from memory: 'A young man apprenticed himself to a master to learn the art of appraising jade. At the beginning of the first lesson, the master thrust a piece of jade into his hands instructing him to roll it backwards and forwards between his fingers. He then began talking about everything under the sun, except about jade. When to the despair of the young man a number of sessions had passed in such a fashion, and at the beginning of the last session he once again obediently rolled the piece of jade between his fingers, he was startled: although it bore a speaking likeness to jade, he felt that it was not jade.'

CHAPTER 10 IN CONTRAST TO THE DANI

10.1 IMPACT ON THE SOCIO-POLITICAL PATTERN

10.1.1 Universal means of exchange

The use of the cowry as a means of payment extends to the whole of the known world of the Ekagi. Writing of the opening up of the Baliem Valley, Broekhuijse (1996: 137) noted: 'We obtained (that is to say bought with *nyerak-ekken*, *Cypria moneta* [sic] shells) everything we wanted.' In fact, the use of the shells was not restricted to the inhabitants of the Central Highlands. They were used for the same purpose in the Keerom area, in the hilly country far north of the Star Mountains, and among the Muyu in the hills between the lowlands and the highlands towards the south coast. A comparison reveals that the importance and the role of the cowry varied per ethnic group. On the basis of personal experience, I can say that in the Ekagi culture it received far greater attention and was accorded a far greater role than in the Ngalum culture in the Star Mountains. Nevertheless, it is known that also the Muyu made intensive use of the cowry. Although, on this account, they form an attractive object to offer a mirror image by which to clarify the exceptional role and significance of the cowry among the Ekagi, I have decided against this because of a dearth of relevant data. In fact, I have opted for an ethnic group in which the cowry was obviously not assigned a dominant role, the Baliem Dani.[1]

An examination of the literature allows the postulation that among the Highlanders the Ekagi stood out just as much for the pivotal role they accorded the cowry in their mutual contacts as the Baliem Dani profiled themselves by their martial feats in their wars against each other. In origin, this cultural difference was based on a choice. That the Ekagi apparently elected to place the cowry and all the activities attached to it in a pivotal position, raises the question of how they made this choice and what they wished to achieve with it. Learning of the explicitly bellicose culture of the Dani and the impact of war on the expansion of their society and of the underlying motives prompting it, leads me to presume that the role war played in Dani society was fulfilled by the cowry among the Ekagi.

10.1.2 From the perspective of the survival of the group

The two ethnic groups are of a comparable size. In both instances they are numerically among the relatively larger ethnic groups of the Central Highlands. As did all Highland groups, both depended economically on horticulture in

[1] By editor. The Baliem Dani to whom Hylkema refers in this chapter are the Dani living in the Grand Valley, a wide valley with a flat floor through which the Baliem flows before it leaves the Central Highlands via the Baliem Gorge. The Grand Valley Dani are an ethnic group separate from the Western Dani who live north and west of the Grand Valley.

which the sweet potato was the staple and, in close connection with this cultivation, both kept pigs. Socially, both monogamous and polygynous families occurred, while the population was segmented into patrilineal, territorial clans. The first point of interest for a comparison is that the male half of the population in both groups was divided up into unimportant -- Grand Valley Dani: *kepu*; Ekagi: *daba* -- and important persons -- Grand Valley Dani: *kain*; Ekagi: *ibo*. This was important because at any given moment an outsider was able to know who within the circle of the important men fulfilled the role of leader, despite the lack of a specific designation for a leader and despite the alternating character of this leadership.

Broadly speaking, on the basis of their horticultural activities, both ethnic groups developed the same sorts of work, including handicrafts, house-building, hunting, trade, and war. But the minute these are compared with each other, remarkable differences are apparent. Although both were populous, horticultural peoples, the Dani, packed into close proximity in the limited space of a large, fertile valley, evolved a methodically intensive horticulture, on territories separated by areas of no-man's land. The Ekagi who were widely scattered in naturally demarcated valleys or regions, practised a partially intensive and partially extensive horticulture on relatively unpromising soil. Despite this difference in habitat and actual culture, both concentrated their interests on the maintenance and the continuation of the group. Whereas the Dani practised birth control, the Ekagi honoured the ideal of the largest possible family. However, in view of these antithetical family policies, what is particularly striking is that traditionally there was so little discrepancy in population growth, in other words, despite the variation in methods, the two results were virtually the same.

10.1.3 Glorification of violence among the Dani

It can be postulated that, within the range of their undertakings, both groups have laid special emphasis on one particular activity, to the extent that this activity in fact served as a dynamic factor in the constitution of social life. I leave aside how the emphasis is related to the distinctive features of their territories. 'The life of the inhabitants of the Baliem was – according to Veldkamp (1996: 91) – dominated by war, the enemy, fear, and taboo.'[2] Corresponding to their predilection for warfare, the Dani maintained [socially and politically] a distinct separation between inner and outer world. In fact, the fertility of the soil of the Dani provided them with a no-man's land to protect themselves against a hostile outer world, to build watch towers in this periphery and to have a clear-cut village formation in the centre of their territory characterised by a communal palisade containing fenced-off groups of houses built close together, reflecting a similarly close-knit, structured community.

---

[2] By editor. Frits Veldkamp established the first patrol post in the Grand Valley in 1956.

Although as a consequence of war it could happen that an enemy was driven from his lands, which opened up the possibility for an expansion of territory, this was not the real motivation. The real danger to the continuation of the group did not come from outside but from within: horizontally by the rivalry between the members of the living generations and vertically because of the vulnerable nature of the bond with the ancestors. Fighting with the enemy continually offered the opportunity to show what a man was worth.

> Social prominence, with the privileges pertaining to this status such as polygyny, plenty of land and pigs, was achieved in this society by being valorous in battle, and by wounding, or preferably killing, many enemies (Veldkamp 1996: 92).

Brute strength, bloodthirstiness and bravery occupied a central position in the system of values. This enabled the society to be divided up into a lower level *kepu*, unimportant people, persons of little account, and an upper level *kain*, prestigious people, people who counted, and simultaneously there was another distinction made within the upper level of this hierarchy, with the top occupied by the actual leading *kain*. Mutual rivalries were settled without people feeling the need to make them explicit or to raise them as the underlying reason.

> It was not – says Broekhuijse (1996: 144) – territorial conquest which mattered, nor was the slaying of as many enemies as possible important; what mattered was the maintenance of the intense relationship between the living and the dead .... Joy was aroused not so much by the slain enemy (he was a mere symbol), but by the significance of that symbol, namely that the *mokat* [the ancestral ghosts], were close by the people and were sympathetic towards them. That meant that the *hiperi* (sweet potatoes) would grow in abundance, the pigs would remain healthy and other matters would prosper. The enemy believed in the same religious ideas. Consequently, this generated an unending series of victimisations. In a nutshell: war was primarily a sacred occasion.

If this relationship between the living and the dead presents us with the motive, and the mutual rivalry among the living the unmistakable reason, the principle we recognise at the basis is an unevenly divided degree of individual ambition.

10.1.4 Distrust of violence among the Ekagi

In contrast, the first fact which strikes the observer about the Ekagi is that they maintained no [such] clearly defined boundary between the inside and the outside world. Instead of there being a clear-cut boundary with the outside world, there was an unmistakable internal division of the inside world. Within the clan or sub-clan, the Ekagi had several layered divisions, according to group and territory. For the outside world, sub-lineages were the smallest units, named after their location. However, they were further divided into extended families. For example, in the sub-clan Tekege of Dimiya, people distinguished various lineages designated by territory, such as the Tekege of Tagatadi, the Tekege of Mogodagi, of Arnokotu and so forth. Within the Tekege of Tagatadi there was yet another sub-division into *iboopa*, the descendants of the most senior, *mabiipa*, the descendants of the middle, and *amooyeepa*, of the most junior branches.

Settlement corresponded to these territorially and nominally far-reaching divisions. Although the Dani of old had settled in villages, among the Ekagi the founding of villages did not take place before the colonial era. Related to the fact that land which would reward hard work was scarce, the Ekagi lived traditionally in family dwellings scattered widely apart from each other. These were divided into a male section and a family section, as in the Mapia region, or into complexes of family dwellings serving as the residences of extended families attached to one communal men's house, as in Paniai. These sorts of dwelling units actually accommodated three, four or five household heads and their families. Segments of clans and sub-clans clashed frequently over discrepant claims to one and the same piece of land, and over misbehaviour of pigs. Moreover, men saw their pigs, not to mention their women and girls, as being under constant threat from each other's undisciplined male youth.

In contrast to the Dani, the Ekagi eschewed the use of spears. Terminologically, they made a distinction between *ara wagii*, fighting with bow and arrow, and *kopa wagii*, fighting with sticks. Bows and arrows were consonant with a conflict in which blood could be drawn or people killed. Hence they were not employed between kin relatives. Sticks were used in fights in which strictly speaking no blood could be drawn, hence between relatives. In fact, such a fight with sticks could readily spin out of control, blood was indeed drawn and it could flare up into a battle to the death in which bows and arrows were used. Although the abolition of warfare dates from the colonial era and the older generation could still remember plenty of wars, also before its abolition war was regarded as a disaster or an evil. On the one hand, many a folk tale, referring to the past, begins with a life and death struggle, but on the other, referring to the present day, people constantly point to the interference of a fine-hungry, omnipotent, foreign government apparatus. Remarkably, in the tales wars are never waged between clans, but they escalate from fights between *keneka*, brothers, in the sense of patrilineally related first cousins, second cousins and so on. Moreover, [they provide] illustrations that brute force does not pay and that, despite initial successes and gains, the most foolhardy attacker in the end is always thoroughly punished, because supernatural figures take the side of the innocent loser.

[For the Ekagi,] armed conflict is inherently demonic, more precisely devilish, in origin. Consequently it is human beings unworthy. Bearing this origin in mind, people were expected not to allow their indignation and anger to get the better of them. They were to exercise restraint and to attempt to resolve any differences which may have arisen in a dignified manner. Instead of wars and fights being encouraged, children were endlessly warned above all not to give any cause for such violence. On all possible occasions in church sermons the theme of preserving unity was hammered upon. According to the nature and attitude of the preacher, instead of revenge and taking the law into one's own hands, the male members of the congregation were exhorted to practise humility, the female resignation. Or, regardless of their sex, they were admonished not to hold grudges, but to state these in the presence of recognised authorities during public sessions so that they could be talked about and the injury be compensated by a fine. Instead of physical brutality, in such meetings oratory, persuasion and diplomacy took pride of place. In order to prevent war with other clans, people even went as far as to kill an adulterous brother themselves. However, it is not surprising that, when that happened, the position which the adulterer had achieved within his group entailed gross legal inequality. And fights or legal quibbles between *keneka*, brothers, demonstrated the importance of being able to call upon matrilineal kin,[3] affinal relatives and others who had been obliged by gifts.

Remarkably, in case of warring brothers, or when an adulterous relative, a sorcerer or a witch were killed, people alluded to the intervention of supernatural powers, beyond the ken of the human world. In the first case, people allowed themselves to be used as their henchmen; in the second people offered to act as representatives. In an exorcism during the ceremonial consecration of a new house in the Mapia region, those present, above all the younger people, were harangued that if they misbehaved they were making a hole in the Earth's crust through which personified Evil could invade the human world from the Underworld and, infiltrating among the people, could drive them to murder and mayhem. In the Paniai region, if there were a quarrel about garden land, those involved were called upon to moderate their behaviour, in order to prevent the earth mother from rising up and planting her 'blood-pole' among them. Although, in the event of an execution, people initially endeavoured to prevent the eruption of a blood feud by including a close relative in the conspiracy and allowing him to shoot the first arrow, the context makes it clear that people did not act of their own accord, compelled by vulgar envy and hate, but as representatives of one of the supernatural or heavenly male deities in his guise as the Avenger of Injustice. Very carefully, they safeguarded themselves against the reprisals of people and spirits. No matter how convinced people may have been that they were right, they were aware that with an execution humans were trespassing across a boundary that they should have respected. In order both to discourage and to justify violent behaviour, the Ekagi resorted to religious arguments.

---

[3] By editor. I suppose that, also in this instance, Hylkema refers to consanguineal relatives via the mother, for instance to relatives belonging to mother's patrilineal clan (See p. 69, note 7).

10.1.5 Survival threatened by internal envy and rivalry

If this meant that specific bellicose characteristics which would be praised in war were met with distrust rather than prestige, it stands to reason that the survival of the group was highly threatened by internal distrust, jealousy, envy and rivalry. Although this differed in each region, on account of their scattered settlement the Ekagi were still able to avoid even their rivals who lived closest by. In the Mapia region an Ekagi man could take up residence among his cousins; in the Paniai region he could retire to his own family home. Nevertheless, this does not mean that he was any less envious or ambitious or less obsessed by a compulsion to prove himself than a Dani man. The observation that people could not only make a success of pig-raising, but also of various other undertakings, and the recommendation that each person should do what he is good at, was the standard conclusion of disputes contended between injured parties about who had earned the designation *ibo*, big man, or even better *tonowi*, successful big man. Each self-respecting man was desirous of making a name for himself and standing out above the nameless throng of the *daba*, low, ordinary men.

Nevertheless, the owners of pigs are not merely convinced in their own hearts that only they should be considered for the title,[4] they also had a tendency to express their conviction by maintaining trade relations with each other to the exclusion of anybody else. The pinnacle of this was exchanging with each other castrated boars which had already been weaned, as *pekanipo*, literally 'apple of one's eye'.

As a matter of fact, the raising of pigs for sale in a world in which the sweet potato was the staple was a vulnerable trade, which only strong, diplomatically skilled personalities were able to manage.

In line with the distrust and envy within the group was the institution of *deeba mege*, traitor's purse, receiving payment for luring a 'brother' into an ambush prepared by an enemy. Mutual distrust, envy and rivalry erupted into murder and mayhem within the group and into executions of adulterers, sorcerers and witches. In a certain sense the Dani had found a radical solution to this problem by creating a common enemy outside their own group and territory. Instead of this, the Ekagi sought to reduce the problem to manageable proportions within the boundaries of the group and the territory, and to steer the existing ambition and rivalry in such a direction that they might be of benefit. Whereas the Dani thirsted for blood and were wont to indulge in 'bellicose language', the Ekagi pondered over and talked about pigs, shells and women. Just as war was traditionally a well-known phenomenon among the Ekagi, so was the use of shell money among the Dani. However, whereas among the Dani it was speci-

[4] By editor. It is not clear to me whether the term 'title' refers to either *ibo* or *tonowi.*

fically war which time and again indirectly restructured the community, both horizontally and vertically, in Ekagi society it was the shell which formed the structural and the dynamic element.

10.1.6 The shell trade dominated by rivalry and cliques

Superficially the primitive shell system does present itself as a pioneer of the modern monetary system, exhibiting all its characteristics such as comprehensibility, universality, objectivity and pragmatism. Closer examination reveals that first of all, eschewing the women's world, the shell was drawn into that of the men. Furthermore, the system was extremely sub-divided and hierarchically ordered, on the basis of characteristics that were not common knowledge. Only acknowledged experts were considered to be able to assess the real value of the shells, while a common man had to be the rival of his partner in order to use them to his benefit. In the course of a process which had perhaps lasted for years, the shell system had finally become so idiosyncratic and complex that it was no longer possible to maintain the analogy with a monetary system.

Their trading journeys, called *duwa uwii*, and following on from this the *duwa yawii*, were characteristic of the Ekagi. *Uwii* means to go thither, *yawii,* in this context, be travelling, making a journey. The origin of *duwa* is uncertain. Preceding *uwii*, *duwa* can be the supine of *duwai*, to go, to cut off. Generally there is no direct object; but sometimes *duwa* is preceded by *ita*, road, path, and in this case it appears that the expression is a binary compound: *ita-duwa + uwii yawii*. Since people gave the appearance of being both vulnerable and guilty when they were travelling on their own, it is obvious that they preferred to be accompanied; an *ibo*, the ordinary big man, by one or more of his peers, each at his own cost and at his own risk; a *tonowi*, a truly big man, by one or more subordinates, exclusively at his expense and his risk. Actually, a *daba* often travelled alone because of his poverty, while, secure in his already established name, a *tonowi* could afford to travel unaccompanied. In the framework of the jealousy fomenting between men and women, a trading journey implied various taboos for a wife on pain that [her husband's] trip might end in disaster. Illustrative of the mutual relationships in the men's house, trading journeys were regarded with mixed feelings. It seems that certain men were afraid of undertaking a trading journey because they feared that, during their absence, business which they did not want to miss out on, would be taken care of by others. Whereas these others watched the departure of a fellow group member with apprehension, scared that he would outperform them with the gains of a successful journey.

In a society in which two uterine brothers were disinclined to be seen walking together while unaccompanied, because of the suspicion this might kindle in others, the unanimity which the trading group exuded quickly assumed the character of a clique, which was in bitter contradiction to the feelings which the members fostered for each other. Associatively, in an extension of the intransitive [verb] *uwii*, to go thither, into the phrase *ita duwa uwii*, to undertake a trading journey, the transitive form *uwai* presents itself: to send thither, with the companion or companions as the direct object. As soon as someone accepted a person as a fellow traveller, he assumed responsibility for that person's life and well-being. Should the companion not return from the journey, the blame for this could fall on the person who had taken the initiative for the undertaking. There was a legal presumption that 'to send thither' should be understood to be 'to let deliberately come to grief', in the active sense of 'to put at risk', 'to sacrifice', or 'to dupe'. An Ekagi preferred to act individually, eager to keep all the advantages for himself, and anxious that he might be duped and exploited by a companion. If this were true of all his activities, it came to a head in his use of the shell. Normally, even a father and son would not disclose their business to each other. Sometimes, people did have an idea of each other's activities, but they were never quite certain about them. If a person seriously wanted to insult another, he should look in his victim's purse/pocket, as it were. There was no room for a third party between a man and his shell. Man and shell were so intimately bound together, their identity and activities could be called identical; they were so narrowly linked to each other that, if the condition of the one deteriorated, simultaneously that of the other visibly declined. Nevertheless, despite his lonely operations, time and again a self-respecting, ambitious man found himself caught up in the competitive, hierarchically structured group.

Comically chosen names for personified shells betrayed more insight into each other's behaviour and motives than people would have permitted themselves to put into words in a normal conversation. Just as men, locked in rivalry, had a tendency to hold others up to ridicule by undertaking a trading journey and then to dupe their travelling companions, it appeared that a shell, on account of its lack of conformity within the hierarchical order of a string, could be designated using the name *Duwauwigipai*, Someone who does nothing but go on trade journeys, and also *Uwagapai*, Someone who dupes others.

By editor. Hylkema does not appear to have finished this chapter. He rounded off section 10.1 with the above. He had started, and restarted, drafting sections 10.2, 10.3, 10.4, 10.5 and 10.6. He later used section 10.2 when drafting chapter 12, and he incorporated parts of sections 10.3, 10.4, 10.5 and 10.6 into chapter 14. Chapter 12 seems to be simply a sketch since it consists in less than one page. Chapters 11 and 13 are missing altogether. Chapter 14 is followed by chapter 18 which consisted of one section numbered 9.3 and which I renumbered. The following chapters are numbers 22 and 25, which is the final one.

CHAPTER 12 DIVIDED OVER CLANS AND LINEAGES

12.1 MYTHICALLY BASED

How to bring structure to a group of people? In order to put together [an image of] its structure, one can examine the group either from the outside or from the inside. Witness the clan names, the division over clans is most conspicuous. Given the two sexes, the Ekagi have patrilineal clans and virilocal marriage. That provides a degree of stability. Above the clan names are phratry names that [however] do not carry practical weight. To a certain extent clans are locally anchored. But they may be found in several locations, as in the case of the Mote. There is a clear transition from relatedness on the basis of descent, and on the basis of territory. While interests on the basis of descent are theoretical or spiritual, relatedness on the basis of territory serves practical interests. They compete. Each clan is subdivided into sub-clans, more or less named. Subsequently sub-clans are subdivided into lineages, and lineages into sub-lineages. The mutual relatedness is given shape in the awareness of common descent. That translates into the possession of a common ancestor and a common tale of origin. It entails more negative consequences than positive ones: members are not to kill, and not to marry each other.

12.2 HISTORICALLY BASED

The character of the group becomes important in the context of face-to-face relationships only. Actually, clans and sub-clans result from an evolution from below. The most conspicuous segment is the local group. As the choice of [marriage] partners makes clear, the attention is focused on the mutual relationships within these local groups. The actual contacts and relationships, framed by the kinship system, follow from marriage relationships. The vertical and horizontal dimensions differ, in close connection with numerical strength. By himself a person cannot form a group. A local group can be simple, on the basis of a monogamous marriage, or compound, on the basis of polygyny. The members of a local group have tangible interests in common with regard to outsiders, but their members' mutual interests conflict. The group's cohesion is made clear by how people live together: [there is] one men's house and [as against] several family houses. It expresses the mutual relatedness, but at the same time everybody's independence. These two have to be brought in accordance. A group appears to be made up of either two generations, so the relationship between parent and child is prominent, or of brothers, so the relationship between elder and younger brother requires attention. Thus the structure is sketched [above]; now we turn to the cohesion. To what extent does cohesion obtain? Structure and cohesion get together in the visible or invisible leadership.

CHAPTER 14 LEADERSHIP AT LOCAL AND REGIONAL LEVELS

14.1 FORMAL STRUCTURE ON THE BASIS OF SEX AND BIRTH

As regards sex, the situation is clear. The male half of the population is born locally; the women born locally are married off: the women present hail from elsewhere and belong by clan name and so on to a foreign group. Unity is created by kin relationships between men. People distinguish four generations in the composition of the local group: the older and the younger generations are central, with in the margins the oldest and the youngest generations. The former is no longer of account, and the latter does not participate in [public] life as yet. Contentious is the relationship between the parental and the younger generations. Who is the more important one is a matter of debate: either the vertical relationship between the generations, or the horizontal one between two or more brothers. The two are interrelated: as the one declines, the other grows. The distinction between older brother and younger brother corresponds to a formal leadership. The structure is expressed in 'head' and 'body', in 'the one ahead' and 'the followers.' Certain relationships are inescapable, which is expressed in kin terms. However, the structure of the group is derived from the position of the leader [within it]. Generally people distinguish between ascribed and achieved leadership.

14.2 LEADERSHIP ON THE BASIS OF SEX AND BIRTH

14.2.1 Terminology

Referring to leadership, current Ekagi vocabulary includes first the term *migouto*, literally head, but originally probably a shortened translation of the Indonesian *kepala kampong,* village headman. More authentic is the term *migouguu uwii*, derived from 'to be at the head', in the meaning of to be in front. The term *ibouto*, literally 'the very oldest of several brothers', is absolutely authentic.

14.2.2 Leadership within the nuclear family, as implied by sex

14.2.3 Leadership among brothers, as implied by birth

14.2.4 Leadership within the family, as implied by birth

14.3 CONDITIONED LEADERSHIP

14.3.1 Bipartition between ibo *and* daba

The impact of sex and birth depends on how people actually perform. It results in the bipartition of a group into *ibo* and *daba.* Leadership has to be supported by recognition and loyalty. People may join a leader and support him in the implementation of his plans, but they may also not turn up and let him muddle on by himself; finally, they may turn against him by joining an adversary. Decisive is what a person can bring in, what a person has to offer.

14.3.2 Individually, within the nuclear family

Brothers all work strictly individually. A man has a say over the members of his nuclear family only. The extent to which a man finds recognition, and accrues appreciation and support for his undertakings, depends on his attitude towards his wife and her interests. These are with both her family and with her children on the other. The birth ceremony is crucial. On that occasion she can parade her husband and her own status before friends, acquaintances and kin. Within the nuclear family a husband may expect absolute loyalty from his wives in relation to all the children who have been born to him. Generally, a man is responsible for his wife. They are jointly responsible for the children and, with the older children, they are jointly responsible for the younger ones.

However, as the head [of the family] he is their sole representative to the outside world to which he represents them exclusively. This situation continues until they [the children] marry and leave the family. The father may further expect absolute loyalty from his children in his dealings with outsiders. Nevertheless, he has to buy loyalty from both his wife and his children. If he wants to enjoy authority, he has to prove himself. His [ability to] supply meat, in daily life, but especially during birth ceremonies and pig feasts, is decisive. This is the only way he can buy the loyalty of the members of his family. To be able to serve meat, it is essential to have shells. Each man is entitled to a wife. If father and brother fail him [in this respect], the local group helps out. The members of the nuclear family co-operate under the husband's leadership. On this level all men are fundamentally equal. They all have the same obligations, towards their families, to their mothers' and sisters' kin, and to their wives' kin.

Ekagi do not work communally. They do not do so, because without fail that results promptly into hierarchical relationships. Everybody works for himself and is supposed to supply his wife and children with the essentials of life.

14.3.3 Ambivalent relationship between father and eldest son

The legal rule is that the father is the exclusive head of the family and that, after his death, [this position is taken by] his eldest son. The positions of father and eldest son are extremely vulnerable. Should there be competition between them, the question is whether the younger brothers support their father, or their eldest brother.

The eldest son enjoys a privileged position. But his primogeniture does not automatically endow him with the capacities required [for leadership]. Remarkable is the affection of the father for his eldest son. In him he sees his true successor. His trust in his son makes him blind to his [son's] deeds and deaf to critical comments. It must be extremely painful for a father when, in her reaction to a second marriage, his first wife alienates his oldest son from him. A case in point is the relationship between the amitiousWeakebo Mote and his equally ambitious oldest son Johannes (Tillemans 1951).

14.3.4 [Mutual relations] between a group of brothers
The eldest brother is in the best position, firstly because of the inheritance, and furthermore because he can oblige them [his younger brothers to him] when their bride prices have to be assembled. However, that is also the time, when everybody can show what he is worth. In some respects people act collectively in the matter of a bride price. However, within the group concerned they act strictly individually. What a person has achieved, becomes clear during [the assemblage and the distribution] of fines and bride prices.

The hierarchy between brothers is reckoned by reference to their mother so, in case of polygyny, there may be several *ibo*, eldest sons. However, the eldest son of the first wife is the real *ibouto.* Younger brothers, for instance the eldest son of a second wife, contest his position. The eldest son has to prove himself in relation to his younger brothers. This requirement emerges when the bride price is assembled. He need not have shells available, but he should have pigs which he can convert into shells. For a person who has assets, it is easy to borrow shells. At least as important is having relations to whom he can appeal. Relations are acquired by marriage. Hence [there is a preference for] polygyny. By marrying off daughters, such relationships are continued. In addition, he should have *ibouto* as relations elsewhere. Pospisil (1963: 31) refers to them as 'best friends'.

14.3.5 Acting communally on local level on account of bride prices
A person's worth within a local group becomes apparent each time a *perkara* is held[1], [and?] especially during the final assemblage of a bride price. On these occasions it is imperative [for an Ekagi man] to show up, with pigs in case of a *perkara,* and with shells in case of a bride price. On the one hand it makes clear what a person can dispose of, on the other what he is prepared to contribute to the group. Participation is extremely graded.

14.4 LEADERSHIP ON THE BASIS OF PRESTIGE
Whether or not a person is a leader, is apparent from the extent to which he meets the needs of his subordinates and also from the relations to whom he can turn to meet these needs plus the number of people whom he is able to mobilise.

14.4.1 Acting communally at regional level during pig feasts
Outsiders may perceive a *yuwo*, a pig feast, as a market, but in fact many interests are at stake. On such an occasion everybody is also respected

[1] By editor. *Perkara* is an Indonesian word, meaning quarrel or lawsuit. I am inclined to have it here translated with moot, as I did in Hylkema 2002: 237-8.

individually. [A man] need not take part, he need not stake his pigs and shells, but, if he does not, he marks himself as an outsider. Firstly people can prove to others what they are worth. [To this end] They are inclined to stimulate and to counsel each other, because wider interests are involved. What is involved, is visible on the *yuwo* terrain. Just as the oldest man builds a men's house, the initiator [of the feast] builds a dance house. Subsequently each of his companions builds a *kewita*, sleeping quarters. Each is working under the umbrella [of the initiator], but is simultaneously expressing his support. He does not want to desert him. What everybody is worth, is made clear on the day of the *yuwo*, by way of the number of pigs brought out and by the amount [of pork] disposed of. What matters is the number of people who feel obliged, who are prepared to 'cover', *apumai*, the initiator, and, in addition, how much they are willing to stake for him, how much they can mobilise for him.

14.4.2 First among equals on regional level

Ibouto are equals, unless the equilibrium is disturbed because one of them begins using his shells to assemble the bride price for young men living outside his proper territory. This obliges them to him, and that gives him authority over them, The loyalty [an *ibouto* receives] from insiders and the recognition [he receives] from outsiders mutually interact. The *ibouto* with the greatest name, is the one who enjoys most prestige. Areas were actually associated with specific names. Therefore, Boelen can refer to Auki as *kepala* [Ind. headman] of Pouna. The name Pouna evokes the name Auki. The name Tigi evokes the name Weakebo. All the more so since the names of both were known far beyond the region, the question arises whether they have acquired their name by their introducing the [white] foreigner.[2]

People got together in the men's house of the leader with the greatest name. His house received the most visitors. Travellers sought shelter at his place. He decided with whom among his subordinates he brought travelling traders into contact. On their part it was important for subordinates to frequent the men's house in which strangers preferably stayed overnight. Who had the greatest name became apparent from before whom the people chose to bring their quarrels [for adjudication]. In this way a man acquired political power, and he was able to exert influence. Possibly, in the past, prominence could become apparent during war by seeing who gathered the most people behind him. Remarkably, the people in the Mapia region said that they did not fight wars on the field of battle, and never ventured beyond assassinations. [As pointed out

---

[2] By editor. Like Weakebo (chapter 2, p. 30, and this chapter, p.101), Auki was a famous leader in the early phase of the colonial era. Boelen discusses Auki and his leadership in Boelen n.d.: 154f, 179f, and he refers to him in that book as the headman of the Mapia, but I do not know where he refers to him as the headman of Pouna. See also Ploeg 1996: 218f.

above], *ibouto* who enjoyed the greatest prestige and loyalty, were able to get together the largest number of people during pig feasts.

14.5 CONFIRMED BY SIGNS

People claim that there were distinguishing badges [for *ibouto*], for instance Weakebo expected feathers. I noticed this during the revolt.[3] But I do not know whether this is original or [just] an elaboration of the right *tonowi* possessed to adorn themselves, among other ornaments with bird of paradise skins. [Matters have now been] scrambled by the institution of the *kepala kampong,* as well as the *hansip* [Ind. village constable]. In some cases the government has in fact appointed the most senior man in such a position. For that reason legal disputes were brought before him.

Just as warfare brought the greatest satisfaction and the ultimate challenge to the Dani, the Ekagi have the opportunity to measure up to their rivals in a restrained and peaceful fashion by participating in pig husbandry, the shell trade and the bride price market. This enables them to aspire to a *tonowi* position, while they are already in the process of surrounding themselves with followers so as to maintain themselves in their position.

14.5.1 Conditioned loyalty

Out of well-understood self-interest, the community was prepared to encourage an ambitious member in his rivalry with other members. Nevertheless, simultaneously its members made it perfectly clear to him which road he had to travel to reach the top. On the basis of specific remarks, I suspect that some members of the older generation took part in this encouragement not simply from simple self-interest, but because they had also analysed and understood the mechanism behind it. Subsequently, they very consciously attempted to curb the existing assertiveness and rivalry so that these would work out constructively, instead of destructively, for both the men concerned and for the community.

A man could limit himself to participation in pig husbandry and hoard the shells he had thus acquired, as if they were an end in themselves. By this strategy he secured his interests against any son, who chose to rival him, but [in doing so] he also knowingly aroused the envy of competing kin, with ahead the not quite inconceivable danger that he would be executed as a sorcerer, since he enriched himself at the cost of the community. He should bring the shells back into circulation. [And he should have done so] not simply for his own benefit by buying meat and so on, but for the benefit of the younger generation, via [contributions to] bride prices, [thereby confirming] their original function as

---

[3] By editor. Hylkema witnessed at least two revolts against the Indonesian government. Since he uses the singular here, I take it that he wrote this part of the text after the first of these revolts. It took place in 1969, during the Act of Free Choice.

link between the pig market and the marriage market. [If he did so,] he offered tangible proof that he was prepared to bear the responsibility commensurate with the position he had acquired and consequently promote the welfare of the community.

One surprising fact about the bride price was that people did not benefit directly from it. They did not act to make an immediate profit. They merely put out, in the certainty that they could not take back. They acted to make friends with the aid of the Mammon of unrighteousness, as in the [biblical] parable of the unjust steward (Luke 16: 9).

CHAPTER 18 SORCERERS

18.1 GLORIFICATION OF THE INTELLECT AMONG THE EKAGI

18.1.1 Normative

A leader has to be endowed with the proper capacities to be assured of the loyalty of his subordinates. In response to this [requirement], the Ekagi have not emphasised bravery, as have the Dani, but *dimi*, intelligence. This is expressed in *gai*, to think, as in 'to imagine', or 'to set a goal', and in *dou*, to look, as in 'to take the measures required', or in 'to realise one's goal'. In short the idea being conveyed is 'to be enterprising'; or, starting from *dougai tai*, a composite of the participle *doo* and the verbal suffix *egai*: 'to consider a matter from all sides and then decide upon a strategy', in other words 'not acting impulsively.' Consequently, using intelligence as yardstick, they divide humankind according to gender into *daba*, small, low, unimportant, voiceless, and *ibo*, great, high, important, with voice. [They do this] presumptively, by referring to natural data. But then they go on to use the same yardstick to divide the male half of the population into two strata, *daba* and *ibo*. This is done not presumptively, but on the basis of experimental selection. As bravery can only be proven on the field of battle, *dimi* only becomes apparent in the successful acquisition and management of shells. Social prestige, with the prerogatives which the Dani derive from bravery shown on the field of battle, such as polygyny and the ownership of many pigs, are acquired by the Ekagi by the intelligence shown in conducting cowry transactions.

18.1.2 In a religious frame

The religious disposition of the Dani is revealed in their attitude towards magic and taboos, and culminates in the efforts to maintain relationships between the living and the dead, in the [seemingly] a-religious context of the field of battle, by means of a seemingly completely a-religious activity as wounding and killing. By those holding such a view of humankind and the world, the greatest violence is not merely an ideal worthy of pursuit, but the person who realises it optimally is simultaneously the benefactor of and the model for his group. There is not a single reason to suppose that, with regard to belief in magic and witchcraft, and the observance of taboos, the Ekagi traditionally yielded to the Dani. Having witnessed the various ritual sacrifices and incantations, there is no reason to suppose either that Ekagi placed less value on a correct relationship with the ancestors or with spirits, even though they were engrossed in such a seemingly purely secular matter as the shell trade. Just as success on the field of battle was a sign, so success in the shell trade was a sign.[1] Indicative of the religious undertone is that a real *tonowi* did not cling to his property by hoarding

---

[1] By editor. I assume that, with the term 'sign', Hylkema consciously alluded to the use of that term in the Bible, as for instance in Mark 11: 12, where Christ says: 'Why doth this generation seek after a sign?'

it, but spent it just as easily as he acquired it, since he believed he had been chosen.[2] As [among the Dani] the significance of the sign that was encompassed in wounding and killing the enemy is a reason to rejoice, so [among the Ekagi] the significance of the sign encompassed in acquiring a shell was a reason to rejoice, both individually and as a group. [By the presence of] this person, the group was favoured by the ancestral ghosts/spirits. In response, the group was prepared to see in him a model and benefactor and to grant him all the prerogatives which accrued to such a position.

A person's intelligence is not of his own making. A person, *mee,* is more or less identical with his body, *mee*, or his figure, *epoo*; a person and his soul presuppose each other for the duration of a life-time, but the link between a person and *dimi* intelligence, is extrinsic rather than intrinsic. Firstly, not all people appear to have been equally gifted with *dimi*, but, moreover, the same ancestral ghost/spirit could both endow a person with *dimi* and take it from him, as a result of which he did not become stupid, but goes mad. Given its origin, *dimi* appears to have been spiritual, or rather divine. A person [gifted with *dimi*] was a sorcerer, but a good sorcerer, provided he let his community share in the benefits which accrued to his gift. If he withheld the benefits, this was tantamount to turning against his community and he degenerated into an evil sorcerer, and consequently had to be executed.

[18.1.3] Jealously guarded specialty

Ekagi did not keep secret from the whites that other ethnic groups were ignorant of the value of shells and hence could be tricked into accepting fake shells in exchange for real ones. Eventually, they were prepared to allow a white person to believe that members of the administrative and church organisations should not know that they turned fake shells into real ones, and that this was a top secret (Pospisil 1958: 127). As becomes quite apparent in Giay (1995), the Ekagi saw themselves subjected to continuous threat from outsiders who wanted to filch their secret from them.[3] It is their specialty. But this attitude towards other ethnic groups and foreigners betrayed more than the Ekagi would like. What they jealously screened off from outsiders, they also, equally jealously, concealed from other Ekagi. They did not seek instruction, because they did not want to be lectured. But that is only half the answer. People knew that [when they resorted to this] they would be rejected, or fobbed off. [For men] Shells were a means to prove they were superior to women, but just as much a means to prove that the older generation was superior to the younger. By all means everybody should [have the chance to] develop his own specialty, to discover what he is good at, but, on account of *dimi*, a man was superior to a woman.

---

[2] By editor. Again, Hylkema seems to allude to a biblical phrase. In this case to 'For many are called, but few are chosen' (Matthew 22: 14).

[3] By editor. But see also the Conclusion, Part 4 of the book.

D*imi* is what allows a distinction to be made between *daba* and *ibo*; and there were no nuances in this. The point was that a person should excel at a specific activity. Everything in which a person excelled came from the spirits. Here the word *dimi* was linked to the word *eguu,* in the sense of specialty and hence of secret. A person had to do his best, so as to give his ancestor the chance to reveal with what he has endowed his descendant. The possession of *kamu* [magic] was a form of *eguu.*[4] It should not be relinquished. But in order to practice *kamu*, a person should have given proof of being among the chosen, of having been able to appeal to a dream, or, preferably, a vision. A person should have a tangible sign of having been chosen.

18.1.4 On the basis of election

On the basis of the behaviour which they [the Ekagi] exhibit towards foreigners, it is tempting to attribute them with a secular vision of life, oriented towards the eager pursuit of gain (Pospisil 1978: 3). In this perception, they had already left the Enlightenment, with its scepticism regarding non-human forces, behind them, and, bypassing rationalism and modernism, had arrived at a pragmatic post-modernism. Possibly readers have been puzzled by the references to such a typically religious document as the New Testament. I have taken the liberty of doing so because, comparatively speaking, it provides a striking characterisation of the atmosphere. Ultimately, people interpret their behaviour religiously.

Whether or not a person succeeds in growing is not purely a matter of intelligence, but [also] of divine intervention. Intelligence and stupidity are both caused by spirits; especially stupidity, [which is interpreted as] having one's ears boxed by the spirits. Deception prompted by anger and envy, theft and destruction of somebody else's goods were bad. Basically, people were equal. For that reason it did not behove the one person to do harm to the other. [Likewise,] It did not behove a person wilfully to curtail another in his development. In this matter Tokiiwiyai was quite clear when the village head-man in Uwebutu, Bobaapiiyawi, confiscated his chickens. He should have left that to non-human/supernatural agencies, and with this [comment] Tokiiwiyai, or: Martinus, had God in mind.

An Ekagi was always searching for omens, in general, to ascertain whether he had been favoured or not, but very concretely, when he was about to embark on some undertaking. Also when he went fishing, he appealed to the ancestors. He knew that he depended upon non-human/supernatural forces and agencies which could thwart him on his path, or, conversely, could clear it for him. Each large undertaking carried out by several people was preceded by prayer: people prayed to the ancestors to obtain shells, just as they prayed to obtain game and wildfowl. This quite apart from the fact that people knew that they had to go to

---

[4] By editor. In this context *kamu* means magic (Steltenpool 1969: 129).

others to get those shells, just as they had to go the forest to catch game and wildfowl. People were already crushed in their hearts [cowed] by this ritual so they were unable to offer resistance.[5] Others took a mythical dog along, which made people so fearful that they were unable to resist its owner. In a ritual, prayer became a conjuration to clear the obstacles from their path. In this case, they accepted the intervention of the *kamu tai mee*,[6] paid him [for his services], but [this was] clearly in the perspective of the entity represented by this *kamu tai mee*. But what they really wanted was contact with the source. Just as they were not content to contact the bishop via the local priest, but wanted to speak to him personally. Thereafter they had to swallow yet another disappointment, because the bishop was also not the source, but merely an intermediary. [The same was the case] when they approached debtors to collect shells which were due to them, or when they accosted others to ask for help to which they were not entitled.

18.1.5 Tonowi *were sorcerers*

Tonowi did not only own shells, they themselves were sacred people. They also performed as *kamu tai mee*, as did, for instance, Weakebo Mote. As long as people benefited from them, they were admired and held in awe. However, as soon as they started enriching themselves at the expense of others, their fellows, they became so despicable that they had to be executed.

---

[5] By editor. Hylkema's wording is unclear. I take it he means: During the prayer, during the performance of the ritual, the hearts of the people one had to deal with were crushed, so they were unable to put up resistance to an unfavourable deal.

[6] By editor. Magicians (Steltenpool 1969: 129).

CHAPTER 22 AS WEALTH ITEM AND AMULET

22.1 THE COWRY AS A WEALTH ITEM

While visiting me at my home, Imoudakebo had assessed my shell and assigned it to the lowest grade of the *yuu,* meaning the shell was worth next to nothing. Nevertheless, he could not resist picking it up from the table again and again, to examine it. The highly developed categorisation and sub-division [of cowries] offered the connoisseur an excuse, and indeed the opportunity, to bring his shells out once again to have a look at them, either alone or in the company of his exchange partners. The idea was not to count them so as to find out how many he had in his wallet, but rather to view each shell as part of a collection of porcelain.[1] He literally never became sated with it. It fascinated him. [To do this] He did not mind to miss out [on an event] or to break off what he was doing. His behaviour easily aroused resentment or sarcasm, especially from women. Many sayings can be traced back to this activity. It is obvious that the people did not value the cowry solely as a means of payment.

The shell did not derive its value from what it could buy, but had an intrinsic value, such as a work of art has, or, more appropriately, a reliquary. Sometimes a person moved heaven and earth to get hold of a particular shell, just like the merchant who sought beautiful pearls and sold everything [he had] in order to be able to buy them (Matthew 13: 45). And once a man possessed a shell, he did not simply stuff it in his pocket, but instead he packed it in a special container and treasured it. The use of the cowry as a means of payment may have been founded in pragmatism, but it had passed into the realms of irrationality.

During the presentation of the bride price on behalf of Isaias Tekege in March 1974, among the spectators I saw a woman, unknown to me, with, I thought, a wonderfully youthful complexion and an attractive face. When I later asked Isaias who the woman was, I noticed at first how extremely difficult it is to describe a person exclusively on the basis of facial features. Moreover, these features said nothing to him. Should I have formed a better idea of her nose? Only when I mentioned: 'The women who at a given moment was leaning ostentatiously against Josep', did he understand to whom I was referring. What had struck him was not her exceptional appearance, but her daring erotic-sexual behaviour. As a matter of fact, it should be mentioned that traditionally, when choosing a partner, what in our eyes counted as a beautiful countenance, was not perceived as a valid criterion. There was no word for beauty in the vocabulary. It is only recently, since people have become aware of this lack, that the Indonesian word *cantrik* has come into use. If people wondered why a boy had fallen in love for a certain girl, the stereotypical reply was that he had allowed

---

[1] By editor. Hylkema was probably inspired to allude here to porcelain since he was aware that the cowry is the house of what in Dutch is called the porcelain snail.

himself to be blinded by her glistening calves or the exceptional pallor of her skin. The supposition that there is a link between an atrophy of the senses and the amount of attention paid to money, power and jewels --including the cowry as it was then in vogue among the Ekagi-- has been mentioned more than once in the literature (Fortmann 1974: 39).

22.2 THE COWRY AS A SACRED OBJECT

22.2.1 Analogous to a charm or amulet

However secular shells may seem in their function as money, they are not money, but valuables [see chapter 1.1.3] and hence they have to be understood as [imbued with] religious significance.[2] When I wanted to take a picture of one of the shells displayed during the presentation of a bride price, panic and protests erupted among members of the younger generation.[3] People have long left behind their initial objection to being photographed personally; usually they appreciate it. But the indefinite, but nonetheless palpable objections that have to do with being robbed of one's *eguu, aya,* inner life force, nucleus or soul, were apparently valid for shells. A shell possessed an inner power and exhibited to the world outside a radiance, of variable strength. Consequently, [it was] also vulnerable. Given that charms and amulets lost their power when they came into contact with water, a shell has to be protected from ground and rain water. That a merchant should have discovered his treasure in the field and then buys the field, is incomprehensible to the Ekagi (Matthew 13: 44). As mentioned in chapter 7.1.1, on one occasion, in Timeepa, when it turned out that the nassa attached to the genital apron of a woman had not been detached when she was buried, there was no question about it, she had to be exhumed so that people could remove the shells. A shell should not be exposed to water, [if so], just as an amulet full of magical power, it would become lifeless or powerless.

22.2.2 Attractive and repugnant

As all of what has just been said shows, the Ekagi were fascinated by the cowry. But this was not shared by all. With the appearance of Zakheus Pakage dissent became manifest. Zakheus condemned the shell and would have preferred to have it replaced by money, but he failed. Certainly, the *Wegee Bagee* movement

---

[2] Religion here should be understood as 'the remarkable human inclination to construct for themselves a non-empirical world which is presented as the true and most profound reality' (van Baal: 1977: 387), or as can be heard in the question: 'What is there in man -- to supplement his empirical knowledge and rational activities with an array of notions and actions concerning a non-verifiable world, which we call religion' (van Baal: 1981: 3) and defined as 'all notions and acts referring to a reality which, though it cannot be verified or falsified, is accepted by the group of believers concerned as true and as relevant to their real life and world' (van Baal 1981: 5).

[3] Bernard Tekege, Tomas Tekege, and Marius Mote; as their names betray, all three Catholics connected with the mission station.

continued to be extremely ambivalent towards the *mege* [the cowry]. There is not one single trend. The shell exerted so much influence on the people that it kept them away from God. [Redundant sentence omitted]. Shells were powerful. They exuded a beneficent influence which made them desirable, but they could also radiate a malicious influence. They were attractive and repugnant, [according to] the use which could be made of them. Shells could make people betray their closest relatives. They were also used as *deeba*, a lure, witness the expression *deeba mege* according to its use and connotation to be translated as 'blood money'. This feature was enacted with great verve in the Holy Week during the stage production of the Passion. [This was done] alluding to the *deeba mege* in a myth of origin like that of the Tekege (Hylkema 1988: 33), but especially to Koyei, a figure comparable to or equated with Jezus, and the central character in the *Wegee Bagee*, with its centre in Idakebo in the Kamu Valley.

It was no accident that Zakheus Pakage abolished the shells, when he urged people to burn their amulets and charms. Again, the attitude to these amulets was ambivalent. They were worth to be pursued, but [nevertheless they] should be thrown into the water. If the Protestant mission was successful with the abolishment of such paraphernalia, this was among other factors because they made people shudder. [In the mid-1950s], at the time Pospisil in the Kamu Valley –the area which later developed into the cradle of the *Wegee Bagee*– had been astonished by the quantitative and secular attitude to life of the Ekagi, in the Tigi area a fight took place over the shell, the first one to be recorded in writing. [When Zakheus Pakage,] who had spent years abroad, first as a member of de Bruijn's group in Australia[4] and then at the mission school in Ujung Pandang, made an undisguised attempt to reform in the village of his birth, he condemned the shells. Not as might have been expected with a purely quantitative and profit-oriented attitude to life, by appealing to the fact that the shells had no value, because they could not be used to buy anything in the *toko,* but by using the religiously inspired argument, that humans were destined for eternal life, if they parted with everything that was related to death: no more mire around the houses, but also no more shells since they were dangerous, affected people's health and were propagated by the devil in the guise of the snake.

22.2.3 The cowry as a ritual requisite

Firstly in the wedding ceremonial in the Mapia region. It will be dealt with below, in the discussion of the wedding ceremony.[5] And then in the head and tail game. Here it appears as a male symbol referring to life and as a female symbol referring to death.

---

[4] By editor. Japanese forces captured the Enarotali patrol post in May 1943. However, de Bruijn escaped with a party that included a number of Me. Months later, the party was rescued and flown to Australia (de Bruijn 1978: 167-269).

[5] By editor. Hylkema has not carried this intention through.

CHAPTER 25 THE SHELL'S MYTHICAL PROVENANCE

Introduction by editor. Notwithstanding its length, this last chapter has also remained a draft. It contains further clues to the genesis of the manuscript. Earlier, Hylkema had numbered it chapter 11, but he had changed this typed number to a handwritten 25. The numbering of the sections and sub-sections with 11 continued up to section 11.6, in the present version 25.6. It was followed by a section numbered 1.27.4 which Hylkema renumbered 11.7, by hand. The final section, which I have numbered 25.11, had the number 1.28 in Hylkema's text. Hylkema had not subdivided all the sections of this chapter into sub-sections. The sub-division of sections 25.3 and 25.7 is my own, as are the titles of the sub-sections. The text of the last sections had remained very much a draft. Yet, it provides significant information so I decided it is an essential part of the monograph and retained it.

25.1 THE MYTHICAL INTERPRETATION OF THE EMPIRICAL IMPORT

Precisely because everybody is perfectly aware that the *ogai* bring the shells from elsewhere, [their importation] should not present a problem; even less so since people have been able to go [to the coast] and pick up the shells on the beach themselves. Nevertheless, the report of the Club of Kotomoma reveals that this is not as easy as it seems. It is all the more remarkable that the origins of the shells are constantly being discussed. People do not want to limit themselves to this empirically traceable origin.

Certainly the importation [in large quantities] has stripped the shell of its sanctity; but to a far lesser degree than might have been expected. The empirical and mythical origins were placed alongside each other; the one did not need to exclude the other. In the report of the Club of Kotomoma we constantly come across the strange fact that the members have integrated the empirical import into their mythical view of the world. At the same time this story of the origin is based on the prophecies made at Kotomoma. In their own words, one group of people and one general source are placed at the origin, not of the shell as such, but of its arrival. It is not a folk tale, but an anecdote from the recent past determined by person, time and place; an account of something which mattered during the time of the previous generation. It is only one of a number of such anecdotes. Generally, they are so specifically connected to the local situation that only a few of them are known beyond the immediate family.

In various anecdotes and stories we find [elements] which in the Report of Kotomoma are situated in a particular locale and with regard to a particular clan, but that actually apply to the territory of the whole ethnic group. [For instance,] People knew *tonowi*, who obtained shells in a miraculous manner. Although it is precisely these people who should know how they actually did acquire the shells, the way they want to present themselves to others requires that this has to be embellished with sacred details. It is noteworthy that only stories about cowry shells appear and disappear again; and only a few of them are generally known.

Generally speaking, these tales seem to be fantastic and bizarre at first glance. As if the people have plucked them out of thin air. However, they are more closely related to one another than might seem. There are certainly remark-able correspondences in details and in fact they are all based on a generally accepted stock of ideas. Nevertheless, the most remarkable fact about these anecdotes is the intermingling of generally accepted conceptions and a specific locale by linking them to particular crops, trees and the like, and to specific persons. In these tales we are confronted with all sorts of reptiles, shrubs and mythical figures. Naturally the presentation of all this information leads to questions about their symbolic meaning, both separate and in context. One symbol evokes the other. For that reason the tales are difficult to categorise or to order. Below are some tales from various regions. In reality they are no more than summaries. In order to experience the sphere in which they were actually told, they should really be heard in their original setting. People hear them from their fathers or their mothers or from good neighbours of the older generation. What happened occurred not long ago at all, in the time of the older generation, in very close relationship to trees and shrubs in the immediate environment, about which people when they were youngsters had known no more than that they were taboo. However, they also reflect the personal relations within [the] families [concerned]. I owe the anecdotes below to my key informant.[1] I refer to the people who figure in them by their kin relationships to him.

25.2 A STORY IN CONTEXT

Once upon a time close to the cliff at Tagatadi,[2] there stood a banana tree. Its stem was used by a *koyo*, an iguana, as a ladder 'to give birth to shells', *mege pai*, at the foot of the tree. It vomited the shells from his mouth. Its whole body was a *pugiuka,* a shell purse, according to his father, Imoudakebo. It began just below its chin and reached right down to its tail. When the reptile raised its tail, its mouth opened and you were able to look right down to the bottom of this purse. When it beat against this bag with its claws, the shells came out automatically. After the reptile had a first time deposited the shells in a small hole chosen at random at the foot of the banana tree, Imoudakebo dug a row of

---

[1] By editor. Since Hylkema in the next paragraph mentions Imoudakebo as the father of his source, I conclude that Hylkema is referring here to Isaias Tekege.

[2] By editor. As mentioned above (Introduction, p. 18), Hylkema employed Isaias while he was stationed in Epouto, located on the eastern shore of Lake Tage. So, I suppose the tale is set near the mountains which border the lake in that area. I do not know the location of Tagatadi.

small holes and in them he planted shoots of the cordyline species *bui*. This is a male symbol. His mother added that around these she had planted shoots of the cordyline species *wokodu*, with narrow, red leaves, a species related to the male demon Teege. After that the reptile had used the last hole in the row, in which he had planted a *bui*. The shrubs had died after his half-brother, Jesaya, had made a garden there. At this point, his mother again passed the remark that good tobacco could be grown in the blood which had remained on the spot after it had given birth [to the shells], whereupon Isaias, who knew about the function of the *koyo* as a male symbol, had wonderingly asked if this event was accompanied by the flowing of blood. His parents answered in unison: 'Did you think that it would not involve any blood? Of course there was blood'. Then his father continued alone: 'Do women give birth if there is no blood in the womb; if the source of blood has dried up?' That is why they also gleamed because of their smoothness, just like shards of a *pakooba*, a *cymbicum* shell.

When they had just emerged, they resembled the slime exuded by taro. People gripped them firmly with a pair of fire tongs so that they could dry in the sun. Only after that could they pick them up. His mother said that his father had used the first shell to buy meat, in other words: it was a good quality shell. However, her remark could also be interpreted as a complaint that he had broken a taboo and his chronic stomach complaints could be traced back to this act. His father denied this and indignantly refused to countenance such a suggestion: of course the first shell should not be picked up. Nevertheless, it was indeed a shell with a high value, a *Tage-bodiya* one. Generally speaking these shells belong to the highly valued categories such as *bomouye* or *bodiya*. He had bought three portions of meat with it.

This reveals that they did not enjoy this [supply of cowries] for as long as might have been supposed from what has just been said above. Fairly soon after the reptile had begun to deposit shells, father's sister's husband Badiituma Mote had taken the first shell away. Since that time the reptile had never returned. With all what it was planning to bear it had disappeared for good. One of the neighbours, Idimabeutuma Tekege, who happened to be present during the conversation, went on to say that he and some others had taken upon themselves the task of seeing that nobody took away the first shell. He had even expressly warned Badiituma not to harvest any sugar cane in the vicinity. From this it can be concluded that, during the harvest, Badiituma had taken the shell away unobserved. Later the banana tree was chopped down by father's father, Bobeukebo. There was still birth blood, *kigi-tagi paga tage*, adhering to the stem. This was the reason that the tree was also *daa*, forbidden, and only adult males could eat the fruit of such a tree, in fact only Bobeukebo could do so. In an attempt to identify this particular clump of trees more closely, Cecilia reminded her son Isaias that she had once asked him to cut a bunch of bananas with a stone knife, *oo*. This bunch was growing on a trunk which had originated from this same tree; as a woman she could not do this.

25.3 NOT FOR PRIVATE CONSUMPTION

[25.3.1 The risks entailed]

In the anecdote above it is said that father's sister's husband Badiituma Mote had taken away the first shell to be deposited, *motii*. This was a terrible breach of good manners, in the first place because it was not his own territory, and the shell was certainly not destined for him. But even if a person found shells on his own land, taking them away was a risky undertaking. This is demonstrated in the following story. Collecting mythical shells was an extremely risky affair, first and foremost because the snake could strike out at the person involved. For instance, in December 1981 Severinus Dou, catechist at Watiyai, said that a story was doing the rounds about a certain Kudiyaikatuma Do of the village Digiuto, near Damabagata in the Takaapa region.[3] He was supposed to have stolen some six shells, which had been laid by a *kigei*, a snake species, on the protective layer of grass sods on top of an embankment. Afterwards he fell ill and died. That is to say, he was still alive, but he rotted away on the outside. He was put in a coffin with a lid on it. But, because people were curious about what would happen, they left his face free. After they had waited for quite a while and had heard no sound, [it was obvious] that he was well and truly dead and he was buried.

It is clear from the choice of words that Kudiyaikatuma had committed an offence against a *kigei* by stealing its shells. Perhaps it had had a completely different purpose for them. Looked at from this point of view, it becomes obvious that [in the previous anecdote] other people like Idimabeutuma had not stolen them, but that they were also not meant for Badiituma. Exercising all due caution, Imoudakebo had taken them away. They had concluded that they were destined for him. However, according to his wife he had not used them properly. In fact, he drew the punishment down on his own head. However, the punishment could just as well have been visited on his descendants. In December 1971 Yan Adii, a catechist at Udaugiida, had said that as a general rule people were not allowed to keep, *makii*, shells which had been deposited by a reptile and were forbidden to use them for their own gain, *mapugai*. If they did so their children would die so that they would have no male descendants left. Not only would the man who committed such a trespass be left childless, even after his death his sin/misdeed would afflict his whole line of descent, even his *epa*, his lineage. In the report of the Club of Kotomoma it is stressed that people did not distribute the shells for their personal use. [One repetitious sentence omitted].

---

[3] By editor. Takaapa is located southeast of Lake Tage.

This is a reference to a more general fact. For instance, men were not allowed to make personal use of the shells which they had acquired during their first appearance as *kamu tai mee*. Sometimes the impression was given that they should be kept, in the same way as *kabo mege*. But that also does not seem to be correct and accordingly Cecelia Degei had not done so. The only correct procedure is to give them away, *wudu*. As a hunter, a man was expected to give away the first game he captured. In this instance, the [way to handle the] shell accords with generally valid patterns of thinking and acting.

[25.3.2 A resulting taboo]
At the foot of the Mogodagi [Stone Face?] there stood a *wau* (*Myrtaceae Eugenia*), a myrtle bearing red, plum-like fruit, which until recently only few people were allowed to eat. The explanation of the [earlier] prohibition was that the tree had grown up on a spot where *mege* was collected, *mege tagiida make podomita wau*. From our point of view, the word *tagi* is ambiguous. In its general sense, it describes the traces, in the form of rubbish, left behind from some sort of activity. It can be used to describe the root hairs of taro or of sugar cane, unripe sweet potatoes, but it can also cover stubble in the field, the rubble of a house which had collapsed, a graveyard. In this sense, the expression does not offer enough clues. In view of the explanation [offered], it can be assumed that in this case *tagi* is used as an analogy for a place at the side of the house where the flattened grass and the flecks of blood betray the fact that a woman has given birth there.

When asked to explain, she [presumably Isaias' mother, Cecilia Degei] said that at that spot a snake, personified by the personal name Yuwo Emaadama, had caused shells to grow and then had rooted them up. The snake only really felt happy when she could nestle down and wallow in the shells, 'Just as we can sleep well only when we have spread out a rain cape, or Europeans when they have wrapped themselves up in a blanket.'

[25.3.3 An alternative way of producing shells]
When Isaias expressed his scepticism about the possibility of reptiles producing shells, his father exclaimed: 'Even humans gave birth to them, then certainly *eniya*, demons, could.' Here he referred to an anecdote told by their neighbour Utuutatuma. In order to procure shells, all his [, Utuutatuma's,] grandfather had to do was to rub them out of his upper arm, via his lower arm and hand so that they emerged between the the flesh and the nail.[4] This is a reference to the custom of massaging the arms of a dying or dead relative with downwards movements, with the intention of rubbing out the *iyoo*, Ind. *bibit*, germinated seeds, in the most extensive sense of the word, locked up inside him/her. This

[4] By editor. Hylkema's wording does not make the point of exit of the shells quite clear. The 'flesh' may refer to either the cuticle or the finger tip.

was to prevent them going to the grave with him/her and rotting away, and also to be able to appropriate them. Although this custom was observed for both a father and a mother, the arm, divided up into upper arm, lower arm and hand, ending with the opening between the flesh and the nail, stands as a symbol for the penis. In the ritual practised when moving into a new house in the Mapia, during which the young people are admonished not to misbehave, this opening is graphically closed off with a shard of a *cymbicum* shell. The following practice unambiguously elucidates the underlying intention. If a dead man's penis were erect – a sign that death had been caused by adultery –, people stirred his underbelly (lower abdomen) with a *tipa*, a stick of oak wood, in itself an object perceived as a male symbol, until semen appeared.

Utuutatuma's father and grandfather had exchanged these shells for meat and sweet potatoes. Utuutatuma himself had preferred to save them so as to be able to buy a sow and a boar or a hog. However, he had actually robbed himself of this opportunity. When he had broken off twigs of the cordyline species *bui* and *magaumau*, the one sort with broad green and the other sort with broad red leaves, both male symbols, he dug a hole at Iigoona, on the south-western shore of Lake Tage. After he had slaughtered a pig, his first action was to put blood and the matter which had collected in his shell purse into the hole. He then refilled the hole with earth and planted the cordyline twigs on top of it. These sprouted roots and are still standing there. A few weeks later, when he and some other people happened to be in the vicinity, he found a snake, an *ugeeniya,* close to a fallen log. Although a snake could sometimes be found which had bumps on its body, traces of where it had been beaten with a stick during exorcisms, this snake had holes in its body, a sign that she had been pierced by the cordyline twigs which had been planted on top of the hole. Seven people died within a few weeks. After the others had first tried in various ways, 'to guess her identity and purpose', *ateine tai*, to get the snake to go away, without the reptile lending an ear to their pleas, she did react immediately when he, as a guess, said: 'You are the snake which ate those seven people and now you have come to show us your belly'. She scuttled away and disappeared into the ground in a hole at the foot of a *dauti*, a cypress, also a male symbol. 'If the entrance to the hole had not been closed off with *bouyo*, with shoots, the present generation would also still be able to press shells out of their fingers.'

[25.3.4 A tonowi *rewarded]*

A tale was told in Mogodagi about Yagoudabedo Pigai, a *tonowi* who lived in Ugapura, in the Kamu region. [He was said] to have placed a body on a death platform and then lain down next to the body on that platform.[5] After this a long

---

[5] By editor. The distance between Ugapura and Mogodagi is considerable, so it seems that the report was widely spread. Ugapura is located in the eastern part of the Kamu

consecutive series of all sorts of crops turned up near the platform for the purpose of devouring the corpse. At the end came the sugar cane variety called, *poogiye*, and the vegetable *digiyo*, *Rungia klossii.* These two ordered the other crops to wait with devouring the corpse until they had paid off what they owed the dead man. After Yagoudabedo had dismissed various offers, including a small net full of acorns, *tipa poo*, a symbol of male offspring, he had finally consented, when *poogiye* and *digiyo* presented him with an exceptional sort of cordyline, the multi-coloured *dedo*, as well as a *daba-diyo*, a round stone with which the body is rubbed to make it invulnerable to arrows and bullets. They advised him to plant this cordyline in the garden after he had slaughtered a pig. Seven days after he had done this, he would be summoned either by the male Spirit, *Deiya ka mee*, who lived either on or in Mount Deiyai.[6] This is what happened. Since then he has been regarded as someone who, without anybody else noticing it, is summoned by the Deiyai with a soft, whistling sound, *Deiyai ka tiu etita mee*, or someone on whom the Deiyai red cloth has set her eye, *Deiyai kagaba ka edoota mee.*

This anecdote is based on the idea that the crops which provide food for the living are in their turn fed by the dead. Among these crops, the sugar cane variety *poogiye* and the vegetable *digiyo* stand out especially. Both are fertility symbols, the sugar cane is a male and the *digiyo* a female symbol. Both are said to lie at the origin of all the other cultivars which can be distinguished [within these two species]. Both are said to grow wild. Although they are neither planted nor cultivated, if a garden is being made, they may not be eradicated. Wherever they are found they should be weeded and fertilised with garden soil. This tale is closed with the quotation: ‘Now that we have said this, go ahead if you want to eat us, just as long as you don’t neglect to fertilize us and keep us free of weeds.’ As a matter of fact, my informant gave the impression that there was a cycle of stories around both these plants; but I did not investigate this any further.

[25.3.5 The story of Kopa-peku]

First, an elderly man in Timida told a rambling tale about an *api*, a girl, who had once brought a certain Mebeu Gobai shells, that is to say she had vomited up shells. But she had taken them back, had disappeared with them, and had changed into the pond [called] Kopa-peku. Subsequently, a man called Markus Gobai retold his story.

---

basin, due west of Lake Tage and separated from the lake by a mountain ridge. Mogodagi is located to the east of Lake Tage.

6 By editor. As mentioned above in chapter 2, note 22, Deiyai is the tallest mountain in the ridge between the three Paniai lakes and the Kamu basin. It appears to be the abode of both male, *Deiyai ka mee*, and female spirits, *Deiyai ka abe.* In the present anecdote the Deiyai red cloth seems to be personified, as a female.

This *api* changed into the pond Kopa-peku; it was a girl who had come from the east. When she came to benefit Kotuudo Gobai,[7] in Timida on the southern side of the Weya Valley,[8] people filled seven bags of shells. Then she travelled on to Bokowa, a hamlet in the vicinity of Badauwo, on the northern side of the Weya Valley. On the first occasion she brought him a box of tinned fish (sauries); on another occasion shells. She appeared four times. Because she shuffled, people could quite clearly hear that she was coming. She vomited the shells out of her mouth between the taro leaves in the vegetable garden at the side of the house. She had curled up her body in spirals, *kotu*, in seven different places. She was so tall that you could not see her tail. It was still at the confluence of the Gado and Iyoopii Rivers.[9] Because she had rolled herself up into four coils there without showing her tail, the water rose unruffled as in a still-standing pond. Nevertheless, she did not follow the course of the river, but came overland. When she arrived, she slithered around the poles of my father's house and then she put her head down in the taro beds to vomit. Because she could not be beaten off with sticks, the people finally slaughtered an adult pig. After this she went away back to where she had come from, very slowly, uncoiling the seven spirals one after the other. The last sound people heard from her was the splash when she took to the water at the mouth of the Gado. No one knows where she lives now. She belongs to the *eniya*, the invisible beings, spirits and demons; she no longer has a visible form as she did during the incident. She visited the father of this old Gobai man here. The snake was usually [called] Kotuudo, 'A certain number of humps, bumps'. Her real name was Maikai-Kotega, 'Wait at the ocean'.[10]

The name of her male partner was Kotee-Pani, 'Two species of thorny liana', or 'Guardian thorny liana'. He betrayed his presence at night by a whistling sound. His foot was broken at the ankle. This had happened spontaneously. He was blue-coloured, like some beads. [And] He always carried an arrow with him, a bamboo arrow made of a species of *koto*.[11] He shot a great many people. I forgot to say that the edge of her pubic apron consisted of only three threads of unspun

---

[7] *Kotu*: rise, bump.

[8] By editor. The River Weya flows into Lake Paniai from the east. Timida and Badauwo, mentioned in the following line, are indeed located in the far east of the Me territories. The lower course of the rivers flowing into Lake Paniai is swampy in many places, dotted with *peku*, small lakes and ponds.

[9] By editor. These rivers are not mentioned on the maps at my disposal. Possibly they flow into the Weya.

[10] By editor. The meaning of Hylkema's Dutch translation of this part of the anec-dote is not clear. It does indicate however that the apparition has left the Me habitat and has gone to live on the sea coast, far away.

[11] By editor. Presumably because he wanted to clarify the associations the associations carried by the word *koto,* Hylkema has added, within brackets:: 1. species of bamboo; 2. bridge; 3. row; *koto-dogiyai*.

bark, like those worn by the Moni women.[12] She was constantly changing shape. She appeared in a number of guises: as a human being, as a canoe, as a canoe with transverse poles on which the scoop nets are laid when catching crayfish, of Maikai-Kotega, or the *yina* snake. This *api* who came from the east is the elder sister of human beings; she came by herself.'[13]

25.4 PORTENTS IN DREAMS AND REALITY

Trying to acquire shells by means of a variety of undertakings was a very cumbersome process. People tried to find an easier way to do this. For instance, people could as it were bring shells closer to their homes by planting various trees and shrubs, such as cordyline. [Or] by not clearing away spider webs in the house, associating these with *gaa* [rope, string]. [But here it should be noted that] spiders produce these webs internally, not externally. Or [it could be done] by dreaming of them. [This was not done only in the case of shells, because] in their dreams people also foresaw pigs, a swarm of children and so forth.

25.5 CONSTRUCTION OF A HOUSE

It is also noteworthy that people proceeded to build a storehouse, Ind. *gudang*, in which to store all the goods expected, but specifically for the cowries. People also believed that, once they had constructed such a building, they had only to enter it [to be enabled] to re-emerge laden with goods. Here we have to do with a kind of sanctuary.[14]

25.6 IN ANSWER TO A SACRIFICE

[Moreover] some sort of sacrifice had to be offered, [because] the building of a storehouse did not solve the puzzle of the origin [of the shells]. The village headman of Abaimaida, who belonged to the Magai clan, 'feasted' in his house with the snake *agai*. When this was related to me, I did not comprehend what the informant understood by feast. Feasting is a sacrificial meal. Each time [during a visit to the Ekagi] the bishop exclaimed enthusiastically what a fine feast day it was, the people felt obliged to put their shells together to buy pigs and poultry and to eat these at a communal meal.

---

[12] By editor. The Moni are the eastern neighbours of the Me. The term 'unspun' is erroneous since the Me did not practise spinning. Probably Hylkema meant 'unplaited'.

[13] By editor. Here, at the end of Markus Gobai's account, Hylkema put a quotation mark, although he did not put one at the beginning. It seems, then, that he rendered the account closely.

[14] By editor. The sentence at the end of this note formed part of the main text of this chapter as the last sentence of section 25.1. Since it did not appear to fit there, I shifted it to section 25.5.

The presence of shells is cosmically betrayed in great swarms of fire-flies around the house or in an enormous number of stars shining down directly above the house.

According to Cecilia Degei, the abundance of shells was due to Yuwo-Emaadama (pig feast-blood-old woman) (p. 59) {Still to be investigated}.

25.7 ADDING TO THE EXISTING SHELLS

There was a whole range of amulets which could augment the number of shells or could produce them. The piece of red cloth has already been mentioned. However, as well as this [there was] a whole range of other possibilities. The *woti*,[15] in which people speculated, must be included.[16]

[25.7.1 Encounters with pito yago*]*

The following anecdotes should be understood against the background which Maarten Gobai, his mother's sister's son, at Timida, told my key informant Isaias Tekege. Once, one night when Maarten returned from visiting the home of the local primary school teacher he saw, on his way home, a *pito-yago* at the side of the road, literally 'someone in possession of a torch', 'a woman with fire in her armpit', approaching through the long grass. Then, he saw to his side, in the long grass, a big woman standing. As soon as she saw him, she crumpled right up. But Maarten sprang on her in one bound. It then transpired that she was a *yina*, a reptile, which had transmogrified into a human being. She told him that she was the wife of a local Gobai and begged him to let her go. But Maarten wrapped her in his shirt and shut her up in a wooden box when he reached home. The whole night through he heard her bumping about. The next day he killed a pig. She devoured the liver and the heart completely. It seemed as if her whole body was hiding under the nassa, and she had very long antennae. Two days later, as they were collecting firewood, Maarten told his bosom friend what had happened to him and how he now kept the reptile a prisoner in a wooden box. When this [friend] had passed this on to the husband of the woman concerned, he buttonholed Maarten: 'You are keeping a *tokapuga*, a lizard, prisoner aren't you? Release it.' Maarten obliged and took the reptile back to the spot where he had caught it. At the end of his story Maarten wondered what would have happened if her *ipuwe mee*, her relatives, had not demanded her back.

---

[15] The *pakooba* shell.

[16] By editor. In this section Hylkema has included the following three notes, probably with a view to elaborating on them at some future date.

Megebeto + mege bugaiya. Giay p. 144.
Boat/shell = woman, but two as in the Mapia marriage ritual-
Ambivalent reaction to the appearance of the invisible

In the first note Hylkema is referring to p. 144 of Giay's 1995 book. Here Giay writes: '*Megebeto* is a tortoise-like being which is believed to be symbol of spirit being. It can deliver cowrie shells.' Giay continues with a mythical tale relating how the *megebeto* had once helped a man and his two brothers to obtain cowries.

The other two notes remain unclear to me.

On another occasion, Maarten saw the light of a *pito-yago*, a woman with fire under her armpit, blinking on and off on the spur of a mountain. After telling his wife that she must keep very still, he sidled up to her, but just as he wanted to catch her off guard, she disappeared through a crack in the clay soil. Maarten had recited this story on various occasions, but the last time his wife was also present and she confirmed his story. They linked these happenings to their recent loss of a small son.

[27.7.2 A failed attempt to conjure up money]
Although the person, place and time were different, the preceding and the following tales should be read in connection with each other. On the advice of others Tokiiwiyai You, who lived in Uwebutu,[17] had once caught a lizard with a forked tail, something like the tail of a fish or of a swallow. The tips were red resembling burning charcoal. He put the reptile and a 100 Rupiah note in a bottle. But when after quite some time, in contradiction to their prediction, no second version of the first note had appeared, he had given the reptile to his brother's son, Arnold You, a primary schoolteacher who had come from the Apmisibil on a holiday. He did not know what the latter had done with it.

[25.7.3 Snakes and their harmful effects]
Yesaya Pigai (who lived in Uwebutu and was a member of the Uwekebo clan segment) claimed that the youngest of seven snakes resided with Imobega Keiya. He kept it in a chest. Because he had sprinkled a sort of powder over the reptile, it kept itself coiled up. A Tatogo [man] who had listened to this brief report had then exclaimed in horrified tones: 'How dared he? I am already terrified when I see a worm or a lizard!' He was conscious of the fact that such a man was playing with fire. This report was understood against the background of the generally know fact that seven snakes live in Lake Paniai, a mother and six daughters. The mother lived in the middle of the lake and each of the daughters had focused on one of the centres of population [surrounding the lake]. They gave birth to shells and money. Since there had been a number of cases of tuberculosis at Epobutu,[18] the people believed that these snakes would manifest themselves. They were already searching for the key that would enable them to escape.

This short report contains the suggestion that the snakes which [once] gave birth to prosperity either will be replaced or instead of prosperity will bring forth disaster. What in this report was a prediction, had become reality in the one below. [This concerns] a report about the time a pig feast was being planned at Epobutu in the Muye Valley. Throughout a very wide area people expressed mixed feelings about this, because of the fact that tuberculosis had been

[17] By editor. Uwebutu is located on the western shore of Lake Tage.
[18] By editor. Epobutu is located near the south-western corner of Lake Paniai.

diagnosed there. People there had seen the mother snake on the spot where the dance house was to be built and a daughter snake at the side of a primary teacher's house. Both could give birth at any moment. That is why – so it is said – the doctor at Enarotali had advised the residents of Epobutu to go to live in another place and to [lay out] gardens there. [Reportedly], this was because through the very air they breathed out, both the reptiles passed the dreaded illness on to humans. The people would only be able to return, when the two of them had been killed.

Dopiimude Adii, of Uwebutu, once named four men, including her first husband, who *mege-piyaimo*, literally: [who] had hidden 'shell-tree leaves' in a bamboo cylinder, for the purpose of creating a snake inside it. *Mege-piyaimo*, by which the Me concretely think of cordyline leaves, are a magical means to lure shells. After three of them, including her husband, had died, as well as one of her children, Okaabii You, the fourth man in the plot, confessed what they had done. He died shortly afterwards. The snake had devoured him.

25.8 PRODUCTION OF SHELLS

From the ambivalent standpoint of both the attractive and the repulsive , the origin is important. But with the storehouse [see section 25.5], the puzzle was still not yet solved. All sorts of tales were in circulation about how people came by their shells. It was said of some that they could make the shells appear from their arm, from between the fingers. [This should be] understood as an analogy to the origin of fire, because that also came from the biceps. However, at the same time, [it can also be] associated with ejaculation. This conjures up the idea of the [cowries] as solidified sperm. Although snakes, for instance the *eguwai*, the python, which lives in trees, can be male, they are usually female. Therefore the *koyo*, a large chameleon-like lizard with a remarkable ridge along its spine, appears as the male partner. With its inflatable cheeks [it is] clearly a male, phallic symbol. If shells did come from a *koyo*, they were found at the bottom of a cordyline bush or of sugar cane.

25.9 BORN IN BLOOD

These amulets once again indicated contact with figures in the spirit world. The red cloth pointed to the *Deiya ka abe* [see p. 37]. These figures could be seen in the animal world, above all as a snake. There were also two more possibilities. If a female being was expressly assumed to be the point of departure, people expected to find the shells under the taro in the garden in the vicinity of the house, the place of residence of the female *manes* [probably Latin: ghosts], manifested in a snake. Just as the web comes from inside the spider, so did these shells emerge from inside the *koyo* or snake. In both instances the word *pai*, to give birth, is used, but then in the sense of producing by depositing.

25.10 ORIGINATING FROM THE DEAD

When a sacrifice is made we see that these are horticultural people who understand that everything grows on what has gone before. While in this case the balance swung to the attractive side of the [Latin:] *fascinosum*, it could also swing back to its horrific character. Then, the origin was not sought in life but in death. People who hoarded shells during their lifetime, turned white when they died and produced shells from their anus.

25.11 AUTHENTICITY AND ORIGINALITY

For this to be understood, it is necessary to broaden the framework. The issue has both a theoretical and a practical side. It is possible to speculate about this, but not without some strings attached. The more people were involved with origin, the more they were esteemed, as if it had earned them rights. What rights [these were,] was another matter. [At issue is] a general problem, which however is continually made concrete. Every phenomenon can be questioned as to its origin, both in relation to the phenomena surrounding it and as a phenomenon in its own right. The inquiry results in a provisional ordering between the matters on hand. They can relate to each other as either resulting or not resulting from each other; in other words in agreement with our biological perception about species. Within a species a distinction can be made between earlier or later, between procreator and that which is created. The relationship between two species is more difficult. Given that no one species is equal to another, the two cannot be equivalent either. [And] if both species are exogenous, this raises the question of which came first. This puts origin centre stage.

However, before a phenomenon arrived, it had originated. Something could have come later even though it originated first. This leads to the question of the place of origin. Something could have originated somewhere else and then arrived, [but it] could [also] have originated locally. Finally, what matters was the genuineness, authenticity and originality. Just as the originality of the clan is set out in the myth of origin, people do this for all other matters as well. In the matter of food crops, among sweet potatoes, people distinguish between the indigenous and the exogenous species.[19] Among the indigenous sweet potatoes, the *kadaga* is placed right at the origin. Among the vegetables and the various species of sugar cane, the *digiyo* and the *poogiye* are so placed. Placed right at the origin of the crop, each first species, even though from the viewpoint of procreation this cannot be traced, was involved in the origins of the rest. In contrast to the cultivated species, these grow in the wild. In fact, this is what gives them their rights. They are not to be uprooted. Wherever people come

---

[19] By editor. This term is a translation of the Dutch term 'soort'. With his use of that Dutch term, Hylkema is imprecise according to the canons of Western biology. He may have followed Me biological conceptions, but this remains unclear.

across them, they have to be cleared of weeds so that they will not be engulfed and suffocate. They should also be fertilised; if this is not done the punishment will be that all the other cultivated species will disappear. The continuation of all those derived from it is at stake with the continuation of this original species. It is possible to go a step farther. If the original species is to survive, the survival of the original specimen must be guaranteed. The same is valid for clans, just as it is for the original dog and the original snake.

Of course, this leads to the problem how the original specimen came into being. Remarkably, for a great many of all the phenomena, the question of the origin of the first specimen is not a matter for discussion. This is closely bound up with the fact that people claim certain localities to be the origin of the original specimens, for instance, the origin of the first sweet potato, and hence also the obligation of ensuring its survival. The origin of the *kadaga* is connected with the Pugo Valley.[20] It is an obvious religious centre. Probably the coming into being of a religious centre in the North Kamu goes back to the origin of pigs. The people concerned have to have a covering story which covers this and a palpable reality. The story can become common property. Although this is threatening, it is not fatal. Ultimately it is up to the people themselves to ensure the safety of the original [specimen], so that nobody [else] can appropriate it.

---

[20] By editor. Hylkema writes *kadega* which I have taken to be a typing error. The River Pugo is an eastern tributary of the Yawei which drains the three Paniai lakes to the south. It is noteworthy that the Me appear not to have a memory of the introduction of the crop. But also the location mentioned, in the south-eastern part of the Me territories, is intriguing given that the sweet potato is likely to have been a late introduction, from the Moluccas, via either the south or the north coast. Since in the Mapia region, close to the south coast, taro long remained the dominant staple (Hylkema 2002), an introduction from the north coast, that is to say from the north-west, is more likely. As in the case of the cowry, the people may have mythified the origin of the sweet potato.

PART 3 BRIDE PRICE, by Sibbele Hylkema

Introduction by editor. It seems that the bride price monograph that Hylkema had in mind was much larger than the extant manuscript. The last version of the table of contents mentions six chapters, while only the drafts of the first two chapters of the manuscript are of chapter size. Of three other chapters he drafted brief sketches. Moreover, he mentions several times that he will return extensively to a topic while in fact he does not do so.

It seems further that Hylkema, while writing, re-canvassed the monograph. The manuscript contained two tables of contents, one of which he had provided with handwritten additions and changes. I assume that this was the last version that Hylkema drew up and I included it in an appendix to part 3, this part of this book. Hylkema discussed some topics more than once; moreover he wrote two drafts for chapter 3; and he skipped some section numbers, while he mentioned others twice. I have merged the two drafts for chapter 3 into one. The last pages of the manuscript consist of many unfinished starts and reformulations that I edited. As I mentioned in Part 1 of the book, I do not rule out that Hylkema planned to fuse the cowry and the bride price manuscripts into one, given for instance the gaps in the cowry manuscript after chapter 10.

CHAPTER 26 A PROBLEMATICAL INSTITUTION

26.1 IN THE CONTEXT OF EXCHANGE

26.1.1 Payment for a woman

Invariably, in the wake of the wilful behaviour of the individualistic younger generation, sooner or later the maxim crops up: 'Where two persons marry, two families marry.' Apparently the maxim assimilates not only experience, but also wisdom. If this is the case in modern society, it is the more valid in a traditional one in which the existence of tight communities on the basis of kinship and affinity is to be carefully nursed. And it is even more valid in a society where the necessity to be a member of a group was daily experienced. In some isolated groups this necessity is still experienced.

Within these traditional societies we come across two related, but at the same time opposite terms of which one deserves our special attention: dowry [Dutch: *bruidsschat*] and bride price [Dutch: *bruidsprijs*].[1] In the light of the recent past

---

[1] By editor. In Dutch the two terms are indeed 'related' but 'opposite'. However in translation the relatedness is lost.

people are still aware of the meaning of the first term, but they are puzzled by the second one. They are easily inclined to view the term as an error, of either the pen or the tongue, and to correct it by replacing it with ‘dowry’. Once both terms had lost their currency, they dropped from the vocabulary and were left to the dictionary.

Since I wondered what a standard dictionary offers the modern reader in this respect, I consulted the Van Dale.[2] Van Dale mentions under dowry ‘the sum of money or goods that the bride brings into the marriage’, and under bride price ‘what the groom has to pay for the bride’. After having taken apart the composite term, the definition first adds to ‘price’ the matching verb 'to pay'. Then, it adds as subject the term 'groom', conceptually the standard opposite of 'bride'. A further designation of the person to whom is paid wisely lacks. With the factual description ‘what the groom pays for the bride’ we are brought to a primitive realm, and, within the context of barter or exchange, to the realm of the market.

Before discussing what characterises exchange or trade, I observe with regard to the definition in the Van Dale, mentioned above, that herein the average Ekagi Papuan finds his own conception precisely expressed. Among them ‘Pay for a woman’ is the standard expression used in everyday language. It posits the woman undisguisedly as an object. Culturally biased, we are inclined not to take that choice of words seriously, but instead to take the words metaphorically. Like we, for instance in the case of soccer, use terms such as attacking and defending party, that directly derive from the field of battle. Nevertheless, it is not the idea that a soccer match degenerates into a bloodbath. Certainly, however, such an interpretation does not accord with what the Ekagi Papuan has in mind. The expression is so common that literally everybody, irrespective of schooling and of one’s personal views of the matter, uncritically uses it both in spoken and in written language (for instance Giay 1995: 211). While the expression reflects the idea that the dominant generation has made its own, it influences in turn the image that the younger generation is conceiving and internalising.

26.1.2 Contrast between the exchange of commodities and of gifts

Until rather recently, it was deemed appropriate in modern society that the groom offered his bride an expensive present. It was possibly also a practical present such as two wedding rings which subsequently were solemnly exchanged between them. Currently, it seems maybe more likely that the bride answers this gesture by giving a more or less equally costly present. This is indeed correct if we have to do here with a gift. Not every gift is a present. What seems to be a present can in fact serve as an illicit commission, or as a tip, as a

---

[2] By editor. ‘Van Dale’ is the name of a much-used set of Dutch dictionaries.

toll or tribute, or as a sacrifice. For a present to become a gift, it has sooner or later to be answered with a counter gift.

The exchange harbours a certain amount of reciprocity and, accordingly, the exchange of gifts reminds of barter. Undoubtedly, exchange of gifts between two persons and exchange of goods in the context of trade or barter have a lot in common. In both cases there are two subjects, two objects, and two acts, offering and accepting, that differ with respect to subject and object, but are similarly made up, thus constituting exchange or barter. Yet, at the same time, the exchange of gifts and the exchange of goods display remarkable differences. Exchange of gifts often concerns expensive goods. By contrast, as soon as such goods are traded they are as it were desacralised or commercialised. In the case of trading one usually distinguishes between objects of exchange, such as goods for consumption, and means of exchange, such as money. Historically it appears that fine metals that were first made into valuables were subsequently used as coins, as means of exchange. The exchange of [for instance] food against food is called direct exchange, of food against money indirect exchange.

Referring to the existing literature (van Baal 1975: 50), we can characterise direct and indirect exchange, or trade and exchange of gifts, as follows. Trade is a matter of pure calculation. On the market buyer and seller are each other's equivalents. In their dealings with each other they are not bothered by pre-existing social relations. They are exclusively interested in the other's goods and what these goods are worth. And they are free to offer these goods for sale and [on the other hand] to buy or accept what has been put on offer. With the completion of the exchange, con-tacts between the two parties concerned are broken off. They are not in any way linked to each other. If the parties do not exchange, either directly or indirectly, but instead arrive at a contract, this contract is legally protected. What is rendered and received is specified in detail, on the basis of the value of the goods and the point in time they are delivered. In that sense we can speak of a balanced mutuality or reciprocity. Trade is guided by a considered weighing of pros and cons, of free and conscious decisions.

In the case of gift exchange, by contrast, participants need not be equals, witness mother and child who give each other presents at their birthdays. Usually strong social relationships already exist between them that the exchange of gifts further reinforces. For both, the person who gives is more important than the object given; the object derives its value often from the person from whom it is received. In many cases, it has more emotional than practical value, hence often valuables are given such as adornments that are displayed or worn occasionally, rather than daily. After having received a gift, there is no need to produce a counter-gift instantaneously. Although mutual gift giving pre-supposes reciprocity, this need not be strictly balanced; the objects [exchanged] need not be strictly equivalent and the moment of repayment is not fixed. But in contrast to the freedom that is implicit in trade, with gift exchange one is, how paradoxically it may sound, both obliged to offer a gift and to accept a gift offered. Gifts link the participants, they result in making the participants committed to each other, turning them into partners.

26.2 ETHNIC GROUPS LIVING FROM AGRICULTURE

26.2.1 Segregation between men and women

Bride price occurs among all ethnic groups in the Central Highlands of New Guinea. It is far from exceptional that an institution, in some or other form, is found among all ethnic groups, witness the use of the cowry, the construction and use of dance houses, and the organisation of pig feasts. The various ethnic groups have a great deal in common. Remarkable is, first, that all of them are dependent upon intensive agriculture for the cultivation of their staple crop, sweet potato or taro. In close connection with their cultivation, they practise pig husbandry. All ethnic groups are subdivided into patrilineal, exogamous, named clans. According to Haviland (1975: 176),[3] the clan organisation is closely associated with a pronounced segregation of the sexes. [Haviland observes that] work is either male or female, so men and women rarely perform a task together. Both boys and girls are actually educated by women, who encourage tractability in their children. But the time comes that boys have to change roles to become men who are to be hard, competitive and aggressive. They have to prove their manhood, while women need not prove their womanhood. Usually this entails that men exert their superiority, and hence their authority, in relation to women.

26.2.2 Both equipped for a life in rivalry

Generally speaking, [Haviland's above] characterisation of agricultural societies is accurate. Hence it strikes the more that with regard to Ekagi education several comments can be made. While [Haviland's] text suggests that women, in contrast to men, educate children of either sex to be tractable, it is noteworthy that among the Ekagi women emphasise the sex difference at the least just as much as men. Instead of one series of terms attributed to children on the basis of birth order only, Ekagi use two separate series in conformity with the sex of the children: a series from eldest to youngest son, next to a series from eldest to youngest daughter. Both series refer to the mother. Hence, in a polygynous family, one may find, in addition to several eldest and youngest children, an *enaago*, an only child. This means that the terms do not show the birth order of children of different sex. Brothers and sisters are each other's *paneka*. The term encompasses the practical interest that the one has for the other, an interest that clearly and fully shows up in the context of marriage.

From early on, each child is educated to carry out the tasks allocated to him or her, according to sex. Remarkable is that boys, once they have become adults,

---

[3] By editor. I was unsuccessful tracing this reference.

appear to be more meek and tractable than girls, while girls appear to be at least as combative and competitive as boys. This can be noticed in disposition and behaviour towards members of the same sex, hence within the confines of the tasks allocated to each sex, but often just as much vis-à-vis the other sex. A case in point is the contrast between the role that each sex has as regards selecting a spouse, and their actual behaviour.

Associated with the notion that men are to be hard and aggressive is the use of weapons such as bow and arrows and, in the case of the Ekagi, clubs. Although the role division between the sexes denies women the use of weapons and of physical violence, and women for that reason cannot train boys how to use weapons, it does not prevent that they incite men to physical violence, or accuse them of cowardice. And while the use of physical violence is denied, there are other forms [of violence] that inflict pain and hurt just as much. Notorious are in this regard the diatribes delivered with a shrill voice and consisting of a series of pithy statements. Women deliver them by preference from a hillside so each word can be understood far and wide. Such events should not prompt the conclusion that socialisation has failed. Instead, it can be said that both sexes are educated and equipped to stand up for themselves and to hold their own in a society marked by rivalry, both among and between the sexes. In response to [Haviland's] comment that women need not prove their femininity, it can be posited that [among the Ekagi] women know they are constantly challenged, in a competition encouraged by men, to prove their femininity, identified with fertility, both by production and by procreation. If they do not, they run the risk of being accused of the negative form of femininity, witchcraft, and, in its wake, of being avoided and excluded.

26.3 EACH GROUP AND EACH REGION IN FLUX

Because the various ethnic groups in the Central Highlands have so much in common, it may be concluded that they continuously borrowed from each other. Simultaneously it is noteworthy that each ethnic group has elaborated these common elements in quite specific ways. This holds for purely material matters such as the string bag. Although these bags are in use everywhere, each ethnic group has its own models and manufacturing techniques. The cowry circulates throughout all of the highlands as a means of exchange or of payment, but the ways each ethnic group uses and evaluates them shows remarkable differences. Members of each group basically wield the same structuring principles as their starting points, witness the segregation between the sexes, the subdivision of the ethnic groups into clans and the bipartition of the male members of the group into social strata.[4] However, within each group they are used according to

---

[4] By editor. Hylkema refers here to the contrast between 'big' and 'small' men. He portrays Ekagi society as inegalitarian, even more than does Pospisil. While the latter

group-specific criteria based on an own system of norms and values. Hence the way people live is characteristic for each group.

In this context, common elements, such as the dance, the dance house and the pig feast, that each ethnic group sustains in its own way demand our attention. Not only do people appropriate foreign elements by integrating them in their own culture, they also change and develop them from generation to generation; they trade them in for something novel, or simply drop them. This means that with society also culture as a whole and the various, separate culture elements are in continuous flux. The process of change need not take place at the same time or equally fast among the regional sub-groups. Influencing factors are differences in population density and population growth, and the intensity of contacts with neighbouring groups and regions.

To return to our topic, there are remarkable differences in the composition of the bride price and the way the price is managed, between on the one hand the thinly populated, isolated Mapia region in the west, and the various, distinct regions round the lakes on the other, with, in the very east, the Paniai region in the vicinity of the Moni people. These differences allow the reconstruction of several recent developments. It seems as if the westerly Mapia region was one or two generations behind the Paniai region. In the Mapia, people practised, albeit sporadically, a wedding ritual of probably older derivation, in combination with transferring bride price. They consciously retarded the drastic development of the bride price that had started elsewhere. In Paniai the traces of a wedding ritual were already completely eliminated, except for a few details such as the exchange of genital coverings and a linguistic expression about a ceremonially made garden. But people had its meaning creatively adapted to the altered situation. At the time of European settlement in the 1930s, the ethnic group was in the process of splitting into two culturally and linguistically distinct groups, witness the two names, Ekagi and Yimogi, which were applied at the time [see Le Roux 1948-50, vol. 2: 658-9].

The successive transfers of bride prices were moments of cardinal significance in the network of continually changing social relationships. The way they were arranged and effected formed a nexus that brought all sorts of conceptions, notions and customs together. Ordering and comparing the various data about this topic from the Mapia and the Paniai regions not only shows what the bride price was like at a specific moment of time and how it developed in recent history; it also shows a social organisation engaged in a process of continuous change, in line with a changeable conception of humankind and of the world.

---

holds that upward, and downward, mobility among the Ekagi is prominent (1989: 25), Hylkema stresses the barriers that hinder social advancement.

26.4 AS PRACTISED IN THE PANIAI REGION IN THE EARLY 1970S

What follows is an account of the event as it unfolds before the eyes of an interested, but guileless spectator. Like in each transaction, two parties are involved in the bride price, the givers and the receivers.[5] Within each party one can distinguish a nucleus. The nucleus of the price givers carries out the preparations. In some cases they deliberate with the nucleus of the receiving party right from the beginning; in others only after they have carried out their task. The one nucleus consists broadly of the groom, his father and often a local elite person, as sponsor; the other one of the father or a brother of the bride, and the person, or his heir, who in the past was sponsor at the marriage of the bride's father. In their full size the groups consist of the various kin relatives and acquaintances of the members of the nucleus groups.

The nucleus of the price giving group is faced with a threefold task, in accordance with the three parts of which the bride price is constituted. They are named *awii,* an amount of money to be given to the mother of the bride; *one,* consisting of several *muto,* strings of cowries, and several single *yoo*, shells of high value, to be given to the father, or his heir, and eventually to the sponsor of the father's marriage; and *kadee*, consisting of several strings of shells and a large number of single shells of miscellaneous value, to be given to brothers, kin and creditors among the price takers. [Because the background to this tri-partition will be made clear below, here a short explanation of the terms suffices].

Before the price givers come into action in full force, and the negotiations that the nucleus has started enter their decisive phase, the nucleus has to have assembled the ingredients of the *awii* and the *one*, and a large part of the *kadee.* When the negotiations are opened, privately, the members of the nucleus can show the price takers, by way of offer, what has been assembled and subject it to their judgment. Not only the single high value shells, but also all the shells of all the strings and also the strings in their entirety are put to the test and given a value. Starting from this concrete offer, claimants can formulate their wishes, first with regard to changes in what has been shown and secondly with regard to additions on the day of the transfer. In this phase the negotiations consist of sounding out what people want to offer and to receive.

Only when both parties have come so close that a last round of talks offers a realistic chance that they will come to an agreement, a day is set when the final negotiations are to take place so the total force of both groups can be mobilised. Usually these negotiations take place in the yard of the house of the groom's father, and sometimes in the house of the sponsor, in close connection with how

---

[5] By editor. Below I use the terms 'price givers' and 'price takers' for these groups. I modeled these terms on 'bride givers' and 'bride takers'.

much each has brought in and thus with their positions within the local community. When most of the expected participants of both parties have got together, around nine or ten in the morning, a mat, rain cape or piece of bark is put out on the yard. It serves to display the strings of shells and the single shells that the nucleus has assembled. The strings are shown in their full length; the single shells are divided over six heaps according to category and quality. Thus, all the mobilised relatives and acquaintances can make sure about quantities, values and qualities. On that basis they decide what they may want to contribute further.

Then hours of bargaining follow. In all manner of speech, in turn funny, serious and indignant, it is pointed out to bystanders that this is a serious occasion and that, hence, they should rise to it. Seasoned remarks, jokes and puns, and sharp impu-tations and reproaches, follow each other in an inscrutable order. A few relatives near the mat receive the single shells that are contributed, evaluate them, and praise or revile them. Finally they put them on the appropriate heap, to either the silent satisfaction or the open disappointment of the contributor.

As long as the price givers are busy, the price takers look on from far or nearby, in silence. When the price givers opine that enough has been assembled, they leave the floor to the price takers to inspect the shells and to rearrange the heaps of shells according to their own judgment. The result is that the heaps of valuable shells shrink and the heaps of worthless shells grow. Since, of course, the dismayed price givers are unwilling to meet further demands, the price takers threaten to break off the negotiations and to return home, with the bride, unless the price givers appeal to their members to produce better quality shells. Usually, both parties finally come to an agreement. Sometimes a session is adjourned to the next day in the expectation that those who have stayed home will yet turn up. It is rare that the final negotiations are broken off irrevocably.

26.5 ANALYSIS AND EVALUATION

26.5.1 The proceedings

In the above I set out the characteristics of the exchange of gifts and the exchange of goods in the context of barter and trade. When we consider the transfer of the bride price in the light of these characteristics, it is clear that we cannot speak of the transfer of a gift. The bride price, with its complex composition, is approached as a means of exchange, deployed in indirect exchange. The transaction is modelled on barter as it takes place on the market. The two parties are not interested in each other, but in what the other has to offer: one in shells of distinct quality and quan-tity, the other in a woman. The woman's quality can be ascertained, but it is fixed. Nothing can be added to it. Possibly, another woman can replace her, if there is an urgent need for shells. The price can be modified in several ways, given its complex composition. The parties face each other as equals. The proceedings give the impression that when the parties cannot agree over the price, they are free to take back the means of exchange that they have on offer and to satisfy their needs by starting negotiations elsewhere. In the context of barter, this means that contacts between the parties are restricted to the length of the negotiations and are subsequently broken off, whether or not the transaction has taken place.

Although the staging of the event logically leads to this conclusion, it is applicable only in case the transaction falls through. In case the negotiations lead to a marriage, it appears that bride and groom can establish relationships with each other's kin. Moreover, given the much wider use of affinal terms, it appears that both families are no longer strangers to each other. For both, the transaction leads to rights and obligations that they earlier did not have. This holds also for the husband even though he continually and emphatically makes it clear to his wife and her kin that he has paid for her. This practice suggests that the above analysis or interpretation of the proceedings has gone astray, as if somewhere an erroneous inference has been made.

By editor. Hylkema continued his discussion with sub-section 26.5.2, entitled, in Dutch, *Onder het aspect of subject and object,* which I translated as 'Subject and Object.' He returned to this topic in chapter 29. So as to make a better ending to the unfinished manuscript, I shifted this sub-section to that chapter, sub-section 29.2.2, the final section of the manuscript.

CHAPTER 27 THE BRIDE PRICE THROUGHOUT HISTORY

27.1 CASES FROM THE ERA 1930-1970

27.1.1 Introductory remarks

Because the bride price has a key role in social life, it is noteworthy that all prices are different in composition, even if they are transferred on the same place and the same day. Within a short period of time and in a restricted area the differences are so small that an average bride price can be calculated as it was then, in that area. But over a longer time period such a calculation is out of the question, let alone if several regions are taken into account. In that case, the changes in the material composition of the bride price are of such magnitude that a comparison has to be restricted to noting specific trends.

To illustrate this change I present a series of bride prices from the recent past. The origin of the data is heterogeneous. Some derive from the extant literature, most of them I collected myself. The literature mentions only average bride prices, pertaining to time and place of the inquiries. Given this restricted validity, I have chosen for a number of cases that occurred over a number of generations, and a number of regions. The data are not based on a focused and wide ranging inquiry. Several result from quite accidental information. In passing, the subject cropped up in the course of a conversation, while the context in which this happened seemed to guarantee reliability. Others result from samples associated with the case of Isaias Tekege, my key informant at Epouto, in the Paniai-Tage region, that I could closely follow. As regards reliability, but especially completeness, it matters whether or not the data are obtained directly, or via one or more in betweens. And also whether or not the details fitted the usual pattern and whether or not they were still of interest to the person concerned. Which gift is part of the bride price and which is not, may be open for discussion. What matters in personal recollections is not the historical importance of these data, in so far as they allow us to glance into the past, but their current value for the informant himself, with an eye to a future discharge. Notwithstanding their qualitative differences, each of the cases can be called sufficiently exemplary for a given moment or period in time in the history of a specific region. Taken together they show how the bride price has developed.

Extensive exposure of the peculiar characteristics and conditions of each separate case is not appropriate in a general survey. Sometimes, nevertheless, I have added details that bear immediately on the case, while I will elucidate them in a following part of the monograph. In the survey the bride price for Isaias Tekege's bride got a central place. Several other bride prices are linked up with this price. They are the ones paid in the recent or distant past on the occasion of the marriages of his close relatives of previous generations, his father, father's brothers and his grandfather. Grouped around these are the various cases that came my way in the margins of my inquiries.

27.1.2 Information regarding the original names of the items

In the absence of precise equivalents for several names, I retained the original names of all the goods in the description of the cases. Here I restrict myself to a short explanation of these original names. For a comprehensive discussion of these names and how they interrelate, I refer to my study of the cowry.[1] The most important part of the bride prices that are here mentioned are the *mege*, the cowry, and the *dedege*, the nassa shell. To start with, Ekagi distinguish within the total stock of cowries several, named categories. With that category corresponds a broad value, going from low to very high. As regards the Paniai-Tage region, the categories mentioned in the cases can be hierarchically ordered in accordance with these values. At the top of the ladder is the *yoo.* About halfway up are successively the *munidagi*, the *yoodagi* and the *kubawi*; although they are distinguished by name, they are, neglecting these names, called *yoodagi*, because they are of comparable value. Several rungs farther down, is the *bodiya.* At the bottom of the ladder are the categories *mitouyautuuya* and *yuu.* Given that there are no identical specimens, each shell can be evaluated separately, on the basis of its formal characteristics, and be ordered hierarchically. Although belonging to a specific category, shells can be placed both higher and lower than its category indicates. This happens in fact only with shells halfway and farther up the ladder. Thus the highest placed *yoo* can slump in value and became equivalent to a *mitouyatuuya* or *yuu,* the lowest categories. Liable to wear, shells are easily damaged.

As mentioned in passing, the above applies to the Paniai-Tage region only. Some of the mentioned categories, especially the *bodiya,* are encountered also in the Kamu-Tigi region. Although I am not certain whether this *bodiya* is everywhere granted the same value, it can be called universally valid on the basis of its use. Other categories occur regionally only. Peculiar to the Kamu-Tigi region is the *bomouye.* Although [there?] the *yoodagi* and the *bomouye* are close in terms of their purchasing power, in the Panai-Tage region the *bomouye* is put on the level of categories at the bottom of the hierarchical ladder. There are data that allow the conclusion that once the *bomouye* was a highly valued category also in the Paniai-Tigi region and only later was devalued to a foreign and practically valueless coin. This indicates that the shell system historically has been continuously changing. The traditional, hierarchically ordered shell system shook on its foundations when, after the settlement of Europeans, shells overran the entire area. In conformity with the scientific distinction between money cowry and ring cowry [chapter 1], people have kept the latter out of the system as counterfeit money. They have granted only the money cowry

[1] By editor. See part 2, chapter 2.

authenticity and made it part of the stock. Although they did so honouring the traditional differences in formal categories, they distinguished, within each category *wei,* old, and *iyaa*, new specimens. Old shells were of higher, new ones of lower value. They were used alongside each other.

All cowries can be individually transacted, on the sole basis of their individual value. Next to this use of single shells, Ekagi use *one* or *muto*, strings of shells that have been laced together. Ideally a string contains 60 shells, however, in the Paniai-Tage region usually only 50 or 40. Only those shells which are halfway the ladder, or a bit lower, are used for strings, and not those at the top and at the bottom. Shells with top value are put next to each other, in accordance with the strict individuality and the value of each of them; those at the bottom are distinguished by category, but handled quantitatively by throwing them in heaps. While making a string, shells are not joined at random. The position in a string shows the category of a shell and its individual value within this category. Mostly on the strength of the age of the shells used, strings are qualitatively distinguished in relation to each other into the qualities *etike,* right, meaning relatively high-valued, and *aka,* left, meaning relatively low-valued.

After cowries have been evaluated by category and by their individual features, they can be added up by category, much like [Americans can speak of] four dimes and five quarters. However, nassa are not even distinguished by category. Nor are they counted. After having been stringed together completely arbitrarily, they are evaluated by the length of the strings. When they are used in the bride price, the human body, from crown to foot, is used as measure.

The distinction between the three constituent parts of the bride price: *awii, one* and *kadee*, has not been observed in all cases. It is possible to hypothesise how the items have to be assigned to the three parts, on the basis of those cases where the distinction has been observed, but I leave it unmentioned given the lack of exact relevant data.[1]

27.1.3 A series of cases

Case 1, Marriage of Nidaikawii Pekei; my notes do not mention the identity of the bride.

---

[1] By editor. After the names of bride and groom Hylkema mentioned a place name, presumably the name of the village or neighbourhood of the groom in which the couple settled. I have added the name of the region in which the settlement is located given the regional differences in the composition of the bride price.

Mostly, Hylkema listed the items of the bride prices vertically. In some instances he arranged some of them horizontally. He did not explain this usage. I presume it has to do with the three categories in which the price is subdivided. That, I think, is also the reason that Hylkema, in case 3, listed *muto,* shell strings, twice.

2 *muto*
10 *kubawi*
10 *pakooba (Cymbicum diadema)*[2]
1 *yika* (a stone axe)
6 strings nassa shells

Case 2, Marriage of Ewotuma Tatogo and Makeepamabii You, Uwebuto, south western tip of the Paniai-Tage region, around 1935.
2 *yoo*
1 *muto* (afterwards another has been added, privately)
10 *yoodagi*
10 *boiya*
4 strings nassa shells

Case 3, Marriage of Gaatiyaawii You and Adiidoge Adii, Uwebuto, south western tip of the Paniai-Tage region, around 1940.
6 *yoo*
3 *muto*
3 *yoodagi* (afterwards another 3 have been privately added)
2 *muto*

Case 4, Marriage of Bobeukebo Tekege and his third wife Dimipugiwo Madai, Epouto, Paniai-Tage region, around 1950
4 *yoo*
2 *muto*
5 strings nassa shells

Case 5, Marriage of Tokiiwiyai You and Degemaga Tekege, Uwebuto, south western tip of the Paniai-Tage region, around 1950.
1 *muto*
3 strings nassa shells
This bride price lacked the *one*, the fundamental part composed of *yoo* and *muto*. Payment of this part was postponed until the bride price for a daughter from this marriage would be paid.

Case 6, Marriage of Imoudakebo Tekege and Cecilia Degei, Epouto, Paniai-Tage region, around 1950.[3]
5 *yoo* (2 *etike*, right; 3 *aka*, left)
2 *muto* (*etike*)
5 strings nassa shells

---

[2] A large oval shell, shaped like a bowl; often only fragments were in use.
[3] By editor. Imoudakebo Tekege and Cecilia Degei were the parents of Isaias Tekege, as mentioned one of Hylkema's key informants.

In her parents marriage, Cecilia was born with only sisters. She had given birth, in a former marriage, to a stillborn son. Widowed, she went on her own initiative to Epouto to the bridegroom, without letting her relatives know. Marking out the irregularity of the event, only her cousin, her father's brother's son Meuwituma Degei, turned up to receive the bride price. He had brought a new and an old string bag, *ute*, with him. As *kadee,* or 'single shells', Imoudakebo put 30 old *yoodagi* and 60 old *mitouyatuuya* in the old string bag, and 30 new *yoodagi*, 60 new *mitouyautuuya* and 120 new *yuu* in the new one. The round figures make it clear they are approximations. The groom claimed that the bride's relatives, by sending one representative only, had deprived him of the opportunity to haggle. He felt that he had been compelled to come down handsomely, lest the bride would be fetched back. When Imoudakebo married a second wife, around 1965 [case 14], he paid his wife's father's sister's husband, Tikiyo Mote, as *kadee*, 1 *bodiya-yoo* (*etike*) and some *bodiya.* Although they were paid on the occasion of his second marriage, he wanted them to be included in the expenses for his first marriage.

Case 7, derived from de Bruijn (1955d) [data presumably refer to the Paniai-Tage area].[4] [5]

1. ONE

Composed of *yoo*, *kobawi,* and *bodiya,* assembled by the groom's father or his substitute, and earmarked for the bride's father or his substitute.

2. DEDEGE

4 to 5 strings nassa shells, assembled by the groom's mother or sister, and earmarked for the bride's mother or sister.

3. OKAAKAI[6]

30 old cowries, assembled by the bridegroom and earmarked for the bride's mother.

4. KADEE

40 old cowries, 1000 new cowries, *pakooba.* The 40 cowries were assembled by the bridegroom and his close relatives and were earmarked for the eldest brother of the bride. He shares with his brothers and gives father's brother(s) and

---

[4] By editor. Also these data are taken from de Bruijn's 1952 *Dienstnota* (see chapter 2, note 14, p. 34). I do not rule out, however, that de Bruijn checked them in the light of information that he got while he was posted among the Me from 1938 to 1943.

[5] Because of the valuable character of the many details, I have added explanations and corrections in footnotes, and used this as a model while slightly re-arranging Dubbeldam's data [case 9]. The author [presumably de Bruijn] is not aware of the distinction between the *yoo,* the most highly valued cowries, that can be transferred as single shells, and the highly valued *yoodagi* that are eligible to become part of *muto*, strings.

[6] The term *okaakai* can be translated with 'to be distributed according to choice,' *in casu* the choice of the mother of the bride.

mother's brother(s) 2 to 3 specimens per person. The 1000 new cowries and the *pakooba* were assembled by the bridegroom, close relatives, distant relatives and acquaintances and earmarked for companions of the bride. The *pakooba* were often earmarked for the bride's mother.

Case 8, from Pospisil (1958: 54), Kamu area, up to 1955.
'An average bride price, on the basis of twenty four cases, is approximately 300 beads, 120 old cowries, 120 white man's cowries three *dedege* necklaces, and one large male pig.'

Case 9, derived from Dubbeldam (1964: 295-6), Paniai-Tage region.[7]
In 1957 the bride price in Paniai consisted of the following two parts'.
ONE
1. One: 1 or 2 *yoo,* 5 to 10 *munidagi* or *yoodagi,* at least 1 *muto* old *bodiya.* Wife's father or wife's brother(s) will receive these shells, unless the bride price has been burdened with a debt of wife's father (in case he had had to borrow shells for his own marriage, to be repaid [one generation later] when his daughter married).
2. Dedege: 1 string *dedege* and/or *wodaago* and *kegeego.*[8] These objects are for wife's mother.
3. Okaakai: 30 old cowries, *pakooba.* These are for wife's mother.
KADEE
4. Kadee
a about one *muto* old shells
b at least one *muto* white man's shells
c beads (a few strings)
d other goods.
These goods are to be received by wife's brother(s) and other relatives and creditors.

Case 10, Marriage of Peubedo Mote and Badiiyeba Gobai, Epouto, Paniai-Tage region, around 1960.
5 yoo

[7] By editor. Hylkema had translated Dubbeldam's English text into Dutch. In addition, he had, unlike Dubbeldam, made *dedege* and *akaakai* separate sub-categories of the *one* part. And finally he had changed Dubbeldam's spelling of Me words in agreement with the spelling he used himself. For this English version of Hylkema's text I used Dubbeldam's 1964 English, while retaining Hylkema's re-arrangement of the *one* part and of his spelling.
[8] As regards the number of nassa shell strings, it may be presumed that the author has misunderstood his informant. He meant *dedege* in the plural, while this did not become clear in Indonesian. *Wodaago* means literally marsupial teeth, and *kegeego* possum teeth; the latter word is a sub-category of *wodaago.*

2 muto
5 nassa strings, 12 cowries

Case 11, Marriage of Tokiiwiyai You with Perpetua Tatogo, a widow, Uwebuto, south-western tip of the Paniai-Tage region, around 1960. The groom is the same man as in case 5.
2 *yoo* (1 *deke-uyoo*, 1 *muka-yoo*)[9]
2 *muto*
34 single *yoodagi*
5 nassa strings, 10 single cowries

Case 12, Marriage of Beemabiipai Tekege and Angela You, Epouto, Paniai-Tage region, around 1960.
4 *yoo*
2 *muto*
40 single *yoodagi*
5 nassa strings, 1 *yoo*, 12 *bodiya*

Case 13, Marriage of Yosep Tekege and Angela You, widow of Beemabiipai Tekege (case 12), Epouto, Paniai-Tage region, around 1965.
2 *muto*
30 *yoodagi*
7 *bodiya,* 1 *yoodagi*
When Beemabiipai had drowned, after the birth of a daughter, kin from both sides instigated that his widow Angela was married to his younger brother. Because they had transferred 4 *yoo* on the occasion of the first marriage, the Tekege stipulated that there was no need to pay *yoo*.

Case 14, Marriage of Imoudakebo Tekege and Mote Degemau, Epouto, Paniai-Tage region, around 1967. This is Imoudakebo's second marriage. See case 6.
4 *yoo* (3 *etike,* right, out of the assets of the bridegroom; 1 *aka,* left, provided by mother's sister's son Mauwadiibega Tekege, in Dimiya)
3 *muto* (2 *etike*, out of the assets of the groom; 1 *aka,* provided by Yesaya, an as yet unmarried halfbrother)
14 *yoodagi* (11 from the groom, 1 *kubawi* from the groom, 1 *yoodagi* provided by mother's sister's son Mauwadiigeba Tekege, in Dimiya)
15 *bodiya* (provided by Eakokobe Tekege, Potibutu).
On the instruction of Imoudakebo noted down by his son, my key informant Isaias.

---

9 By editor. The words specifying the *yoo* refer to the shape of the shells (see chapter 3, sub-section 3.1.2).

Case 15, Marriage of Titus Degei and Bibiana Kotouki, Tigi area, Kamu-Tigi region, around 1970.
2 *yoo*
3 *muto*
nassa 'on rain cape', which means that the quantity had not been fixed beforehand
4 pigs
IB 5000
Head decoration made of cassowary feathers
The bridegroom, born in the Mapia region, received a reasonable salary of the Department of Agriculture. He abducted the bride, while she was a boarder at the domestic arts school in Enarotali. The unprecedented size of the bride price made the Mapia people decide to close their borders for bride seekers from other regions.

Case 16, Marriage of Bernard Tekege and Anna You, Epouto, Paniai-Tage region, around 1970.
6 *yoo*
2 *muto*
60 *yoodagi*
4 pigs (1 adult, 2 young adults, 1 half adult)
IB 1000 (instead of 20 *bodiya*)
The bridegroom received a, minute, salary of the government in Enarotali. The bride, daughter of the well-known *tonowi* Bobaapiiyawii, in Uwebutu [, on the western shore of Lake Tage], had finished the house keeping school. Both belonged to the elite of the younger generation. On account of this extraordinary high bride price, the Tekege at the east shore of Lake Tage still wait for a chance to get restitution.

Case 17, Mapia region, around 1970. Officially, the bride price in the Mapia region consisted of 1 string of cowries and 7 strings of nassa. The actual prices appeared to be higher.
a. Marriage of Isaias Tebai and Marta Wakei, Timeepa, around 1970, 2 *muto*, 7 nassa strings, 1 *muto,* IB 5
b. Marriage of Mateus Wakei and Albina Tebai, Timeepa, around 1970, 1 *muto* (*aka,* left), 1 *muto* (*etike,* right), 8 nassa strings

Case 18, Marriage of Vitalis Mote and Adolfina Muyapa, Wotai, February 1974
6 yoo
3 *muto*
± 30 *yoodagi*
± 40 *bodiya*
± 120 *mitouyautuuya*
± 200 *yuu*

20 *bodiya*
IB 1500
According to the bridegroom these amounts had been demanded by the bride givers on the eve of the transaction. I did not get to know how much was in fact transferred.

Case 19, Marriage of Isaias Tekege and Natalia You, Epouto, Paniai-Tage region, March 1974.
6 *yoo*
3 *muto*
33 *yoodagi* (*wei,* dry)
21 *yoodagi* (*iyaa,* fresh)
± 60 *mitoutyautuuya*
± 60 *yuu*
20 *bodiya*
IB 1000
These were the amounts assembled by the bride takers. I could closely observe the assemblage of this bride price and I gave it a central place in this study.[10] At the time substitution of the cowry by money was to be expected. Using the average exchange rates, I calculated that this bride price came to somewhere between IB 15,000 to IB 17,000, or Rp 300,000 and Rp 340,000.

27.1.3 Evaluation: the cowry is central
The cases mentioned show that during the period of, roughly, 1930 to 1975, the material composition of the bride price was in a continuous process of change. While novel items were included, old ones were discontinued. The stone axe is mentioned in case 1 only. It is noteworthy that the *pakooba* appears, apart from case 1 (± 1935), also in cases 7 (± 1950) and 9 (± 1957). Some time in the past this shell was required for ritual conjurations. I add that, as late as 1970, an informant noticed the shell in the string bag of an old woman, next to other traditional objects, such as stone knives. Together, they formed traditionally the gift that a woman's relatives, after her death, expected from her son. At the time that tradition had fallen into complete disuse. Pospisil (1958) does not mention the shell in his inventory of average bride prices. Nor does it appear in the previous cases. Accordingly, it may be surmised that the information that Dubbeldam got, did not distinguish between recently discontinued and still current practices.

Both authors mention beads which were current in the 1950s. Given that the information that I got in 1973 consistently mentioned the nassa, while it never mentioned beads, their use appears to have been a transient fashion to the extent

[10] By editor. Hylkema refers here to his 1974 monograph dealing with the bride price (Hylkema 1974b).

that my informants did not find it worth mentioning. From the beginning to the end of this period the nassa occurs, at least regionally (cases 15 and 17). By the end of the period, their use had ceased completely in the Paniai-Tage region. Although already Dubbeldam [1964: 302] reports that shells were commonly bought with money, it does not appear as a part of the bride price until the end of the period, be it in the margin, in the *awii*, the part earmarked for the bride's mother. At first it replaces shells, later it becomes a steady item next to shells (cases 17 and 18).[11]

It is remarkable that the pig is mentioned in a few cases only; first in case 8 with regard to the Kamu area (one adult boar), subsequently in case 15 with regard to the Tigi area (four pigs), and finally in case 16 with regard to Uwebuto, a valley in between Paniai-Tage, Tigi and Kamu. To start with, the considerable differences in number are noteworthy. Moreover the animal is absent in all the other cases, also in Dubbeldam's detailed account (case 9). It contrasts with the use of pigs in compensation: in Paniai-Tage, but also elsewhere, pigs were persistently asked and given in case of blatant violations of law. The phenomenon of legal disputes is noteworthy, because their organisation shows little difference [with bride price negotiations]. In both cases the negotiations are soon accompanied, on both sides, by the intimidating fury dances; incidentally, a privilege reserved for elite men of repute. As mentioned in the comments on the cases concerned, the transfer of four pigs was seen as a risky excess. In both cases the price takers presumed that the bridegroom was prepared to pay whatever was asked because he was deeply in love or highly ambitious, while his kith and kin would not fail him. It is questionable whether or not the transfer of a pig is part of the bride price. In Tige, the bridegroom traditionally donated a pig to his wife's relatives when the marriage was completed [consummated, or: after the birth of a (male) child?].

Throughout the entire period the cowry has a continuing and central place in the bride price, both in the form of single shells and of strings. Complete strings are used in the bride price only. The cowry has such a dominant position that the technical terms that were usually employed can be explained only with the cowry as reference point. In the Mapia people remembered that in the past the expression had been used, *api reu makii*, literally ' to lay down a girl'. The word *reu* was known in this expression only. What it meant was not known. In the meantime people, also there, have shifted to using the expression used elsewhere: *kadee makii*, probably an abbreviation of *api mege kadee makii*, literally 'girl …

By editor. Hylkema's manuscript has a gap here. His text resumes at the point where he recapitulates how the composition of the bride price has changed. He

[11] By editor. Hylkema seems to refer to low value shells.

returns to the topic in sections 2.3 and 2.4. Hylkema's review neatly complements what is known about trade in the highlands of eastern New Guinea. For instance, Hughes (1977: 184f) and Healey (1990: 236f) note the increase in shells traded into the highlands of eastern New Guinea. In their trading the Me appear to have focused on exchange items, primarily cowries, while they showed little interest in objects for self-decoration such as feathers. In a handwritten comment on de Bruijn's paper dealing with Me land tenure (1952, 1955b), Hylkema points to the seeming paradox that the Me combined their intense pre-occupation with cowries with a materially very sober way of life.

… valuables such as the *pakooba*, body decorations such as feathers and beads, and tools such as the stone axe, at the end of the period the bride price consisted only of items that functioned as means of exchange in social life. Although they were all reduced to means of exchange, not all categories of cowry were treated similarly. The highly valued *yoo* could be transacted, for a pig or for other shells, but in fact this happened only in view of future use in the bride price. The reduction of the means [of exchange] to the cowry brings very clearly to the fore that the transactions were controlled by an elite. By providing services and by selling craft and agricultural produce, and caught crayfish and game, the common man could take part in the shell economy, but these transactions usually involved small numbers and shells that were halfway the hierarchical ladder. To participate successfully in the shell economy, one had to belong to the limited group of pig owners.

27.1.4 Required size of the bride price

It should be noted that calculating the average size of bride prices is typical for a quantitatively oriented western approach; traditionally such an approach is foreign to the Ekagi. Comparison shows that they are aware of average bride prices in specific time periods and specific regions. Approximately, prices are the same. Hence it is the more interesting that people do not justify their demand or their offer referring to comparable cases in the same area. On the contrary, they are inclined to ignore them. Although bride prices are paid frequently, people tend to present each bride price as a strictly unique event, in conformity with how they experience the proceedings. Calculating an average price would, however, undo the uniqueness. If people nevertheless want to place the price in a series, then that series is to be conceived vertically instead of horizontally: what matters is what has been paid for the bride's mother. The price for her daughter should be just as large. Especially in the Mapia this rule was emphasised. The continuous change in constituent items, both in kind and in number, demonstrates that in fact the principle is not honoured.

27.2 *SUBSEQUENT DEVELOPMENT*

27.2.1 *Efforts to do away with the bride price*

In the area east of Lake Tigi, during the first half of the 1950s, a [religious] movement started, within the Protestant church, that aimed at replacing the cowry with money (Giay 1995). It was part of the current usage to burn amulets, magical objects, and so on, during massive meetings. Given the revolutionary character of both the endeavour and the behaviour of the leaders of the movement, it does not surprise that from the start people called them and their followers, purely negatively, *Wegee Bagee*, Ind. *perusak*, 'smashers'. With the cowry, the support, or the pivot, of the social organisation would be removed. By doing away with the cowry the continued existence of the bride price came under threat. As regards the situation in eastern Tigi at the end of the 1950s, Grootenhuis reported

> The bride price is no longer paid or received in cowries, but in paper money. In Kokobaya the price is 100 guilders, one sow, 2 or 3 boars, depending on size, to be paid to the parents and the brothers of the bride. The male marriage candidates in the village do not benefit from this arrangement, since they usually have to marry a partner from outside the village, given the exogamy rules. Respecting these rules, their choice is restricted to those women whose relatives are prepared to accept a bride price in money. It does not restrict their choice to Wege followers, since also among others paper money drives out cowries. However, they do not want to subject themselves to the increases of the bride price, since they did away with it in Kokobaya (1960: 12).

This movement, and the regional protestant church society, have for decades contested the bride price (Giay 1955: 154) and abolished it, at least officially. The indigenous leaders were straightaway involved in the matter, It is said that, among prominent Ekagi, marriages have been contracted without payment of a bride price. At the base level the endeavour was unsuccessful: the prohibition was in fact ignored.

27.2.2 *Efforts to regulate the bride price*

While they were personally not directly involved in the matter, the foreign, Catholic pastors had regularly, though indirectly, to do with bride prices, in view of the validity and durability of the marriages that they had to bless. They were aware that, due to the bride price, the bride's free will might well be curbed, while free will was required for the marriage to be valid. On the other hand, they realised that, once the transfer of the bride price was completed, the durability of the marriage was guaranteed. In case the bride price was still pending, durability could not be guaranteed. Consequently, so as to deal with the matter of free will, they asked the bride, before consecration, whether she agreed with the marriage. So as to deal with the matter of the bride price, they asked the bride's parents and guardians whether the price had been fully paid and thus had been completely settled. Because they were not at home in these culture-specific matters, they had in fact often to fall back upon the local catechist when coming to a decision. The catechist was witness and often a participant and so could be relied upon to know the ins and outs of the case. This pastoral practice made the pastors aware that this complex institution [i.e. the bride price] placed people often for extremely complex financial and social problems. Some were inclined to help financially, especially in the case of employees; others to remain aloof, sceptical and weary as they had become due to the many intrigues. To my knowledge, the matter has never been discussed during general meetings. Possibly this was because the awareness lacked how deeply concerned the people were about the matter; possibly because the opinion was that it was typically a matter that was not to be resolved from above, or rather from the outside, but by the people themselves.

More in general, van Baal (1977: 276) warns against codifying current legal conceptions, because such rules continue existing once they have been put on paper. He points out that a procedure for changing customary law is lacking, so codified customary law brings about a lack of changeability. It has become clear that interference by outsiders has adverse effects. As regards the bride price, Fischer (1952: 106) calls to mind an interference from above that took place on Nias. Because the bride price there was ever increasing, young elite women in their late twenties were often not yet married. That was by itself socially unacceptable, moreover it resulted in irregular relationships. To bring this undesirable state of affairs to an end, the Dutch colonial administration, after deliberations with indigenous leaders and representatives of the mission, laid down fixed amounts for each stratum of society. The results were negligible, because nobody stuck to the rules, and the matter mostly escaped administrative control. The measure resulted even in a further increase of bride prices, because people started paying the official bride price on top of the current ones.

How large the problem loomed for the population, and how much they desired that the administration would regulate the matter, became clear during a forum discussion on the last evening of a massive gathering of representatives from the various parishes during a Pastoral Council held in Waghete, on the east coast of Lake Tigi, in the second half of the 1970s. For three days the various regions had discussed a range of topics that had been put on the agenda from above. They concerned matters of current interest, such as the relationship between husband and wife in Christian marriage. While attendance had been sizeable, that evening it was overwhelming. It soon became clear that the forum discussions had been seized upon to make a prominent member of the DPRD, the regional council, and also a member of the forum, aware of the bride price issue. People hoped that he would discuss the matter in the council and would enforce an administrative regulation. Notwithstanding the verbal pressure to which he was exposed for hours, he proved himself to be an experienced diplomat and did not make any promises.

A few years later the parish council at Waghete proposed that another Pastoral Council be held. Although this time the proposal did not come from outside and from the top, it soon became clear that it did not come from the base either. It originated from the local Catholic elite, a small group of salaried public servants and teachers. The spokesmen had only one topic for the agenda: a universally valid, strictly uniform ruling concerning the size of the bride price. Soon it became also clear that it was not the idea to analyse and evaluate the institution in keeping with all its ethnically and regionally diverse forms, meanings and values. Discussions were not desired. What they had in mind was a massive meeting during which the delegates were to declare as universally valid the practice that was at the time current in the Tigi area. Subsequently they would have to implement this declaration, each in his own area. It transpired that the entire *kabupaten,* the entire district, with all its subdivisions, was to be mobilised to end the rivalry that prevailed among the elite, both within and between the regions. All this had to happen at the expense of the Catholic community. The initiative was not accepted.

27.2.3 Exchange of the cowry for money
The above shows that the development of the bride price was heavy on people's minds. Sensational reports repeatedly aroused commotion. The general tenor can be sensed from the short summary that Pospisil presents of the situation in the Kamu

> In 1975 the average bride price has become almost astronomical for a young Kapauku: 300 old cowries, 600,000 rupees (!), five pigs, sometimes even a sowing machine (or a typewriter!), ten or twenty pants or shirts, two blankets, five pots, one or two machetes and an equal number of axes, and neither glass beads or *dedege* [nassa] shell necklaces were acceptable. In spite of these stiff increases in the value of brides, some intellectuals boasted more wives than ever. My best friend Jokagaibo probably set a record in this respect, apparently being happily married to thirteen wives! (1978: 119)

In an earlier record of an average bride price, Pospisil had mentioned the size of the sample on the basis of which he had calculated the average (1958: 54; case 8 in this chapter), but here he does not do so. As regards items that had been discarded, he names nassa shells and beads only, while the qualification 'old' going with cowries suggests either that by then the recently imported shells also had been discarded, or that their number --given the large number of old shells– had grown to such astronomical proportions that it could not be expressed numerically. Apparently, the sensational stories have not been checked. Instead of a record of an average bride price, the text offers an enumeration of goods that incidentally, and not in relation to each other, were transferred in the context of the bride price. They were novelties the impudence of which shocked people the more.

But the enumeration brings the trend to the fore: besides the traditional cowry shell, goods gained in importance that could be acquired only with money. The demand implies that the price givers had money at their disposal. In analogy with the traditional goods, the transfer of these new fashioned goods showed in the first instance the solvency rather than the wealth of the price givers. They are all consumption goods some of which were in general use, such as axes and bush knives. Others, such as the pots, blankets and pieces of clothing, pre-supposed a way of life that went beyond the traditional one, given how they were used and stored. At the least, people had to have a wooden chest that could be locked; more properly a house without a wood fire, hence a second house where people did not live, not during the day, but also not during the night. Because these conditions often were not met, these goods were not put to their functional use and degenerated into ostentatious status symbols. The excessive character of the mentioned typewriter and sewing machine illustrates the offensive folly of the developments. Typewriters were in demand. When a cooperative received its first income from coffee, in the early 1970s, a typewriter topped the list of the goods that people wished to buy with that money. From then on, they did no longer depend on the local government office. Instead they could independently submit reports, including requests for subsidies, to the authorities at the coast. However, a sewing machines was put on the list, not because it was to be handed back, as if it were a dowry, and also not because a person belonging to the bride givers –not to mention the father and the mother of the bride– was going to put it to good use. It referred purely to the education that the bride had received and the future revenues that that implied for the bride takers.

Against this background it should be seen as a victory of common sense that rather abruptly, from the mid 1980s, the bride price had to be paid in money only. At the moment that the cowry disappeared from the bride price, the cowry was finished. Extremely pragmatically, my key informant explained the change by remarking that cowries were not accepted in the local shops. Towards the end of the 1980s the curtain fell for the cowry. Debts from old bride prices were paid in money, new ones exclusively in money. As regards in the Paniai-Tigi area, my key informant told me that a *muto* was equated with Rp 100,000 and a *yoo* with Rp 30,000.

27.3 PREVIOUS HISTORY

27.3.1 Remembered data

The development [recorded in the previous section] makes credible all sorts of remarks of which one otherwise might have thought that they were based on fantasy rather than reality. Not just in general, but also concretely, people in the

Mapia region named cases in which a bride price had not really figured. There, people maintained that the bride price, as practised in the early 1970s, was rather recent. Formerly, broadly referred to as 'before the war', the bride price would have been paid by handing over a string bag full with shoots of the green *dade, Hibiscus manihot.* Subsequently stone axes would have been added. When a Bayatuma Wakei, before the war, had made gardens on land belonging to the Tebai [clan] and hunted small game [there?], his father was said to have gone from Dipa to Timeepa, and to have settled the marriage of his son with a Tebai daughter, by transferring two stone axes and the wing of a red bird, possibly an *odiyai,* a Fire-maned bowerbird.[12]

27.3.2 Data used in the tales

In tales, people refer back to this [state of affairs regarding the bride price?] without further explications, as if it concerns facts that are well known and need not be explained.

27.4 OFFICIAL AND NON-OFFICIAL TRANSFER

27.4.1 One, kadee and *awii*

[As already pointed to in section 26.4,] the bride price has three parts: *one, kadee* and *awii.* The division has to do with the goods that make up the bride price, the size of the group or the person responsible for assembling the goods [on the one hand], and the size of the group for which the goods were meant [on the other]. In the context of the event, *one* can be translated with string or skein, referring to a series of interlinked cowries. The word *kadee* is an abbreviation of the expression *mee kadii makii,* to put down single cowries, meaning that the shells are not tied together, in contrast to the *one. Awii* can be translated with to take hold of. Originally it was probably meant as the opposite of the verb *wudii,* to distribute.[13]

---

[12] For the sake of completeness it should be added that in the Mapia people were very much aware that all phenomena had taken their current form after having passed through all manner of stages. This applies to the surface of the earth, for the various artifacts such as weapons and houses, but also for institutions and customs. Everything results from a gradual development. People are inclined to concretely apply this tenet to all things existing, just as they write about the emergence and further development of a clan.

[13] By editor. Hylkema had added the following note to his text. Although it bears only indirectly on the matter at hand, I have retained it because it shows how he went about drafting his monograph. He recorded field notes on numbered index cards that he consulted while writing.

III.70 Imouda made the following calculation: he would pay IB 1200 for a pig, as *mune*, as pay for looking after it, IB 200, and as *kadee* another IB 100 (an extra, due to a kin relationship via the wife). Some time ago, Imouda and his wife had been the guests of Geiyaibedo Adii, in Atouda, an older brother of village headman Adii. On

27.4.2 Several other titles

The shift from cowries to money that can be historically traced is a clear illustration of the continuously fluctuating character of the bride price. It is a phase of a process. At the same time, the appearance of money, first in the margin, then in the periphery and finally in the centre, draws our attention to the fact that the category of goods did not imply functional equivalence. It is possible to distinguish between goods that, in a specific phase, were essential, those that were central and those that were marginal, and between those that belonged to the kernel and those that were seen as extras.

With the distinction between essential and adventitious we get on a slippery slope. The distinction central and marginal entails that the bride price does not have clear boundaries. It does not stand separate from other prices and gifts, transferred both before and after a wedding. To make the distinction one might use the terms official and public as against non-official and private. But people do not strictly maintain this distinction either. What now generally count as parts of the bride price, have presumably become so as the result of the slow recognition of a custom to present gifts to the mother [of the bride]. Under the general denominator of exchange objects, valuables were displaced by consumption goods and utensils; then these goods were displaced by typical means of exchange, first nassa and cowry shells, and subsequently money. Whether or not goods were considered to belong to the kernel or to the margin, was closely related to whom they were given, and who was held responsible for their contribution to the bride price.

It should not be overlooked that the groom, or his parents, often have gone to great expense to lend force to the agreement that their son will marry a specific girl. Before Theo Petege married Mariana Kotouki, Theo's father had successively given an adult male pig, an axe, a bush knife and a string of cowries to Mariana's father. At the time Theo himself lived at the coast. On his return he felt morally obliged to marry this girl, even though he had set his eye on someone else. It is my impression that no return gifts can be expected as an answer to such gifts. They remind of 'earnest money'. It has to be reimbursed by the bridegroom.

When Isaias Tebai married Marta Wakei [case 17a], her father's brother, Set Wakei, was paid one string of cowries and seven strings of nassa shells; moreover, Barnabas Wakei was paid one string of cowries. Marta's mother had married him after the death of her husband. IB 5 was paid to mother's brother, Goheke Petege, as *mune,* 'look after money', because mother and daughter had lived in his place for some time, before Marta's mother remarried.

---

this occasion Adii had given him pork, valued at IB 100, and a *bodiya.* At a later stage Imouda had paid him for the pork, but he had not paid anything in return for the shell.

The surplus can also be meant to reimburse a young man who had provided a married couple goods or services, hoping that he would marry their daughter. Her parents had promised Monika Petege to Kuyaikebo Wakei. On the basis of this promise he had shared game with them and had helped them with building a house and making gardens. When Monika was married to Yohanes Tebai, the latter paid Kuyaikebo Wakei six strings of nassa shells and beads. The conclusion is that the groom is obliged to reimburse all expenses, whether in goods or in money, that other suitors have made for the girl or her parents.

By editor. Hylkema continued with a section 27.6 in which he again dealt with the tri-partition of the bride price, the price givers and the price takers. I have shifted this section, just like sub-section 26.5.2 that concluded chapter 26, to chapter 29, the final chapter of this part of the book. But I made an exception for a summary in which he lists the factors that bear upon the size of the bride price. He describes these as follows:

1. The price paid for the bride's mother.
2. Status of the woman concerned: *api* [girl] and *miya* [widow].
3. Expenses made. To justify these, people are inclined to appeal to extra-ordinary conditions having to do with the bride.
4. The benefits to be expected from the woman concerned.
5. Status of the bridegroom.

CHAPTER 28 THE WOMAN IN EXCHANGE FOR THE PRICE

28.1 INEQUAL EXCHANGE OF PROPERTY

If one, as the Ekagi do in their everyday speech, defines the bride price as what the bridegroom pays for the bride, several incongruities arise. Certainly the ownership of the goods making up the bride price passes from the giving to the receiving party. The price givers do not retain any say over its use. Nor can people make claims on them on account of the manner in which the price takers have handled the price. Against this, the ownership of the bride does not pass from the bride-givers to the bride takers. Significantly, the bride retains both her clan and her own name, although she marries a member of another clan and she moves from the one location to the other. Even though she has married in, for the rest of her life her clan name marks her as a local stranger, not belonging to the we-, but to the they-group.

True, in exchange her relatives transfer both authority over her and care for her to her husband. His role is exclusive, at least with regard to third parties. Turning to her own relatives, in this case the father and the brother, we have to deal with an irritating discrepancy in interpretation. According to the husband, he alone can be held responsible for her actions. Therefore he has to pay all costs she incurs, whether these are purchases or fines. This means that after the transfer she has to obey him and nobody else. Should she disobey him, he is the only one entitled to chastise her. She is not entitled either to receive goods from others or to give goods to others without his knowledge. Strictly speaking, he alone is entitled to receive from her and to give to her. Nobody else is. Even her relatives are not permitted to do so. Rather than sending claimants to her relatives, the husband is usually prepared to reimburse all expenses which she incurs, so as to reinforce his interpretation that he alone has the right to receive from her and to give to her.

But the interpretation that, apart from third parties, her own relatives are also excluded is hard to maintain. Although her relatives, in exchange for the bride price, have transferred the authority over her and the care for her to her husband, the wife is conventionally entitled to appeal to her relatives if her husband neglects or maltreats her. Her relatives are entitled to turn to the husband and claim damages. Whether they are prepared to do so is another matter. Usually this would not be in their interest. Eventually they can even take the wife back, but then the bride price presents a problem. In the extreme case, avenging her life, in so far as such vengeance is mooted in the case of a woman, this is a matter for her relatives and not for her husband. By itself, this is evidence that the final responsibility for her life and welfare rests with her own kin, even though she has been given in marriage. [To sum up, t]he complete transfer of the ownership of the bride price goes with an incomplete transfer of the ownership over the woman concerned.

28.2 CONDITIONAL TRANSFER OF THE BRIDE PRICE

With the transfer of the bride, the matter of the bride price is not settled. This happens when she bears a child. When it is common knowledge that a man is impotent, he will not be given a wife. But when he can beget children, and the wife does not become pregnant, the infertility is blamed on the woman. In such a case, however, bride and price are not exchanged again; the marriage is not dissolved. The relatives of the wife have no interest in having her back, while the return of the bride price presents only problems. If the husband sends her away, in exchange for the bride price, her relatives can give her in marriage again. However, no man wants to witness his wife in the possession of another man and bearing him children. Retaining his wife, he marries a second one. If, however, a wife dies young, without having borne children who are still alive, the husband can claim a return of the bride price. Instead, the interests of both parties are best served by transferring another wife [to him], if not a girl then a young widow.

Strictly speaking, the bride price is settled by the birth of a male child only. But, in fact, this distinction is irrelevant. At the most it can be an argument [put forward] to reduce the bride price, should, after the husband's death, his widow be given in marriage to his brother. If a mother has died without having borne a son, and her husband and his kin want the bride price back, they relinquish, implicitly, possession of her daughter, and hence a claim to her bride price. However, possession of the daughter assures them that in the future they will settle the loss they have incurred. In the case of a daughter, the bride price for her mother is squared, one generation later, by the bride price for the daughter. In case of a son, the bride price is squared directly, since the son 'replaces' the father. While in the first case the expense is squared by the receipt [of another bride price], in the second reimbursement is realised by the person who embodies life being passed on. Or, as the Mapia Ekagi put it, the string of cowries expended form the son's spine, or the bundle of nerves, or the marrow within his spine. The metaphor is based on the traditional conception that during intercourse semen flows as fluid marrow through the bundle of nerves from the brain to the penis.

Against this, the bride givers are entitled to take her back when she has become a widow and give her in marriage again, for a bride price. This may happen regardless of whether she has borne children in the first marriage. She may be given in marriage to the group to which the first husband belonged, but also outside that group. However, irrespective of who marries the widow and irrespective of whether the child remains with the father's relatives or follows the mother in her new marriage, the bride price for a daughter from the first marriage belongs to her father's relatives.

Naturally this arrangement does not satisfy everybody's sense of justice, so people constantly seek *ad hoc* solutions. When, after the death of Lukas Butu in Timeepa [in the Mapia region], the Wakei gave his widow, Yuliana Wakei, in marriage to the widower, Severius Tigi, the Butu were not a party to the marriage negotiations. However, they retained the rights to the bride price for the daughter born to the marriage to Lukas Butu. Moreover, because Yuliana did not remarry into their own clan, they claimed and received 300 IB from the Wakei as *waka-abu*, literally spouse compensation. It seems as if they recognised that it was fair that the widower, Severius Tigi, was given a chance to remarry, a widow, in accordance with his own status. But, on the other hand, it seems they did feel passed over since their entitlement to remarry her into their own clan had been the primary one. According to my informants, this *ad hoc* arrangement was not founded on tradition. They had mixed feelings about it. Probably they sensed that it undermined the maxim that in principle each man has an equal right, while the acceptance of the bride price offered is the decisive moment. But it is generally accepted that the bride price for a woman who has followed her mother into the latter's second marriage, is paid to the relatives of the deceased first husband. In this case, the groom pays the stepfather an amount as *mune*, a looking-after remuneration, analogous to the older usage of remunerating a woman who had fed somebody else's pig sweet potato scraps, at the time the animal was killed or sold.

28.3 NO EXCHANGE, BUT A CONTRACT

Recently married men frequently claim that acceptance of the bride price means that ownership of the bride passes from her father or brother to him, her spouse. This claim goes against the essence of the bride price institution.

28.4 DIFFERENT FORMS

28.4.1 Without bride price

The bride price institution, as the Ekagi envisage it, presupposes a tight-knit and vital group of people. Each case challenges its members anew to demonstrate what they are worth. It tests whether and to what extent the small group of the groom and his closest kin are valued members of this wider group. In other words: whether and to what extent they have proved themselves members of that group. In answer, the bride price offers the wider group an opportunity to express its appreciation, or its disapproval, [towards the groom and his closest kin,] but before all [it offers its members an opportunity] to show their potential at group level.

Ekagi are aware that they can arrange weddings, and thereby secure the continuity of the group, in less complicated ways. Many folk tales recount that a man marries his daughter to an *enaago*, a young man without brothers, without demanding a bride price. Concomitantly, he might take it upon him to assemble *akaato mege,* a bride price of sorts, to satisfy claims by third parties. However altruistic and unselfish this arrangement might be presented, it means in practice that the son-in-law so benefited is obliged to his father-in-law for life. This method does not satisfy the fundamental principle of reciprocity. It results in a status which is unworthy of both the husband and his wife. While the Ekagi know about this modality through the medium of folk tales, I do not have any examples that they in fact practise it.

28.4.2 Marriage by exchange

A second, plausible arrangement is marriage by [sister] exchange. A young man gives his sister to another man in exchange for the latter's sister.[1] This modality is in fact used, but only sporadically. For instance, Eniyakebo Tekege arranged that Yesaya Tekege, of Taagatadi, the son of his half-brother, married Yosina Pigai, of Mogoya, in 1968, while Yesaya's sister married Yosina's brother, Musa. Even so, a minimal form of bride price changed hands on this occasion. Yesaya's eldest (half)brother, Imoudakebo, who was responsible for him, handed the Pigai a *muto-aka-muto* for the benefit of Yesaya, after Yesaya had given him a *muto* on the occasion of his second marriage (see chapter 27, case 14). For the benefit of their candidate, Musa, the Pigai gave, in their turn, Imoudakebo fifty cowries, without making the effort to string them together [into a *muto*]. After the wedding, Yesaya left his natal settlement and took up residence at Mogoya, near his brother-in-law, Musa. Accordingly, it could be presumed that Musa and Martina had themselves taken the initiative to get married, while the marriage between Yesaya and Yosina was arranged by Eniyakebo, the (half-)brother of Yesaya's [and Martina's] father. Probably Yosina had demanded an uxorilocal marriage.

The fact that this modality is practised only sporadically, justifies the conclusion that people do not see a marriage by exchange as ideal. Given their individual personalities, two women are rarely equivalent objects of exchange. Hence, the exchange can easily turn out to be an unfair one. Ignoring the underlying element of personal preference or mutual love, people argue that one marriage will contrast unfavourably with the other. Irritated, but helpless, a brother has to look on passively, while his sister carries out her tasks with diligence and energy, to the benefit of her husband, while [at the same time] the latter's sister behaves lazily and is uninterested; although they had been exchanged as if they were equivalents. In the opinion of the Ekagi, the two marriages are too directly linked. They will elicit regret and envy in one of the men concerned.

Folk tales often present this modality as a plausible solution. In general, they mention it with approval and appreciation. Previously, however, was usually mentioned that the couples concerned were not part of larger groups. Given this

---

[1] Exchanging women for each other: *wakaiya aka-ume tiyaawii;* to give a sister in marriage to enable one's own marriage: *akatagime tai.*

situation, the question arises: how can people in such a situation maintain themselves and foster a vital community with a solid network of outside relations? Notwithstanding the argument of those directly concerned that the arrangement has eased the obligations of the group, these exchange marriages arouse resentment. The arrangement ignores the continuation of the two groups. Both feel passed over. Making the marriage an affair of those most directly concerned only wrongs other members of the group who would have benefited from the bride price. There is a maxim: an exchange marriage is initiated either because the bride giver is unable to distribute the shells, *mege wudii kaga*, or because the bride taker is unable to get the shells together, *mege ubai kaga*. We return to this phenomenon at length. For ultimately the marriage of my key informant [Isaias Tekege] to his bride was resolved by some sort of exchange marriage between the Tekege of Mogodagi and the You of Poteuwa. The Tekege had prepared a bride price for Isaias, but the You did not take it with them. They did not do so, according to the Tekege, because the price taking You would have had to hand over the shells to the rightful claimants. Instead, they returned it to the Tekege in exchange for a young widow so as to benefit an older candidate within their own ranks. The Tekege ridiculed them: 'Because the You are unable to assemble a bride price, we assembled one for two women.' To resort to an exchange marriage is an admission of poverty and incapacity. By giving a preference to the direct interests of the small group concerned, people commit a betrayal and disqualify themselves as members of a much wider group.

28.4.3 Use of the bride price in succession.

Closely related to the exchange marriage is the successive use of a specific bride price. While the negotiations between the Tekege and the You over the marriage between Isaias Tekege and Natalia You dragged on laboriously, the Mote of Wotai accepted a bride price to the benefit of Alex Pekei of Kebouya without much publicity. In exchange Tomas Mote, of Wotai, acquired a second wife from the Tatogo of Dimiya. In their turn, the latter used this bride price to marry a Tetege woman of Dimiya. Finally, the Tetege had, on 17 March 1973, broken up and distributed the bride price, probably because of the absence of a marriage candidate among them.

Before Wodeiwii Tekege, of Mogodagi, distributed, on 26 April 1973, the bride price that he had received from the Gobai for Bomeyakupa, the second daughter of his first wife, he had first offered it to Isaias [Tekege], on the condition, however that he would marry without further delay. According to Isaias this offer probably did not concern the bride price in its entirety, if Wodeiwii intended to honour rights of third parties, but certainly a substantial part. Because such a speedy marriage did not accord with his own plans, Isaias had declined this offer. In any case, he would have had to add shells [to what he had been offered]. After Adolfus Tekege, of Potibutu, had added several *yoodagi* to the price which he had received from the Kayamee, of Yagai in north Paniai, in exchange for his sister Teresia, the Mote of Wotai found it acceptable. Thus Adolfus' marriage was sealed.

In the bride price that the Tekege of Mogodagi had received when Henrikus You, of Epouto, married Isaias father's half-sister, Rubeka, quite a few shells had to be replaced before Rubeka's brother, Bernard, had been able to use it for his marriage to Anna, the first daughter of the first wife of Bobaapiiyawii You. It was no wonder that the price received for Rubeka had been undersized, given that Rubeka formerly had been married to Adakutuma Mote of Wotai as his second wife. However, appealing to the fact that she had been baptised into the Roman Catholic Church, she had divorced him. The bride price was not returned since she had borne Adakutuma a son. The idea had been that, after the divorce, she could marry an as yet unmarried, Roman Catholic man, again in exchange for a bride price. Some twenty years later, incidentally, this man in his turn married a second wife, besides Rubeka. It is not surprising either that the price [which Henrikus paid for Rubeka] did not meet Bobaapiiyawii You's demands. Appointed as village headman and married to six wives, he was widely known as the *tonowi* in the Uwebutu area. The affair marks the ambition, cunning and vigour of Rubeka's brother, Bernard. Several years later, when he himself had entered the ranks of the administration, he took a second wife, besides Anna, although he had been baptised into the Roman Catholic Church. Roman Catholic public servants were forbidden to marry a second wife, but he evaded this successfully by listing her as his eldest daughter on the pay roll.

In view of the nerve-wracking course of the bride price negotiations which are the focus of this study, it seems a sympathetic idea to have several marriages contracted by means of a single bride price. All the more so since this occurs relatively frequently, at least outsiders get the impression that the parties concerned approve of such a smooth arrangement of several marriages. It contrasts sharply with the once-only use of a bride price, during which all phases are passed through successively: the assembling, the transfer and the breaking up and distribution of the shells concerned. But it is by no means at all certain that this successive use really satisfies all parties. Notwithstanding the bother which a once-only use of the bride price entails, it should not be overlooked that the people themselves have created and developed the institution and have set the rules of the game. Since he was directly concerned as bridegroom, the reserve that my key informant [Isaias Tekege] showed was elucidating. His impression was that the procedure reduced the groom to a case. The transaction has to be finalised rapidly, as it were to be squeezed in, so the next case can be taken on. While the bridegroom becomes a mere pawn in the group, his closest relatives and the members of his local community make it apparent that they are incapable of assembling a bride price under their own steam and having it accepted without having to appeal to previous transactions.

CHAPTER 29 THE PARTIES INVOLVED IN THE TRANSACTION

29.1 TWO OBJECTS WHICH CAN BE EXCHANGED FOR EACH OTHER

People experience and interpret a marriage differently, reacting to their own personal involvement. Normally a marriage is virilocal. Hence people traditionally use the verb *uwii*, to go away, to refer to the act of the bride, who leaves her parental family, and the verb *bukii*, to take in, to refer to the act of the bridegroom who provides a home. While bride and groom start from quite different positions, in this approach they both play an active role as two free and independent individuals. The group from which the girl departs and the one of which the young man is a member are not taken into consideration.

A closer look at these two groups reveals that, strangely enough, the groom still has an active role, while the bride is relegated to a passive one. In this framework, bride and groom are no longer poised against each other as free and independent individuals, but, instead of two persons, two groups emerge, the one bride giving and the other bride taking. The party which gives in marriage accompanies the girl to a home elsewhere, an action referred to as *eumai.* In that home she is admitted as a co-resident, an action referred as *bukii.* She is not bereft of her personality, but in this interpretation of the events she changes from subject to direct object.

Her status changes even more drastically when the transfer of a bride price provides the context for and the essential element in contracting a marriage. Remarkably, where the bride price enters the picture, the nature of that institution causes it to dominate the proceedings. The way the bride price is institutionalised is a gauge from which to deduce the status both are given within their own communities. In this context the terms 'to give' and 'to take', and 'to give in marriage' and 'to marry' no longer appositely cover what is going on. Actually, people do not give and take. They exchange objects. At stake is an exchange of two objects, of an object of exchange against a means of exchange. Although each transaction presents itself as a discrete event, the system presupposes a continuing series of consecutive transactions of two equivalent objects. The transacting parties remain the same, but they continually change position. At one time they have a bride to offer, at another a bride price.

The bride price system has puzzling consequences for the individuals directly concerned. The bride price means that the girl no longer acts as a subject, not even as a personal direct object, but as an exchange object with the bride price as the equivalent counterpart. Although people usually operate less strictly than the above comment suggests, excesses make it clear that the girl is reduced to an object. She risks her life if she does not comply with this position.

29.2 [THE STATUS OF THE BRIDEGROOM]

The bridegroom, on the other hand, is not reduced to an object, but does not act as a free and independent individual either. The bride price is so high that the average young man is unable to raise such an amount. He has to rely on the support of his community. That group is not amorphous, it is structured and the way the bride price is constituted affirms the existence of this group, in its ideal form. It also makes explicit the status that the groom has within this group. Speaking in general terms, a young man who is not yet married is not free and independent; and also if he were to aspire to be so, in traditional society he lacks the means to act freely and independently. Actually marriage provides the normal avenue for this transition. Previously [before he is married], all outside relationships are regulated via the father and, subordinate to the former, via the mother. This is the way he is related to father's and mother's parents, to their brothers and sisters, and to their children, distinguished as parallel and cross cousins. At that age[1] the young man has probably activated one or more of these potential relationships. He may, for instance, have started a personal relationship with his mother's brother, or, beyond the circle of relatives proper, have contacted affines.

The constitution of the bride price presupposes a complete nuclear family, consisting of father, mother with one or more sons and daughters, preferably in equal numbers. Moreover, the father represents the family to outsiders. Each nuclear family is in continuous development. But, at the time sons and daughters have reached marriageable age, we can leave grandparents out of consideration and assume that the parents belong to the older generation. Such a family is not a separate group; it forms part of a wider group of married brothers, both real and classificatory. However, not all nuclear families are actually complete at the time a son or a daughter gets married. This matters especially when the father has gone and somebody else, preferably father's elder brother or an elder brother, assumes his role. Father's younger brother is deemed less suitable. Apparently, the bridegroom comes first, so he is to play an active role. That is only correct in so far his role is compatible with his position in the nuclear family represented by the father.

29.3 A PERCEIVED TRI-PARTITION

29.3.1. From uxorilocal to virilocal

Above I suggested a development from a situation in which the father of the bridegroom hands over feathers and vegetables to the father of the bride, to one in which a complexly constituted bride price changes hands. In the first case an uxorilocal marriage was envisaged, in the second a virilocal one. Further examination shows that the roles of groom and bride have been reversed:

---

[1] By editor. I suppose Hylkema refers to a man who is about to get married.

formerly the groom had to present himself at the bride's house, whereas the current procedure assumes that the bride is presented at the groom's house.

29.3.2 The tri-partitions

As mentioned above, three parts or categories can be distinguished within a complete bride price: *awii*, *one* and *kadee*. The partition runs parallel with a tri-partition among both the price givers and the price takers. The table presents the tri-partitions schematically.

This was the situation in the 1950s and still continued into the 1970s. Although the information which I obtained does not make it quite clear when the tri-partition was institutionalised, some cases are sufficiently explicit to provide some elucidation. At the pinnacle of the development, handling the bride price was modelled on the direct exchange of two objects between two complexly constituted groups: an object of exchange [the bride] and a means of exchange [the bride price]. Only the object of exchange is unitary, while the means of exchange and the exchanging parties are plural.

TABLE

TRANSACTIONS IMPLICATED IN BRIDE PRICE TRANSFER

donors	receivers`
object	object
bride price	bride
subjects	subjects
awii bridegroom	*awii* mother
one bridegroom	*one* ---
father/substitute	father/substitute
sponsor	sponsor
kadee bridegroom	*kadee* ---
father/substitute	father/substitute
sponsor	sponsor
action group	action group

When there is a direct exchange, both parties are generally completely equivalent. They face each other as two action groups, formed in relation to bride and groom [respectively]. When we consider both parties from this point of view, it appears that their structures are parallel, on the proviso that we give the bridegroom his correct place.

In respect of the bride price, I distinguish within the action groups a core and a remainder group, and within the core between the father, brother, sponsor and bridegroom. The father is central. He has the primary responsibility, and the brother and the sponsor act in his name. In this order they operate for the benefit of the bridegroom. It is usually assumed that the groom acts as a subject and that the others co-operate with him. It is questionable whether this is a correct interpretation of what happens. It is not the bridegroom, but his father who is the principal person, or, in the father's name, the brother or sponsor, while the bridegroom is relegated to a co-operative role. He has a stake, but he is, at the same time, an object. In many cases he resigns himself to the facts. Similarly, the bride adopts a co-operative role, in accordance with the behaviour of her father, brother and sponsor.

In contrast to the wider groups, the two cores are remarkably asymmetrically composed. Father and brother, and the quasi-father and sponsor, of the bride and the groom can be seen in strict symmetry. But although the bridegroom appears among the price givers, the bride is not among the price takers, but her mother is.[2] Neither as a subject nor as an object is bride or the groom in analogous positions. As an object, the bride is set against the bride price; as a subject the groom is set against the bride's mother, under the denominator *kadii*, while under the denominators *one* and *kadee* there is no such counterpart [for the groom].

By editor. At this point Hylkema's analysis breaks off. He had dealt extensively with this last topic and had broached it in several parts of the bride price manuscript. Although he had not finished his analysis, it seems important to me that Hylkema draws attention to the asymmetric composition of the core groups. In my view, it refers to the enchainment of the bride prices over the generations.

---

[2] By editor. In a handwritten gloss added to a draft table of contents, Hylkema has observed: '*awii*: a woman who does not get her share [of the bride price], can make the woman infertile. Her demands are unreasonable, yet it is better to accede to them than run this risk. It looks as if she is bought off. This aspect pervades the bride price.'

Because the *awii* is transferred to the bride's mother, I take it that Hylkema refers to her when he writes about the woman who does not get her share. The woman whom she makes infertile is most likely the bride, her daughter. This infertility prevents getting a bride price in return in the next generation.

This entails that the price for a bride should not be less than the price paid for her mother. While a woman acts as an object rather than as a subject on the occasion of her wedding, one generation later, when the bride price for her daughter is transferred, she becomes a subject, as a member of the core group of the price takers, poised against the future husband of her daughter. Her passive role during her own wedding, hence at a time that she still has to prove her reproductive potential, contrasts sharply with the privileged position she has one generation later, when, and if, she has realised that potential.

APPENDIX

The following table of contents of the bride price manuscript appears to be the last one that Hylkema prepared. Most likely, it was a provisional one. The version as presented here combines a printed list with handwritten glosses. But Hylkema kept changing also these glosses. He had, for instance, written extended versions of the content of chapters 2 and 3. But he also kept changing these. Thus, he had changed the typed sub-division of chapter 2 by a few handwritten glosses. Subsequently he wrote, again by hand, a revised division of that chapter, only to keep making changes afterwards. In the process, sub-section 2.2.2 became section 2.3, and section 2.3 became 2.4. Nevertheless, that section was followed by another section 2.3. In this appendix I have renumbered that section making it 2.5. Hylkema summarised the topics he planned to discuss in chapter 3 extensively. His numbering of sections and sub-sections is obviously provisional, but I have left the numbers as they were.

CHAPTER 1 A PROBLEMATICAL INSTITUTION
1.1 In the context of exchange
1.1.1 Payment for a woman
1.1.2 Contrast between the exchange of commodities and of gifts
1.2 Ethnic groups living from agriculture
1.2.1 Separateness of men and women
1.2.2 Both equipped for rivalry
1.3 Each group and each region in flux
1.4 As practised in the Paniai region in the early 1970s
1.5 Analysis and evaluation
1.5.1 The proceedings
1.5.2 Subject and object

CHAPTER 2 THE BRIDE PRICE THROUGHOUT HISTORY
2.1 Cases from the era 1930-1970
2.1.1 Introductory remarks
2.1.2 Cases
2.1.3 Evaluation: development as to numbers and goods, the cowry central: *mege makii* / *kadee makii* instead of *api tau makii*
2.2 Subsequent development
2.2.1 Subsequent history
2.3 Previous history
2.4 Official and non-official transfer
2.4.1 *Awii, one* and *kadee*
2.4.2 Several other denominators, as mentioned, not fixed
2.5 Rules for the determination
2.5.1 On account of mother
2.5.2 Actually, the woman's status

2.5.3 Costs incurred
2.5.4 Advantages expected
2.5.5 Status of groom
2.6 Comparison, left unmentioned

CHAPTER 3 THE WOMAN IN EXCHANGE FOR THE PRICE
3.1 Woman: desired in so far she brings in a bride price. Hence she enjoys the care of the male relatives. She is the possessor.
3.1.1 Possession; is in the care and the responsibility of the father, and is consequently under his authority. Mindset focused on possession.
In fact, people often follow the initiative of the girl, but not always.
They are the ones to avenge her. But at the same time they have the right to kill her.
Premarital sex is not a problem; at least, if there is payment.
Does not influence the bride price. Actually precedes the bride price. But there should be payment.
She should not fall in the hands of another man. During marriage; death in childbirth.
Possession of the man.
Dissociation from the father.
Dissociation from the lover. Questioning with whom she has had intercourse / dreams. He himself eventually prepared to confess his sins. Women know this. Women also know that they play with fire when they do not allow themselves be chaperoned.
Jealous; he is not happy seeing her with other women.
Certainly not with other men, let alone lovers.
He himself convinced that she is entirely his.
3.2 Legally:
3.2.1 When he chastises her, her relatives will retaliate
3.2.2 She keeps her own clan name. But she remains the property of the original clan.
3.2 [Hylkema's duplication] What then did he acquire:
3.2.1 Her industry and her womb. But not unconditionally. It is usually posited that husband and wife have the task of satisfying their most fundamental needs. The father is not able to do so, the husband [has moved into the status of] her father.
3.3
3.3.1 What balances the bride price? Becomes clear when woman dies without having borne a child.
3.3.2 Why does one marry? Because one needs a child.
3.3.3 In the foregoing is already mentioned that it is essential that everyone gets his due, lest they prevent the birth of a child.
Consequently the groom feels called upon to pay off the investments of the rivals.

PART 4 HYLKEMA'S DATA IN COMPARATIVE PERSPECTIVE,

by Anton Ploeg

Whereas Hylkema, in the cowry and bride price manuscripts, had started comparing his data with the reports of other ethnographers and scholars, he had left several topics out. Moreover, since Hylkema died, Stéphane Breton has started publishing about his research among the Wodani, neighbours of the Me. These two circumstances allow me to deal with two issues in this conclusion. I discuss first the contribution that Hylkema makes to the disagreement between Pospisil and Gregory (p. 12-3). Secondly, I compare his data with Breton's reports about the Wodani. By no means do my comments exhaust the comparative scope of Hylkema's reports. But more extensive comments do not seem to be called for in this book because its primary aim is to present Hylkema's ethnography. That is also the reason that I conclude with a quotation from another of his manuscripts.

THE MISSIONARY / ETHNOGRAPHER

Throughout his association with the Me, Hylkema remained a Catholic missionary, convinced of the value of the Christian message, even though in his letters to his family he does not show a strong urge to proselytise. As regards his ethnographic work, his being a missionary offered him the advantage that he could extend his inquiries among the Me for almost 25 years and in various parts of their habitat. Consequently he could observe both cultural changes occurring over time and cultural variety across the Me habitat.

His mission work entailed that he had to deal with the Me in the various projects that the mission undertook. It provided him with additional insights into the Me way of life, insights several of which he found difficult to deal with. While an anthropological field worker is a participant observer, my impression is that Hylkema, who spent most of his working life among his parishioners, Ngalum and Me, saw himself more as a participant, as a member of the church parish that he had helped set up and/or maintain. That would, then, be the reason, it seems to me, that he felt entitled to comment on the Me way of life as an insider, a Catholic insider. It must have been difficult for him to have to conclude that the continuity of the Me groups was 'threatened by internal mistrust, jealousy, envy, and rivalry' (chapter 10). Likewise, he must have been bothered by their compulsive gambling and their propensity to spend money entrusted to them for a specific purpose on purposes of their own instead (chapter 8).

Commenting on Giay's 1995 book, Hylkema writes (chapter 18) that it shows how anxious the Me were that strangers wanted to filch their secret. The comment seems to be prompted more by his long-term interaction with Me than by the content of Giay's book. Because the impression that Giay gives is that the Me were intent upon holding their own against the influx of material and immaterial novelties introduced by *ogai*, colonial outsiders. Joop Sierat comments (pers. comm. 2004) that Hylkema was a persistent questioner. Accordingly, he was inclined to assume that always there remained matters and aspects of matters that he still had to get to know about. This attitude is noticeable in his comment mentioned above that the Me seemed intent upon fathoming the secret of individual cowries. As regards the Biak, Freerk Kamma (1954: 190; 1972: 211) pointed out how difficult it was for the people to put the essence of their belief into words, if they were at all able to do so. During her much later field work among the Biak, Danilyn Rutherford (2003: 204) noticed the same phenomenon. But in the cowry manuscript (chapter 9), also Hylkema himself acknowledged that people, and not only the Me, perceive more features than they are able to verbalise.

In his Ngalum monograph Hylkema writes that he subordinated his ethnographic to his missionary work:

> What follows makes it clear that I engrossed myself in matters that were important to me from a missionary point of view .... This study results from an ongoing effort to acquire insight in their own view of man and in the place of man in the world surrounding him (1974b: 15).

Of the two topics discussed in the present monograph the first one does not result immediately from Hylkema's role as a missionary. In my view he chose the cowry as a topic because of its central role in the Me way of life, albeit during a short period of time. In the case of the bride price manuscript, his missionary concerns are clearer, if only because he, mostly implicitly, questions whether the institution and the social arrangements going with it are in accordance with Catholic marriage. Yet, such questioning made him very alert to the proceedings and thus added to his descriptions.

THE HISTORICAL PERSPECTIVE

As he did in his book about the Ngalum, Hylkema shows throughout both manuscripts his awareness that the people concerned, in this case the Me, had effected changes in their way of life also before first contact with Europeans. As noted in the Introduction, he was first posted among the Mapia Me about whom he writes in a footnote to chapter 27 that they were very conscious of the fact that all phenomena had gone through various transformations before reaching their current form (p. 151, note 12). That he noticed their conception most likely reinforced his attentiveness for change.

Hylkema's view that the Me obtained their cowries from the north deviates from Pospisil's statement that they were imported from the south (1978: 19), probably via the main trade route from the southwest — where access to the coast was the easiest — via the Mapia area further eastwards (1963: 337). On present evidence

I prefer Hylkema's report. If cowries had reached the Me via the Mapia Me, it is to be expected that their use and their appreciation would have been most intense in the west, among the Mapia Me. But Hylkema found the opposite. Jan Pouwer (pers. comm. 2004) and Kalman Muller (pers. comm. 2004) support Hylkema: the muddy coast south of the Me habitat is not conducive to the presence of cowries. Moreover, Pospisil also mentioned contacts with people living to the north, viz. those from whom the Me obtained their extensive counting system (1989: 21). Finally, Kugapa Moni living east of lake Paniai told van Nunen that they obtained their cowries from the east (1973: 20). With his argument Hylkema also accounts for some of the regional differences in the descriptions of Pospisil (1963: 301f) and Dubbeldam (1964: 298f).

However, Hylkema's claim that the number of cowries among the Me had at least sharply increased due to the increased scope for exports, notably of bird of paradise feathers, is harder to settle. Hylkema himself does not quote Me sources. Van Nunen (pers. comm. 2003) does not back the claim. But in a cursory remark Giay concurs with it. Giay relates a prediction cherished by the Me population of the Debei valley, part of the Kamu Valley basin. He writes that the prediction was made when 'the population was small and only few who [sic] had cowry shells' (1995: 218). Another cursory remark concerns the Damal, living to the east of the Me, northeast of Puncak Jaya. The resident missionary-linguist John Ellenberger writes that the Damal have changed from using the small *wailamo* shells, most likely nassa shells, 'to the larger cowry shells in the first quarter of the twentieth century' (1996: 184).

In broad agreement with Hylkema's view are also the outcomes of Ian Hughes' and Christopher Healey's studies of pre-colonial and early colonial lowland-highland trade in eastern New Guinea. They noted the increase in shell trade in the course of that period (1973: 184f; 1990: 236f). There is no sign that Hylkema was aware of their reports. So it seems plausible to me that Hylkema is correct in arguing that in the late pre-colonial era the influx of cowries increased. Consequently, the *yuwo* as witnessed by the first European observers was likely to be a relatively recent development. The same holds for the large number of cowry transactions that the Me engaged in, and also the character that they had given these transactions. Consequently, the capitalist element in the Me economy may have been on the increase and might have increased further, also if the colonial intervention had not occurred.

In contrast to what Hughes and Healey reported, the Me, in their trading, appear to have focused on exchange items, primarily cowries, while they showed little interest in objects for self-decoration.[1] Moreover, the Me habitat was for centuries at the extreme periphery of the Southeast Asian trading network. In the course of the nineteenth century the Cenderawasih Bay area became more and more annexed into this network (Ellen 2003; Rutherford 2003: 181f; Swadling 1996: 126). Export of bird of paradise skins increased in the course of the second half of the 19th century. In 1905 they were the main item of trade in Manokwari (Swadling 1996: 131). Intriguingly, Barry Craig and Pamela Swadling put forward that the Muyu (Schoorl 1993 [1957]) increased the number of cowries at their disposal by trade with ‘plume hunters’, in this case operating from the south coast (1983: 121, n22). Given the early increase of long distance trade in Cenderawasih Bay, Hylkema may have underestimated the time period during which cowry imports increased.[2]

Joel Robbins & David Akin (1999: 5) quote Arjun Appadurai to the effect that partial acceptance of extraneous, state-backed currencies may ‘constitute the Trojan horse of change’. Among the Me an analogous process may have taken place with regard to cowries. If there was indeed a sudden influx of cowries in the recent past, it seems likely that both the number of cowry owners increased and also the occasions on which cowries were transacted. For instance, it may have been a recent innovation that during a *yuwo* bundles of pork were sold for cowries instead of given, as gifts, to exchange partners.[3] The accompanying restructuring of exchanges, and the increased number of men who took part in them, aspiring to become Big Men, made people apprehensive about cowries, made them 'start worrying', as formulated by Robbins & Akin, 'about [their, the cowries'] power to breach the transactional boundaries they [had] erected' (1999: 8). This may be a reason why Zakheus Pakage, the leader of the *Wegee Bagee* revival movement that Hylkema frequently referred to above, urged his followers to get rid of them (Giay 1995: 176f).

---

[1] As mentioned above, in a hand-written comment on de Bruijn’s land tenure paper (1952, 1955c, 1970), Hylkema points to the paradox that the Me combined their intense pre-occupation with cowries with a materially very sober way of life.

[2] Apart from plumes, dammer and other tree products have to be considered (van Zon 1935: 294f).

[3] This speculation is prompted by two sets of information. The first concerns a feast that I observed in 1962, among Western Dani in the Konda valley in the upper catchment of the river Toli. During the feast pandanus nuts were distributed, simultaneously and without *éclat,* by the participants to exchange partners present (Ploeg 1969: 86f). The donees did not immediately respond. The second one is presented by Hylkema in his monograph dealing with the *yuwo.* There he argues that eating together rather than the sale of pork was the most important part of the proceedings (1974c: i).

HYLKEMA'S CONTRIBUTION TO THE POSPISIL - GREGORY DISAGREEMENT

Money

Hylkema's data show, in my view, that Pospisil's characterisation of cowries as money has to be qualified, even though Giay, himself a Me with experience of the currencies used by Europeans, refers to Me cowries as money (1995: 20). To start with, Hylkema, in the last but one chapter of his cowry manuscript, denies that cowries constituted money, given the supernatural power that the Me perceived in them (chapter 22).

However, as far as I can see, and as I have argued elsewhere (Ploeg 2004: 295ff), the way in which the Me used their cowries made them resemble money. Consequently, it seems useful to compare their use of cowries with the use of money in industrialised countries. A feature of the latter is that material money: coins and bank notes, is used less and less (Klamer & van Dalen 1998: 39f), and immaterial forms of money: bank accounts and drawing rights on banks, more and more. John Kenneth Galbraith, noting this process, declared material money, including coins, 'obsolescent' (1977: 164).[4] Among the Me cowries functioned as coins. However, given their fascination with the physical properties of cowries, it seems unlikely to me that substituting them for immaterial forms of money would have appealed to them.

Another feature by which Western coins differ from cowries as the Me perceived them, is that the former are easily recognisable, by look and/or by touch, and are designed to be such, so transactions can proceed quickly. But for the Me, recognising the value of cowries was a matter of expertise, and their appreciation shifted over time. What Hylkema writes about this state of affairs confirms Robert Foster's general observation about Melanesian currencies. Foster writes

> Money forms will always be subject to sceptical reception, an awareness that these forms harbor within them unrevealed possibilities for the future, hidden agencies and identities that might be exploited or might engender exploitation in as yet unimagined ways (1999: 230-1).

Hylkema lends further support for Foster's observation by commenting: 'One gains the impression that [a Me], while examining a cowry, wants to fathom its individual secret' (1974). This perception of cowries made them exemplary signifiers as Hylkema attests above (chapter 22). Just as cowry categorisations, such significations likely shifted over time. That the Me were ignorant of the ultimate provenance of cowries makes it understandable that they closely examined them searching for hidden qualities. This, in turn, facilitated the discernment of thus far not noticed categories.

---

[4] At least in the official, 'white' economy (Hobsbawm 1995: 416).

A third difference is that in some cowry transactions, especially marriage payments, the total value of the cowries transferred was not decisive. In addition, the payment needed to contain cowries of specific types. For this reason, I do not use the term 'denomination' to refer to different grades of cowries, as does Pospisil (1978: 18), but 'category'.[5] Hylkema states that the Me valued the cowry qualitatively and the nassa quantitatively (chapter 3), but from what he writes it seems that the qualitative approach to cowries varied in relation to the category the Me assigned them to. They gave names to cowries that they regarded as exceptionally precious. But the bottom category or categories they referred to collectively as din, Dutch: *gejoel*.[6]

Moreover, the metals out of which western coins are currently made, are worth a fraction of the nominal value of the coins. In contrast, Me regarded their cowries as valuable precisely because of their physical properties and the significance they accorded these. Especially the more valuable categories of shells acquired the character of gems, Dutch: *kleinoden,* or, in Dubbeldam's term, valuables. That is because they did not have the anonymity that, in Western monetary systems, coins and bank notes have in order to function as a medium of exchange. In Dubbeldam's terms: 'valuables have more 'individuality' than other media of exchange' (1964: 293). But, unlike Pospisil, de Bruijn and Dubbeldam, Hylkema (chapter 1) points to the individuality of especially the most valuable cowries to some of which the Me gave individual names.

Finally, among the Me there was no central agency, such as a reserve bank, issuing coins, in fixed quantities and fixed denominations. On the contrary, the Me had no say as to how many cowries they could acquire and put into circulation. They themselves validated their cowries, by popular consent. Appraisements, however, shifted over time. Gregory (1997: 265f), tongue in cheek (pers. com. 2005), has coined the term 'savage money' for currencies the value of which are determined by 'market forces', by changes in demand and supply. He uses the phenomenon of savage money to contrast it with domesticated, state-backed currencies such as the American dollar, up until 1971, when president Nixon stopped backing it with gold at a fixed rate. If market forces include changing appreciations, and hence changing demands, for the various manifestations of a currency, then the Me cowry currency was a 'savage' one. Me appraisements of cowries changed by region which explains

[5] Earlier I had adopted the term 'rank' as used by Lorraine Bariĉ (1964) and John Liep (1999) in their discussions of valuables on Rossel Island, at the eastern tip of the Massim. I dropped that usage, because Breton (pers. comm. 2009) pointed out to me that ranks of valuables on Rossel are not inter-convertible, unlike what is the case with categories of cowries among the Me.

[6] I find Hylkema's term 'gejoel' hard to translate. The term refers primarily to the uncoordinated sound produced by a group of talking and shouting people.

the differences between Me cowry categories as reported by Pospisil and Dubbeldam respectively. It seems likely to me that by discerning new categories among cowries, the Me created new sources of scarcity and thus held off the devaluation likely because of profuse imports.

Capitalism

For Pospisil, Me 'live in a wealth- and profit-oriented society'. He adds: 'This orientation forms a logical complement to their individualism and secularism' (1978: 93). For part of the way Hylkema goes along with these characterisations. In his analysis of the *yuwo*, he mentions how keen men were to make what he calls 'profits' and tried to accumulate cowries. But he qualifies the individualism that Pospisil ascribed to the Me. A passage in the paper that he presented at the 1990 conference in Seewiesen makes it clear how his perception of the Me differs from Pospisil's.

> In general the Ekagi is characterised as an individualist. I can agree with this characterisation, provided the word individualist is specified after the image of a soloist in an orchestra. And if this characterisation is further completed by the addition that his typical individualism with regard to the group is explained by a remarkable [attitude] towards offspring procreated by him personally. Whether an Ekagi must be called a success or a failure in life is ultimately decided by [his] having or not having male offspring. … Generally an Ekagi considers it his task … to put his property beyond the reach of the "brother" and to secure it for the "son" (1990b: 7).

In their introductory chapter to *Money and Modernity,* Robbins & Akin argue that the introduction of state-backed currencies has promoted individualism, be it in particular, Melanesian forms (1999: 31). This point underpins Hylkema's conclusion that the number of cowries among the Me had recently at the least sharply increased. In their case too, the increase may have led to the individualism that both he and Pospisil noted. In line with this tendency is that the individualism was most pronounced among the Paniai Me who were most exposed to the new influx of shells (Hylkema 2002: 233f).

Whereas for Pospisil the 'secular and profit-motivated outlook [of the Me] on life' replaces a 'preoccupation with the supernatural and ritual' (1978: 4), for Hylkema the one does not exclude the other. As appears above, he concluded

> There is not a single reason to suppose that, with regard to belief in magic and witchcraft, and the observance of taboos, the Ekagi traditionally yielded to the [Grand Valley] Dani. Having witnessed the various ritual sacrifices and incantations, there is no reason to suppose either that Ekagi placed less value on a correct relationship with the ancestors or with spirits, even though they were engrossed in such a seemingly purely secular matter as the shell trade (p. 105).

And Giay, himself a Me, wrote in his dissertation: 'The people's past history and religion are closely related. Such history interpreted from religious view point become the foundation for their existence' (1995: 253).[7]

Gifts or Commodities

As for Gregory's conception of the Me economy, Hylkema did not quote him and *Gifts and Commodities* was not among the small number of books that he left behind. But, like Gregory, and in the tracks of van Baal (1975), he used gift in the sense coined by Mauss. Anyhow, his data on Me transactions make me conclude that the gift element in them varied. Many Me transactions conformed at least in part to the Maussian model according to which donors have to offer gifts, while the donees have to accept and later to reciprocate. For example, about *yuwo* transactions of pork Hylkema had written earlier that most took place between kin and that sellers know beforehand which buyers they can expect. Killing a pig and offering pork for sale at a *yuwo* 'challenges buyers to live up to their obligations'. 'Buyers feel obliged, but also authorised to buy from specific sellers' (1974c: 74f). I tend to regard the pork offered as conditional gifts putting further pressure on prospective takers to come forward with their cowries. The important point of the exchange was to acquire cowries. However, sellers were not obliged to accept the shells offered, attempting to get a better deal and thus maximising their 'profits', in other words the number and value of the cowries they would receive for their pork. It does not seem that sellers expected an increment in cowries in excess of the value of the pork that they sold. Because the Me assembled cowries of various ranks into strings, it seems plausible to me --although Hylkema does not discuss this point-- that in either accepting or rejecting a shell offered, they took into account whether it would fill a vacant place in the string of cowries they were getting together.

In the 1974 manuscript in which Hylkema describes the *yuwo*, he writes that only rarely a stranger showed up to sell pork, presumably to persons whom he did not know beforehand and who were not obliged to him (1974c: 76). Nevertheless, he reports that it did occur which suggests that men might turn up at a *yuwo* as individual entrepreneurs selling goods as commodities. However, the occurrence of such commercial transactions at the *yuwo* does not entail that the overall Me economy was a capitalist one. Hylkema presents transactions at the *yuwo* as contests of strength. A *yuwo* was for him a 'fight without weapons' (1974c: 56). Given that buyers and sellers were often related and felt an obligation to transact, it seems likely that they were to transact again at future *yuwo* with a view to building up, or continuing, a series of mutual contests. While the transactions showed opposing interests, they were not agonistic, a characteristic that Mauss (1990: 7) ascribed to gifts, because they were private

[7] Due to faulty translation from the original Bahasa Indonesia, the English in Giay's book is quite idiosyncratic.

transactions that were not necessarily conducted in public. Hylkema emphasises that prospective buyers had to remain anonymous. They approached a seller from behind and offered their shell over his shoulder without uttering a word (1974c: 65; this vol. chapter 6). Even though Hylkema doubts the efficacy of this procedure, this was an intriguing aspect of the transaction, or, in Hylkema's term, the contest. It seemed it was an attempt to give it a one-sided anonymity that impeded its role in fashioning the relationship between seller and buyer.
The transaction that Hylkema observed and recorded took place in the early 1970s. Boelen gave the following description of *yuwo* transactions as he observed them in the early 1950s.

> The pig feast proper is more like a fair. The pigs are tied on poles, on show. Two by two, the men withdraw very secretively to talk business. They discuss which piece of pork one of them will buy and what it should cost. The prospective buyer tries to sell the pork to others in smaller quantities and calculates if he can get a small profit. The person who has secured a smaller piece, tries in his turn to hawk it and explores whether it will bring him a few shells to complement the bride price which his son needs, or to buy himself a new penis gourd or a skirt, for his wife.... All this, while the animal concerned is still grunting at its pole (Boelen n.d.: 167-8; also quoted in Ploeg 2004: 299).

The differences between Hylkema's and Boelen's descriptions show variations among *yuwo* transactions. It is not clear whether the differences resulted from the time interval, or from the various types of transactions that *yuwo* attendants could pursue simultaneously. The differences reported open the possibility that yet other types of transactions did occur. As Gregory pointed out in his 1994 paper that I quoted in the Introduction (p. 13), dichotomising gift and commobity transactions does not cover the variety (1994: 928f).

Both Hylkema and Pospisil report that *yuwo* were thrown by what I regard as Big Men, in the sense coined by Godelier (1991; Ploeg 2004) *Yuwo* were the more successful, the more men brought in pigs and sold pork. In Pospisil's opinion, Big Men acquired followers by what he calls their 'generosity', that is to say by extending 'credit'. But the description that Hylkema gives of how Me men attempt to acquire prominence and that I quoted in the Introduction, seems to me more penetrating.[8]

Thus a *tonowi*, a Big Man, might oblige his followers –or his followers might feel obliged– to become sellers of pork at his *yuwo*. The relation between a Big Man/organiser and a follower can be phrased as a phase in a gift relation. So the

---

[8] Men who are ambitious enough to seek the essential goal in life, namely prestige, accumulate hardly any [cowries and other wealth items]. Real prestige one acquires once one dares, and has mastered the art, to put others under an obligation by letting them share in one's wealth (unpublished comment on de Bruijn 1955b, 1973).

sellers were not there merely as individual entrepreneurs. At the same time the *yuwo* was a communal undertaking and its appeal was such that people, notwithstanding their individualism, were prepared to work together in order to get one organised (Hylkema 1974b). Moreover, Hylkema gives the impression that for the Me successive *yuwo* were linked because they expressed competition between Big Men. Hylkema describes *yuwo* transactions as contests between individual men, and, implicitly, *yuwo* in their entirety as contests between Big Men. While at a *yuwo* pork is exchanged for cowries, apparently always one per transaction, of apparently equal value, *yuwo* themselves differed in size as regards the number of men who bring in pigs and the total number of those pigs.

What kinds of gifts

Whereas in many gift economies donors attempt to challenge their partners by their munificence, by the size and/or the quality of their gifts, among the Me there seems to have been a presumption that donors attempted to stint and accordingly had to be urged to step up their gifts. And whereas Pospisil wrote that generosity was the 'highest value in their culture' (1958: 80), Hylkema's descriptions make it clear that there was a great deal of pressure for generosity, in Peterson's expression: of 'demand sharing' (1993), both at the *yuwo* and while assembling bride prices. People also demanded such generosity from their Big Men, a feature in my view incompatible with a capitalist state of affairs.[9] The credits that Big Men extended were means to secure followers rather than investments to increase output or productivity, in other words, socio-political investments rather than economic ones.

The transfer of the bride price, as described by Hylkema, was agonistic in that it was a public occasion with the bride givers contesting the value of the price offered. While this went on, individual members of the groom's party contributed cowries and, as described also by de Bruijn, they were made in the spirit of competition that Hylkema views as characteristic for Me sociality.

> Emphatically everybody throws or puts his contribution on [the readied pandanus rain cape or strips of bark]. If the *kade* is not assembled rapidly enough, explosions of *wainai* (the traditional fury dances) follow, during which others are loudly reproached that they have contributed not at all or not enough (de Bruijn 1955d: 535).[10]

---

9 Me expected analogous generosity from Europeans and frequently asked for gifts, often exasperating the hoped for donors (Boelen n.d.: 211). In reverse, they were often generous with the food they had produced.

10 Pospisil's description of how a bride price is assembled and transferred mentions exclusively discontent among the members of the bride's party about what the groom's party has to offer (1956: 54f). The different descriptions may well reflect cultural differences among the Me themselves.

Such gifts had to be returned. However, as Hylkema observes, returns were delayed by one generation (similarly: Pospisil 1963: 350), while in case the bride would not bear daughters they might not be forthcoming, because of the enchainment of marriage payments across the generations (chapter 27).

Hylkema's descriptions show that among the Me gift and commodity relations intermingled. These two elements of their social life did not, however, carry the same weight since it was by giving gifts that a man gained prestige. Hylkema reports that there were two standards to assess the status of Me men. First, he states that a man failed in life by not having a son. Secondly, he comments that the 'essential goal' is life was gaining prestige and that a man achieved this by giving gifts. The two standards were heterogeneous, yet they were interlinked: a man who has the wealth to make many gifts has a better chance to marry more than one wife and so has a better chance of fathering at least one son.

In his introduction to number 162 of *L'Homme*, entitled *Questions de Monnaie,* Money Issues, Breton (2002b: 18), following Gregory, draws a sharp contrast between exchanges in the market place in which the transactors aim at economic equivalence and gift exchanges in which transactors aim at identity of objects. Breton describes this contrast as one between the economy of things as against the economy of persons. I find it hard to place transactions at the Me *yuwo* in one of these two categories. It seems more apposite to analyse the *yuwo* sales of pork against cowries in terms of equivalence than of identity, even though the transactors often held different opinions about the value of the cowry offered. In this respect the sales resembled market exchanges. Yet, as Hylkema argues, what mattered also was the effect of the sale, or the attempted sale, on the relationship of the transactors, as in gift exchange.[11]

THE ME IN CONTRAST TO THE WODANI

From the mid 1990s Breton has carried out fieldwork among the Wodani, living north of the Kema river and north east of the Paniai area. They form a far smaller group than the Me. Breton (pers. comm. 2009) estimates there were between 3,000 and 4,000 Wodani speakers during his research. The Wodani language forms, with Me and Moni, a single language family. But Breton's publications point to major differences between the ways of life of the Me and the Wodani. To begin with, he describes the Wodani as more 'egalitarian' (2002c: 198), than the Me appear in Hylkema's analyses. As appears above, and below in the Epilogue, he views the Me as inegalitarian, even more so than does Pospisil (1998).

---

[11] In this discussion I focus on *yuwo* and bride price transactions. The emphasis may well be undue. However, the ethnography, Hylkema's included, is most elaborate with regard to these two institutions.

Like the Me, the Wodani were fascinated by cowries. They too categorised and sub-categorised them (Breton 2000: 561; 2000c: 225f), while, in addition, valuing them on the basis of 'aesthetic considerations, often of a personal nature and open to endless debate' (Breton 2000d: 138). And like the Me they gave names to highly valuable specimens (Breton 2000d: 133). Cowries were an integral part of their life, such that they held that when people originated, they already had cowries. For the Wodani cowries were imagined persons who were immortal (2000: 567; 2002d: 137). While Me did have the idea that cowries were indigenous, it would have been hard for them to maintain that cowries were immortal given their frequent breakage. In the mid 1990s the Wodani, unlike the Me, held on to cowries using them for marriage payments and compensation. In everyday transactions they used Indonesian money and, decreasingly, cowries. Only among Christianised Wodani money had become part, a small part, of their marriage payments (Breton, pers. comm. 2009). When the Me abandoned cowries in the 1980s, the Wodani got cowries from them, especially high quality ones (2000: 561). Breton points to the great speed with which cowries changed hands among the Wodani (2000: 568). From what Hylkema writes, it seems that this did not occur to the same extent among the Me. For instance, when cowries were assembled so as to make a *muto*, a string, they were withheld from circulation. Breton (pers. comm. 2009) points out that there were only a few high value cowry strings among the Wodani, on rare occasions used as a component of the bride price.

Breton (2000) argues that the cowries that form part of the bride price were an iconic representation of especially the 'paternal' part of the bride. As regards the Me, Hylkema does not hint at such a conception. Rather, the tri-partition of the price specified categories of contributors and of receivers. This contrast likely paralleled another: unlike the Me, Wodani practised sister exchange (Breton 2000: 579), hence exchange of persons. Also among them it was not highly valued since there was no exchange of valuables and since it negated the enchainment across the generations. But for Breton marriage by payment provided the model for marriage by sister exchange (2002c: 208; 2002d: 134). Furthermore, Wodani bride prices were assembled primarily by the members of a single clan (Breton 2002c: 203f), assembling was a clan affair, although friends and allies joined in (pers. comm. 2009).

Clan organisation among the two ethnic groups seemed quite different. Breton describes Wodani clans as corporate groups with a strong totemic identity (2002c: 203; 2002d: 137f). Hylkema does not stress totemism and mentions the dispersed, if not fractured, character of Me clans (2002: 243f, 249f). While Wodani bride prices were brought together by clans (ibidem), Hylkema describes the persons contributing to a Me bride price as forming an 'action group' (p. 164), as it seems an *ad hoc* grouping centred on the nuclear family of the groom and including patrilineal and, presumably, matrilateral kin. For

Hylkema this was in keeping with the individualistic character of the Me way of life. The difference in clan organisation can be related to the differences in size of the two ethnic groups. But I do not rule out that it is also a matter of cultural choice.

In what he has published so far about his research, Breton stresses that shells were used to reproduce human life. The point applies as well to the Me. But Hylkema stresses that the use of shells was hybrid: men used the shells also to achieve prestige and prominence, especially by throwing *yuwo* during which they collected shells by selling pork and, possibly more importantly, allowed the other participants to collect them as well. Thus the institution enabled men to improve their prospects of becoming leaders, which is another way in which the Me had made cowries instrumental in the 'reproduction' of their society.

EPILOGUE

To conclude this book, I present a quotation from Hylkema's monograph discussing the role of pigs in the life of the Me (Hylkema 1974c). In this monograph Hylkema describes the extensive socialisation process that the Me applied to turn young pigs into compatible human companions (similarly Pospisil 1963: 205-6). Hylkema observes that pigs were the least ones in a Me household, destined to be killed and consumed for the sake of humans. In the quotation below he widens the scope of his argument to social stratification among the Me and its impact on their lives:

> With its willingness to be sacrificed for the sake of humans, a pig reflects a girl's willingness to be married off, irrespective of her personal preferences, in order to enable her brother to amass the shells needed to marry the girl of his choice ... And just as parents point out to their sons not to be stingy towards their sisters, people say with regard to pigs: 'Let us care well for them. Because when we are ill, it says "You go back home, I will pass on on your behalf'.
>
> While a pig is on the lowest rank in human society, the comparison with a girl, insofar she is prepared to sacrifice herself for her brother, puts into sharp relief what prominent Ekagi expect from those of lower status. It is only fair that these people bear the brunt in order to protect and shield their betters.

BIBLIOGRAPHY

Alua, A.A. (ed.) 2006 *Nilai-nilai hidup masyarakat Hubula di lembah Balim Papua.* Jayapura, Papua; Biro Penelitian STFT Fajar Timur.

Akin, D. & J. Robbins (eds) 1999 *Money and Modernity. State and Local Currencies in Melanesia.* Pittsburgh, PA; University of Pittsburgh Press.

Bariĉ, L. 1964 'Some aspects of credit, saving and investment in a 'non-monetary' economy (Rossel Island)', in: Firth, R. & B.S. Yamey (eds) *Capital, Credit and Saving in Peasant Societies.* Pp. 35-52. London; Allen & Unwin.

Bijlmer, H.J.T. no date (1938) *Naar de Achterhoek der Aarde.* Amsterdam; Scheltens & Giltay.

Boelen, K.W.J. 1954 'Rapport Dienst Gezondheidszorg', unpublished document.

Boelen, K.W.J. no date (presumably 1955) *Dokter aan de Wisselmeren.* Baarn; Bosch & Keuning.

Boelen, K.W.J. 1955 'Begrippen "stam" en "tuma" (clan) bij de Ekagi's', Part 1, *Tijdschrift "Nieuw-Guinea"* 16 (1): 1-6.

Breton, S. 2000 'Social body and icon of the person', *American Ethnologist* 26: 558-82.

Breton, S. (ed.) 2002a *Questions de Monnaie.* Special Issue of *L'Homme. Revue Française d'Anthropologie,* no. 162.

Breton, S. 2002b 'Monnaie et économie des personnes', in Breton, S 2002a: 13-26.

Breton, S. 2002c 'Tuer, manger, payer: l'alliance monétaire des Wodani de Papouasie occidentale', in: Breton, S. (ed.) 2002a: 197-231.

Breton, S. 2002d 'The spectacle of things. A Melanesian perspective on the person and the self', in M. Jeudy-Ballini and B. Juillerat (eds) *People and Things. Social Mediations in Oceania.* Durham, NC: Carolina Academic Press.

Broekhuyse, J. 1996 'De Harvard-Peabody expeditie in de Baliemvallei', in: Schoorl, P. (ed.) 1996: 129-48.

Craig, B. & P. Swadling 1983 'Trading Spheres in the Ok Tedi impact region', in: Swadling, P. 1983 *How Long have people been in the Ok Tedi Impact Region?* Papua New Guinea National Museum Record no. 8: 111-21.

de Bruijn, J.V. 1952 'Korte notities over de verwantschapsterminologie en het grondenrecht bij de Ekagi (Wisselmeren)', an unpublished *Dienstnota [Official Memorandum].*

de Bruijn, J.V. 1955a 'Volksordening bij de Bergpapoea's (1951-1953), *Adatrechtbundel* 45: 324-6.

de Bruijn, J.V. 1955b 'Het grondenrecht der Ekari of Ekagi der onderafdeling Wisselmeren', *Adatrechtbundel* 45: 417-29.

de Bruijn, J.V. 1955c 'Verwantschapsterminologie der Ekagi in de onderafdeling Wisselmeren (1952)', *Adatrechtbundel* 45: 460-8.

de Bruijn, J.V. 1955d 'Huwelijk bij de Ekagi der Wisselmeren', *Adatrechtbundel* 45: 532-5.

de Bruijn, J.V. 1970 'Ekagi land tenure', in: Ploeg, A. (ed.) 'Land Tenure in West Irian', *New Guinea Research Bulletin* 38: 13-23; English translation of de Bruijn 1955b.

de Bruijn, J.V. 1978 *Het Verdwenen Volk.* Bussum; Van Holkema & Warendorf.

Dubbeldam, L.F.B. 1964 'The devaluation of the Kapauku-cowrie as a factor of social disintegration', in: Watson, J.B. (ed.) *New Guinea. The Central Highlands.* Special publication of *American Anthropologist* 66 (4, part 2): 293-303.

Ellen, R. 2003 *On the Edge of the Banda Zone. Past and Present in the Social Organization of a Moluccan Trading Network.* Honolulu; University of Hawai'i Press.

Epstein, T.S. 1982 *Urban Food Marketing and Third World Rural Development. The Structure of Producer-Seller Markets.* London & Canberra; Croom Helm.

Eyma, P.J. 1940 'Verslag van den tocht ten Noorden van het Paniai-meer', 3 October – 4 November 1939', *Tijdschrift van het Koninklijk Nederlandsch Aardrijkskundig Genootschap* 57: 423-41.

Eyma, P.J. no date (probably 1940 or 1941) 'Iets over de middelen van bestaan van de Bergpapoea's in het Wisselmerengebied, Nieuw Guinea, Westelijk Centrale Bergland', unpublished text of a presentation.

Fischer, H. Th. 1952 *Huwelijk en Huwelijksmoraal bij Vreemde Volken.* Utrecht; de Haan.

Fortmann, H. 1974 *Als Ziende de Onzienlijke: een Cultuurpsychologische Studie over de Religieuze Waarneming en de Zogenaamde Religieuze Projectie.* 2nd Edition. Hilversum; Gooi & Sticht.

Foster, R.J. 1999 'In God we trust? The legitimacy of Melanesian currencies', in: Akin, D. & J. Robbins (eds) 1999: 214-31.

Galbraith, J.K. 1977 *The Age of Anxiety.* London; BBC / A. Deutsch.

Galis, R.W. [K.W.] 1953 'Geschiedenis', in: Klein, W.C. (ed.) *Nieuw Guinea.* Vol. 1. 1953: 1-65.

Galis, K.W. 1963 *Bibliografie van Nederlands-Nieuw-Guinea.* Third edition. The Hague; no publisher mentioned.

Giay, B. 1995 *Zakheus Pakage and his Communities. Indigenous Religious Discourse, Socio-Political Resistance, an Ethnohistory of the Me of Irian Jaya.* Amsterdam; Department of Cultural Anthropology / Sociology of Development, Free University.

Godelier, M. 1991 'An unfinished attempt at reconstructing the social processes which may have prompted the transformation of great-men societies into big-men societies', in: Godelier, M. & M. Strathern (eds) *Big Men and Great Men. Personifications of Power in Melanesia.* Pp. 275-304. Cambridge etc.; Cambridge University Press / Paris; Éditions de la Maison des Sciences de l'Homme.

Gregory, C.A. 1982 *Gifts and Commodities.* London, etc.; Academic Press.

Gregory, C.A. 1994 'Exchange and reciprocity', in: Ingold, T. (ed.) *Companion Encyclopedia of Anthropology. Humanity, Culture and Social Life.* Pp. 911-39. London and New York; Routledge.

Gregory, C.A. 1997 *Savage Money. The Anthropology and Politics of Commodity Exchange.* Amsterdam, etc.; Harwood Academic Publishers.

Groenewegen, K. & D.J. van de Kaa 1964 *Resultaten van het Demografisch Onderzoek Westelijk Nieuw-Guinea.* Vol. 1, *Nieuw-Guinea als Gebied voor Demografische Onderzoekingen.* The Hague; Government Printing and Publishing Office.

Grootenhuis, G.W. 1960 'De "wege"-beweging in Paniai in Oost-Tigi', unpublished typescript. Hollandia, west Nieuw Guinea; Kantoor van Bevolkingszaken.

Healey, C.J. 1990 *Maring Hunters and Traders. Production and Exchange in the Papua New Guinea Highlands.* Berkeley and Los Angelos; California University Press.

Hobsbawm, E. 1995 [1994] *Age of Extremes. The Short Twentieth Century 1914-1991.* An Abacus book. London; Time Warner Books UK.

Hughes, I. 1973 *New Guinea Stone Age Trade.* Terra Australis 3. Canberra; the Research School of Pacific Studies, The Australian National University.

Hylkema, S. 1971-2 *Mapia Studiën.* Unpublished manuscript.

Hylkema, S. 1974a *Mannen in het Draagnet. Mens- en Wereldbeeld van de Nalum (Sterrengebergte).* Verhandelingen van het Koninklijk Instituut voor Taal-, Land- en Volkenkunde 67. 's-Gravenhage; Martinus Nijhoff.

Hylkema, S. 1974b *De Bruidsprijs bij de Ekagi.* Unpublished manuscript.

Hylkema, S. 1974c *Het Grote Varkensfeest. De Juwo in de Practijk Onderzocht op zijn Existentiële Betekenis in de Ekagi-Samenleving.* Unpublished manuscript.

Hylkema, S. 1975 *Het Varken. Onderzoek naar de Maatschappelijke Functie en Betekenis van het Varken bij de Ekagi.* Unpublished manuscript.

Hylkema, S. 1988 *Ekagi Texts: Myths.* Unpublished collection of oral texts, in Ekagi and English. The English version is a translation by W.Wolke from a Dutch translation by Hylkema. Leiden.

Hylkema, S. 1990a *Ekagi-Teksten, Volksverhalen.* Unpublished collection of oral texts, in Ekagi and in Dutch, in a translation by Hylkema, and with an introduction by Hylkema. Three vols. Hylkema 2002 is an English translation of the first part of the introduction to the texts.

Hylkema, S. 1990b 'Transaction of the ownership of land with the Ekagi around the Wissel-lakes', unpublished paper presented at the conference 'The Mek and their neighbours', Seewiesen, Bavaria.

Hylkema, S. 1996 *Mee-Mana. Kamus Bahasa Ekagi-Belanda-Indonesia.* Unpublished Mee dictionary.

Hylkema, S. 2002 'Paniyai, Kamu-Tigi and Mapiya, Paniai District, Papua', introduced and translated by Anton Ploeg, *Bijdragen tot de Taal-, Land- en Volkenkunde* 158: 225-52.

Hylkema, S. n.d. *Oorsprong en Leven.* Unpublished manuscript.

Kamma, F.C. 1972 Koréri. *Messianic Movements in the Biak-Numfor Culture Area.* The Hague; Martinus Nijhoff.

Kepper, G. & L.H.W. van Sandick 1938 'Het arbeidsvraagstuk voor Nieuw Guinee', in: Klein, W.C. (ed.) *Nieuw Guinee,* vol. 3: 900-46.

Klamer, A. & H. van Dalen 1998 *Het Verhaal van Geld.* Amsterdam; Amsterdam University Press.

Klein, W.C. (ed.) 1935-8 *Nieuw Guinee.* Three vols. Amsterdam; J.H. de Bussy.

Klein, W.C. 1938 'Dwarsdal door het sneeuwgebergte. Berichten van luitenant Van Arcken over de Amerikaansch-Nederlandsche expeditie naar het gebied tusschen

Idenburg-rivier en Wilhelminatop op Nieuw-Guinea', *Tijdschrift "Nieuw-Guinea"* 3: 479-85.

Klein, W.C. (ed.) 1953-4 *Nieuw Guinea. De Ontwikkeling op Economisch, Sociaal en Cultureel Gebied, in Nederlands en Australisch Nieuw Guinea.* Three vols. 's-Gravenhage; Staatsdrukkerij- en uitgeverijbedrijf.

Leach, E.R. 1962 [1958] 'Concerning Trobriand clans and the kinship category *Tabu*', in: Goody, J. (ed.) *The Developmental Cycle in Domestic Groups.* Pp. 120-45. London, etc.; Cambridge University Press.

Liep, J. 1999 'Pecuniary schismogenesis in the Massim', in: Akin, D. & J. Robbins (eds) 1999: 131-50.

le Roux, C.C.F.M. 1948-50 *De Bergpapoea's van Nieuw-Guinea en hun Woongebied.* 3 vols. Leiden; E.J. Brill.

Maddock, K. 1976 Review of Hylkema, S. 1974a, *Oceania* 47: 165-6.

Mauss, M. 1990 (1924) *The Gift. The Form and Reason for Exchange in Archaic Societies.* Translated from the French by W.D. Halls. London and New York; Routledge.

Peterson, N. 1993 'Demand sharing: reciprocity and the pressure for generosity among foragers', *American Anthropologist* 95: 860-74.

Ploeg, A. 1969 *Government in Wanggulam.* Verhandelingen van het Koninklijk Instituut voor Taal-, Land- en Volkenkunde 57. The Hague; Martinus Nijhoff.

Ploeg, A. 1996 'Huge men in the highlands of Irian Jaya', in: Levine, H. and A. Ploeg (eds) *Work in Progress. Essays in New Guinea Highlands Ethnography in Honour of Paula Brown Glick.* Pp. 213-32. Frankfurt am Main, etc.; Peter Lang.

Ploeg, A. 1997 'P.J. Eyma', *Oceania Newsletter* 19: 12-3. University of Nijmegen; Centre for Pacific and Asian Studies.

Ploeg, A. 2000a 'Inventory of the scholarly writings of Sibbele Hylkema ofm', *Oceania Newsletter* 24: 11-14.

Ploeg, A. 2000b 'Dr. P.J. Eyma's writings on agriculture in the Paniai area, central highlands, western New Guinea', *Journal of the Polynesian Society* 110: 401-20.

Ploeg, A. 2004 'Wealth items in the Western Highlands of West Papua', *Ethnology* 43: 291-313.

Pospisil, L. 1958 *Kapauku Papuans and their Law.* Yale University Publications in Anthropology, 54.

Pospisil, L. 1963 *Kapauku Papuan Economy.* Yale University Publications in Anthropology, 67.

Pospisil, L. 1964 *The Kapauku Papuans of West New Guinea.* Case Studies in Cultural Anthropology. New York, etc.; Holt, Rinehart & Winston.

Pospisil, L. 1978 *The Kapauku Papuans of West New Guinea.* 2nd Edition of Pospisil 1964.

Pospisil, L. 1989 'Traditional egalitarian society, its loose structure, emerging inequality and other widely held myths', in: Haenen, P. & J. Pouwer (eds) *Peoples on the Move. Current Themes of Anthropological Research in New Guinea.* Pp. 18-30. Nijmegen; Centre for Australian and Oceanic Studies.

Robbins, J. & D. Akin 1999 'An introduction to Melanesian currencies. Agency, identity and social reproduction', in: Akin & Robbins (eds) 1999: 1-40.

Rutherford, D. 2003 *Raiding the Land of the Foreigners; the Limits of the Nation on an Indonesian Frontier.* Princeton, NJ; Princeton University Press.

Schoorl, J.W. 1993 *Culture and Change among the Muyu.* KITLV Translation Series 23. Leiden; KITLV Press.

Schoorl, P. [J.W.] (ed.) 1996 *Besturen in Nederlands-Nieuw-Guinea 1945-62.* Leiden; KITLV Press.

Schumacher, C. 1964 'Exploratie', in: Klein, W.C. (ed.) 1953-4, vol. 3: 1-120.

Sierat, J. 2000 *Rapádaba. Mensen aan de Wisselmeren, Irian Jaya.* Bergen, North Holland; Bonneville.

Silzer, P.J. & H. Heikkinen Clouse 1991 *Index of Irian Jaya Languages,* 2nd edition, a Special Publication of *Irian. Bulletin of Irian Jaya.*

Stewart, P. & A. Strathern 2000 'Transformation of monetary symbols in the Highlands of Papua New Guinea', in: Breton, S. (ed.) 2000a: 137-56.

Swadling, P. 1996 *Plumes from Paradise. Trade Cycles in Outer Southeast Asia and their Impact on New Guinea and Nearby Islands.* Boroko, PNG; Papua New Guinea National Museum / Coorparoo DC, Queensland; R. Brown & Ass.

Tillemans, H. 1951 'Gebruiken op Nieuw-Guinea. Regenverdrijving bij de bergbewoners van Centraal Nieuw-Guinea', part 3, *Tijdschrift "Nieuw-Guinea"* 11 (5): 183-9.

van Baal, J. 1954 'Volken', in: Klein, W.C. (ed.) 1953-4, vol. 2: 438-70.

van Baal, J. 1974 'Woord vooraf', in: Hylkema, S. 1974a: v-viii.

van Baal, J. 1975 *Reciprocity and the Position of Women.* Assen/Amsterdam; van Gorcum.

van Baal, J. 1977 *Geschiedenis en Groei van de Theorie der Culturele Anthropologie (tot ±1970).* Leiden; Bureau Indonesische Studiën.

van Baal, J. 1981 *Man's Quest for Partnership. The Anthropological Foundations of Ethics and Religion.* Assen; van Gorcum.

van Baal, J. 1989 *Ontglipt Verleden.* Vol. 2. *Leven in Verandering: 1947-58.* Franeker, the Netherlands; van Wijnen.

van Baal, J., K.W. Galis & Koentjaraningrat 1984 *West Irian: a Bibliography.* Dordrecht, Cinnaminson; Foris.

van der Horst, J. 1995 '*Amakane*, een kennismaking met de Moni stam', unpublished monograph.

van der Veer, K. 1937 'Land- en tuinbouw', in: Klein, W.C. (ed.) 1935-8: 457-523.

van Eechoud, J.P.K. 1939 'Verslag van de exploratie naar het Wisselmerengebied van 13 mei tot 14 november 1938 en van de doorsteek van Paniai tot aan de monding van de Siriwo van 15 november tot 1 december 1938', unpublished patrol report. Excerpts in *Tijdschrift "Nieuw-Guinea"* 4 (1939-40): 121-37, 181-92.

van Nunen, B.O. 1973 *The Community of Kugapa.* Issue of: *IRIAN. Bulletin of Irian Jaya Development* 2 (2).

van Zon, P. 1935 'De bosschen van Nieuw Guinee', in: Klein W.C. (ed.) 1935-8: 271-316.

Veldkamp, F. 1996 'Bestuurlijke dilemma's bij de openlegging van de Baliem', in: Schoorl, P. (ed.) 1996: 73-116.

Verschueren, J. 1953 'Missie', in: Klein, W.C. (ed.) 1953: 160-229.

Vos, B. 1992 *Naar het Sneeuwgebergte.* Amsterdam; Nijgh & van Ditmar.

Vriend, 2003 *Smoky Fires. The Merits of Development Co-operation for Inculturation of Health Improvements.* CIP-Data Thorpe Bibliographic Services.

Wentholt, A. (ed.) 2003 *In Kaart Gebracht met Kapmes en Kompas; met het Koninklijk Nederlands Aardrijkskundig Genootschap op Expeditie tussen 1873 en 1960.* Heerlen; ABP Public Affairs / Utrecht; KNAG.

Wirz, P. 1932 *Im Lande des Schneckengeldes. Erinnerungen und Erlebnisse einer Forschungsreise ins Innere von Holländisch-Neuguinea.* Stuttgart; Strecker & Schröder.

INDEX